UNIVERSITY OF NORTH CAROLINA AT CHAPEL HILL
DEPARTMENT OF ROMANCE LANGUAGES

NORTH CAROLINA STUDIES
IN THE ROMANCE LANGUAGES AND LITERATURES

Founder: URBAN TIGNER HOLMES

Distributed by:

UNIVERSITY OF NORTH CAROLINA

CHAPEL HILL

North Carolina 27514

U.S.A.

NORTH CAROLINA STUDIES IN THE
ROMANCE LANGUAGES AND LITERATURES

Number 184

THE STRUCTURE OF REALISM
THE NOVELAS CONTEMPORANEAS
OF BENITO PÉREZ GALDÓS

THE STRUCTURE OF REALISM:

THE NOVELAS CONTEMPORANEAS OF BENITO PEREZ GALDOS

BY
KAY ENGLER

CHAPEL HILL
NORTH CAROLINA STUDIES IN THE ROMANCE
LANGUAGES AND LITERATURES
U.N.C. DEPARTMENT OF ROMANCE LANGUAGES
1977

Library of Congress Cataloging in Publication Data

Library of Congress Cataloging in Publication Data
Engler, Kay.
　　The structure of realism.

　　(North Carolina studies in the Romance languages and literatures ; 184)
　　Bibliography: p.
　　1. Pérez Galdós, Benito, 1843-1920. Novelas españolas contemporaneas. 2. Realism in literature. I. Title. II. Series.
PQ6555.Z5E56　　　　863'.5　　　77-5148
ISBN 0-8078-9184-3

I.S.B.N. 0-8078-9184-3

This book is dedicated to Professor Ricardo Gullón, in appreciation of his invaluable guidance and encouragement.

TABLE OF CONTENTS

	Page
REALISM AND THE NOVEL	1
The Nature of the Problem	1
Descriptive Theories	3
Explanatory Theories	6
Realism as a "Formula of Art"	14
Realism and the Novels of Pérez Galdós	17
GALDÓS AND THE CRITICS	25
POINT OF VIEW	39
A Theoretical Basis	39
The Narrator: Creation of an Autonomous Reality	44
Selection and Summary	48
The Narrator: Language as Image	52
The Language of Irony	56
The Language of Familiarity	60
Interpretation	62
The Characters: The Language of Perception	69
The Characters: Language as Image	72
Indirect Free Style	74
The Characters Speak	78
Interior Monologue	84
The Language of Dreams	90
Conclusions	96
DISTANCE	101
Some Preliminary Considerations	101
Modes of Presentation	106
Narrative Pace	120
Time	123
Space	125
Tone	129
Characterization	132
Conclusions	134
THE UNRELIABLE NARRATOR	137
Unreliable Narration in Galdós' Novels	140
El amigo Manso	141
Unconscious Irony	143
Manuel Peña	146
Irene	149
Máximo Manso	154
Lo prohibido	160
José María: Idealist and Materialist	160
José María as Narrator	164
José María: The Technique of Demythification	168
Conclusions	182
CONCLUSIONS	185
SELECTED BIBLIOGRAPHY	189

Chapter I

REALISM AND THE NOVEL

The Nature of the Problem

Any critical study of the works of a nineteenth-century novelist like the Spaniard Benito Pérez Galdós must ultimately come to terms with that *béte noire* of critical concepts, realism. The terms "realism" or "realistic," or their counterparts "romanticism" and "romantic," have been used with such vagueness and imprecision by critic and layman alike that there are those who would simply throw up their hands in despair at the prospect of ever getting beyond a purely intuitive understanding of them. How can anything approaching a rigorous definition be formulated for a concept which has been applied to works as diverse as the *Odyssey* and Beowulf, the *Satyricon* and *Père Goriot*, to authors as diverse as Fielding and Henry James, Petronius and Balzac? Even within Spanish literature, how can the same term be applied to the *Cid, La Celestina, Don Quijote, Lazarillo de Tormes* and the great novels of the nineteenth century?

There have been attempts to deal with the problem, to sort out the mass of confusion, to find some path through the labyrinth of contradictory terms. Most notable, of course, is Erich Auerbach's now classic *Mimesis,* which aims at nothing less than the study of the representation of reality in the whole of Western literature from Homer to Virginia Woolf. Auerbach's careful textual analyses trace "in what manner realistic subjects were treated seriously, problematically or tragically"[1] throughout the history of Western literature. His studies reveal how the ancient doctrine of the levels of style: that extraordinary persons and events were to be treated in the sublime, serious, or tragic style; and that ordinary persons (of low social class) and ordinary events were to be treated in the grotesque or comic style was broken down first, by the influence of Christianity in the Middle Ages, and secondly, by the novelists of the nineteenth century, who for the first time accorded serious treatment to "everyday" reality.

Yet, as René Wellek points out, even Auerbach's extraordinarily erudite and sensitive study falters, for Auerbach's definition of realism is based on an irreconcilable contradiction. Auerbach sees realism, first, in "the agonizing revelations of reality in moments of supreme decisions, in 'limiting situations',"[2] of an existential nature. But when speaking specifically of nineteenth-century realism, Auerbach insists on its essentially historical character which represents man "immersed in the dynamic concreteness of the stream of history."[3] Herein, says Wellek, lies the contradiction, for the existential situation which constitutes the basis of realism is unhistorical, even anti-historical, in nature.

On a lesser scale, C. S. Lewis has attempted to discriminate between the "realism of presentation" and the "realism of content."[4] Realism of presentation is "the art of bringing something close to us, making it palpable and vivid, by sharply observed or sharply imagined detail."[5] This kind of realism may occur in works as diverse as *Gulliver,* the *Divine Comedy, Beowulf* or the *Canterbury Tales,* works not often thought of as "realistic in the sense of being probable or even possible."[6] In contrast to this realism of presentation stands realism of content. In C. S. Lewis' words, "a fiction is realistic in content when it is probable or 'true to life',"[7] reflecting that everyday reality of which Auerbach spoke. As Lewis goes on to point out, "the two realisms are quite independent. You can get that of presentation without that of content, as in medieval romance; or that of content without that of presentation, as in French (and some Greek) tragedy; or both together, as in *War and Peace;* or neither, as in *Furioso* or *Rasselas* or *Candide.*"[8] Nineteenth-century realism exhibits both realism of presentation and realism of content.

Both Auerbach and Lewis deal with realism as a concept which transcends any narrow historical period or particular literary movement. For them, "realism," like "romanticism" or "classicism," seems almost to define an existential attitude on the part of the author toward his work and toward the world, the whole epistemological problem of the relation of art to reality. But, certainly, equally valid, if not more so, are those critical theories which deal with realism as a "period" concept, which deal only with the realism most familiar to us all, that of the nineteenth century. René Wellek defends the validity of this period concept of realism, which he defines as "a regulative concept, a system of norms dominating a specific time, whose rise and eventual decline it would be possible to trace and which we can set clearly apart from the norms of the periods that precede and follow it."[9]

Existing discussions of historical or nineteenth-century realism, whether they occur in essays dedicated exclusively to that subject, or in the course of comments on particular works of nineteenth-century novelists, generally fall into two basic categories. First, there are those comments which are merely descriptive. They attempt no more than an exhaustive description of the subject matter characteristic of realistic works and the innovations in style or technique which distinguish realistic works from their predecessors or successors. Then there are those discussions which attempt to explain what is known to be descriptively true about realism by relating it to the historical, social, political or philosophical background of the period in which realism as a literary movement first appeared. Finally, it should be pointed out that theories of realism are inextricably linked to theories of the novel as a genre. The novel is the realistic genre *par excellence,* the primary vehicle in the nineteenth century for the expression of the realist sensibility. Theories of the novel, therefore, shed invaluable light on the nature of realism. Indeed, they offer the best theoretical model of the realist mode.

Descriptive Theories

Descriptive concepts of nineteenth-century realism can best be summed up in René Wellek's working definition of realism as "the objective representation of contemporary social reality,"[10] a definition with both thematic and stylistic implications. The realists insisted that the material used in their novels should be the product of direct observation. This doctrine necessarily limited the reality depicted to one they could have known directly, from their own experience: the society in which they lived, a narrowly defined region in time and space. The realist doctrine also implicitly carried with it a rejection, on the one hand, of "the fantastic, the allegorical and the symbolic, the highly stylized, the purely abstract and decorative . . ."[11] and on the other, of "the improbable, of pure chance, of extraordinary events. . . ."[12] For the realist, then, the world he could portray was limited to that which he and his reader know best, a reality which was least susceptible to transformation by his own or his reader's fantasy, a reality which seemed least subject to the will of pure chance.

The world the nineteenth-century novelist knew best, of course, was that of the middle class. All students of the period are quick to point out the predominantly bourgeois character of realism.[13] The nineteenth-century novel is a novel written by, for, and about the middle class. Most novelists of the period are themselves members of the middle class. Their works chronicle the economic, political, social and spiritual struggles of the middle class throughout the period. The middle class itself was the primary consumer of these works, despite the fact that, in the course of the century, novelists became increasingly bitter in their criticism of the bourgeoisie. The realists reflect the capitalist-positivist ethic of the bourgeoisie, and their own disillusionment with that doctrine. The setting of their works is predominantly urban, reflecting the increasing industrialization and urbanization of society at the hands of the bourgeoisie.

The representation of contemporary social reality indicates the realists' strong interest in society itself, in the mass, in collective reality. One has only to think of the grandiose design of Balzac's *Comédie humaine* or the extraordinary range of Galdós' *novelas contemporáneas* and *episodios nacionales* to be convinced of the realists' desire to represent the whole of a society as an entity in and of itself, almost as a kind of organism—living, growing and dying. This concern with the portrayal of society as a whole is certainly what gives to nineteenth-century realism the distinctively historical character which so many critics have noted. It is, in fact, this historical character, "the embedding of random persons and events in the general course of contemporary history, the fluid historical background,"[14] which in Auerbach's opinion, sets nineteenth-century realism apart from the realism of other periods. This extensive presentation of the social and historical background in most nineteenth-century novels has even led Arnold Hauser to state that the real subject of Stendhal's novels, for example, is "the political system of his own age."[15] This weaving of public events into the fabric of private lives, of history into fiction, seems essential to the realist mode. It is certainly also reflected in the historical novel cultivated by many realists where, conversely, private events are woven into the fabric of public life, fiction into history.

An inevitable by-product of this concern with the portrayal of the whole of society is the concern with the relationship of the individual to society. As Arnold Hauser explains it, the novel becomes the leading literary genre of the period precisely because it gives "the most comprehensive and profound expression to the cultural problem of the age—the antithesis between the individual and society."[16] He continues, "With Stendhal and Balzac the social novel becomes the modern novel and it now appears quite impossible to portray a character in isolation from society and to allow him to develop outside a definite social milieu."[17] This means that realism exhibits, paradoxically, a simultaneous interest in man as a social animal, man as a member of the species, and an overwhelming interest in portraying the individual man in conflict with society.

Hauser explains, for example, that for Balzac, "a character in itself is unimportant; he only becomes interesting and significant as the agent of a social group, as the bearer of a conflict between antithetical, class-conditioned interests. Balzac himself always speaks of his characters as of natural phenomena, and when he wants to describe his artistic intentions, he never speaks of his psychology, but always of his sociology, of his natural history of society and of the function of the individual in the social body."[18] A realist like Balzac's interest in fixing the individual man's place in the social scheme of things is revealed in the important realist doctrine of type. As George Becker states, "the realistic novel rests on its typicality. It must be characteristic in its uneventfulness, its mediocrity."[19] The realist novel presents the typical "slice of life," assuming that that slice of life is representative of the society as a whole. The individual character type is a kind of concrete universal, uniting the general, the typical, and the particular, the individual. As René Wellek explains, the concept of type is "of critical importance for the theory and practice of realism, because 'type' constitutes the bridge between the present and the future, the real and the social ideal."[20]

At the same time, however, there is no denying the realists' interest in the individual man whose own desires are often in direct conflict with those of society. The typical hero of the nineteenth-century novel is *in* but not *of* society. As Arnold Hauser says, all the great figures of the modern novel, "from Balzac's Lucien de Rubempré, Stendhal's Julien Sorel, Flaubert's Frédéric Moreau and Emma Bovary to Tolstoy's Pierre, Proust's Marcel and Thomas Mann's Hans Castrop . . . suffer from the discrepancy between dream and reality and are the victim of the conflict between their illusions and practical, commonplace, middle-class life."[21] This conflict of the individual with society becomes the central theme of the modern novel. In Harry Levin's terms, the realist novel is "the novel of disillusionment," which chronicles the hero's loss of innocence, his "sentimental education" in a demythologized world.[22]

The realist doctrine of "the objective representation of contemporary social reality" also required certain basic innovations in technique. The principal tenet of realist doctrine was "objectivity," an elusive and ill-defined goal which, as René Wellek has shown,[23] few realists ever achieved. Only if objectivity is made equivalent to authorial self-effacement can the realists claim to have achieved their goal. In fact, objectivity to the realist meant "something negative, a distrust of subjectivism, of the romantic exaltation of the ego:

in practice often a rejection of lyricism, of the personal mood."[24] It meant that the realist was primarily interested in the objective world, the world outside of himself, rather than in the world within his own mind.

As Ian Watt has shown, the illusion of contemporary social reality was also created by certain changes in narrative technique: the abandonment of traditional plot, new methods of characterization and presentation of background, and the largely referential use of language.[25] Characters are "individuated" by their realistic proper names and by their placement in a particular temporal-spatial framework. That framework is so extensively materialized that the illusion of physical density in the nineteenth-century novel is overwhelming.[26] The illusion of temporal particularity and of the relentless passage of time is so characteristic of the novel that E. M. Forster can speak of the novel as the portrayal of "life by time."[27] The increasingly referential use of language reflects the realists' preoccupation with representing 'objective' reality, while his use of colloquial language indicates his concern with accurate portrayal of all aspects of human behavior.[28]

Yet, how can what is known to be descriptively true be explained? What relationship exists between the realistic novel's subject matter: the picture of ordinary people living their everyday lives at a particular moment in history in a certain corner of the universe; its theme: the individual man's "sentimental education" or disillusionment in a demythologized world; and its style: the abandonment of traditional plot for the "original" and typical life, the individuation of character and background, and the increasingly non-rhetorical use of language? Critics have variously sought the explanation in the changes which were taking place in society during the period when the modern novel first appeared, in the major philosophical currents of that period, and in the narrative tradition which preceded the novel's appearance.

Explanatory Theories

Arnold Hauser, in *The Social History of Art,* traces the beginnings of the modern realistic novel to the rise of the middle class and the formation of a new reading public.[29] The existence of a new, educated, reading public with the money to buy books and the leisure time to read them freed the author from his patron and subjected him to the demands of the free market composed, in fact, of that same social group. His work necessarily, then, reflected the interests and outlook of the middle class, of which the novelist himself was often a member. Even the fact that, in the course of the nineteenth century, the realist gradually proceeded to shatter the bourgeoisie's image of itself, only reflects the middle class's growing malaise and dissatisfaction with the world it had created.

Hauser sees the novel as a vehicle for individualism which parallels the individualism of the bourgeoisie in its revolt against the authority of the aristocracy. The bourgeois taste for domestic scene in art, for the portrayal of the ordinary and the everyday in literature, is a strong rejection of the purely decorative, ornamental quality of the baroque art and literature of the aristocracy.[30] The strongly didactic, moralistic tone of much of realist literature is a reflection of the "moral rigorism of the middle class ... another weapon directed against the aristocratic outlook ... a protest against the frivolity and extravagance of a social stratum whose levity has to be made good by others...."[31] The sentimental quality of the first modern novels of Richardson, Fielding and Sterne reflects the middle-class revolt against the cold intellectualism of aristocratic literature, the repudiation of aristocratic aloofness.[32] The autobiographical form of the modern novel expresses the same spirit of individualism as does the cult of *laissez-faire*, the principle of free competition and the right of personal initiative manifest in the economic liberalism of the middle class, a movement which denied the inherited right to wealth and power of the aristocracy.

Hauser goes on to explain, however, that the individualism characteristic of the modern novel "is not simply the translation of economic liberalism into the literary sphere, but also a protest against the modernization, levelling down and depersonalization of life connected with an economy left to run itself."[33] It is only since the eighteenth century that individualism "as a challenge and protest against the depersonalization inherent in the process of civilization"[34] has existed. Never before had the antagonism been felt to flow from the individual character of the person in conflict with the collective unit. As has been pointed out, it is precisely this conflict between the individual and society which is the central theme of the realist novel.

Hauser discusses in some detail the new relationship between the author, the characters and the reader which developed in the modern novel, and was particularly evident in the novels of the late eighteenth century. The author begins to treat the reader as an intimate friend, addressing him directly. As Hauser says, in the these early novels "the author and the reader become the principal actors in the novel; they flirt with each other all the time and maintain an illegal relationship in which all rules of the game are broken."[35] Obviously, as the novel develops during the nineteenth century this close author-reader-character relationship becomes less and less obvious as the author becomes more and more self-effacing. But the fact that the teller of the tale continues to appear to be a part of what he is describing maintains the impression of "the immediacy and personal quality of the experience described. . . ."[36] This feeling of immediacy is also a reflection of the illusion of physical density, of materiality, manifest in the modern novel, which so many critics have noted.

Hauser's comments do serve to explain much of the realistic novel's subject matter and theme, but his comments do not really form a coherent theory of realism. They do not adequately explain the relationship between the novel's form and content. The best and most coherent theory of realism and the novel form is offered by Ian Watt in *The Rise of the Novel*. Watt seeks the explanation for the rise of the novel in the philosophical climate of the late eighteenth century created by such men as Locke and Descartes. He argues that the novel's realism "does not reside in the kind of life it presents, but in the way it presents it."[37] The correspondence between a literary work and the reality it presents is essentially an epistemological problem: the reality a work of art presents depends on the current philosophy of truth and knowledge, what can be known and how. The novel arose in a period characterized by its rejection of universal truth, a period in which the growing tendency, evident from the Renaissance onward, for individual experience to replace collective tradition as the ultimate arbiter of reality reached its zenith. Modern philosophical realism, says Ian Watt, "begins from the position that truth can be discovered by the individual through his senses."[38] "But," he goes on, "the view that the external world is real and that our senses give us a true report of it, does not throw much light on literary realism."[39] Rather, the importance of philosophical realism to the novel lies in its concept of the pursuit of truth as an individual matter: how truth is known rather than what is truth. Truth is no longer absolute, but relative, reflected in the consciousness of the individual.

For Watt, the primacy of individual experience in the novel is manifest in its formal realism, "the narrative method whereby the novel embodies the circumstantial view of life."[40] The circumstantial view of life, says Watt, is the characteristic outlook of the novel. It implies the portrayal of those aspects of reality attendant upon the circumstances of the individual. Concretely, the circumstantial view of life is manifest, for example, in the presentation of a world of particular people in particular circumstances, the individuation of character and the detailed presentation of his environment, the early subordination of plot to autobiographical memoir—all essential characteristics of the modern novel's subject and style.

Harry Levin's comments[41] on the subject matter of realism parallel those of Arnold Hauser. For Levin, too, the novel is the representative of the bourgeois age. Its preoccupation with money, property and things and its representation of the urban life, for example, mirror directly the middle-class experience. But more significantly, Levin finds a stylistic and thematic prototype for the realistic novel in Cervantes. In *Don Quijote,* says Levin, Cervantes found the formula for realism in the literary technique of systematic disillusionment.[42] In Don Quijote and Sancho, Cervantes had embodied the eternal duality of the human experience: *engaño* and *desengaño,* illusion and disillusion, innocence and experience, sensibility and sense, appearance and reality. In parodying the world of chivalric romance Cervantes had created the model for the realistic novel. All heroes of the modern novel, like Don Quijote, go out into the world of reality with their heads full of illusions. The world of romance is still present in the real world of the novel. Levin quotes a passage from André Gide's *Les faux monnayeurs* which epitomizes the world of the *Quijote* and of the modern novel: "The way the world of appearances imposes itself upon us, and the way we try to impose our own interpretation on the external world, shape the drama of our lives. The stubbornness of the facts tempts us to transpose our ideal construction into dream, hope, future life, and our belief in these is fed by all our disappointments in this life."[43] For Levin, realism then becomes "a synthesis: the imposition of reality upon romance, the transposition of reality into romance."[44]

Levin's theory of realism is remarkably similar to that expounded by Ortega y Gasset in the second half of his *Meditaciones del Quijote.* Ortega points out that while the epic describes the past world of idealized essence, the novel describes the present world of actual existence. In spite of this, the novel always carries within it the epic world of adventure and romance. Adventure, in the novel, however, has become purely psychological, the illusions in the minds of its heroes. The hero of the modern novel has a will to adventure, a desire to transform reality to conform to his illusions, to lift himself out of his own prosaic reality to the level of the epic hero. The result is inevitable: the violent clash of his illusions, his will, with reality.

Reality in the novel, says Ortega, has a generic function, the destruction of the myth, the ideal: "La realidad adquiere un movimiento, un poder activo de agresión al orbe cristalino de lo ideal."[45] Ortega believes that myth is the point of departure for all literature, including realist literature. But, with the realists, says Ortega, "acompañamos al mito en su descenso, en su caída. El tema de la poesía realista es el desmoronamiento de una poesía."[46] The realistic novel, then, in essence, describes this process of demythification. Ortega's theory of demythification is clearly the equivalent of Levin's theory of realism as systematic disillusionment, the synthesis of romance and reality.

All of these theories of realism: Hauser's theory of the "individualism" of the novel as a reflection of the bourgeoisie's struggle against the aristocracy, of the individual's conflict with society; Watt's theory of the "formal realism" of the novel and its embodiment of the "circumstantial view of life" presenting a world apprehensible by the individual consciousness through the senses; Levin's theory of realism as the synthesis of romance and realism; or Ortega's theory of realism as "el desmoronamiento de una poesía" in a process of demythification all exhibit the same theoretical model: the Hegelian dialectical process.

René Girard, in his *Mensonge romantique et verité romanesque* (the English title, *Deceit, Desire and the Novel,* is more indicative of the book's content), a study of the metaphysical character of the novelistic hero from Don Quijote to Dostoyevski's underground man, accepts the Hegelian dialectical process as the basic model for the hero's relationship to the world in the modern novel, but argues that the basic dialectic is altered by the presence of a "mediator" who determines the nature and direction of the hero's desires. Girard, like Ortega and Levin, sees Cervantes' woeful knight as the prototype of all which follows. Don Quijote lives a life of imitation, of complete subjection to the chivalrous codes of behavior expounded by his idol, Amadís. In Girard's words, "Don Quijote has surrendered to Amadís the individual's fundamental prerogative: he no longer chooses the objects of his own desire. Amadís must choose for him."[47] All of the great heroes of the modern novel: Stendhal's Julien Sorel, Flaubert's Madame Bovary, Dostoyevky's underground man—exhibit the same pattern of behavior, a life determined not by Self, but by Other.

The really important implications of Girard's theory for the theory of realism have to do with the obvious parallels between the character who acts as mediator between the hero's desire and its object and the narrator who acts as mediator between the reader and the world of the novel. Thus the dialectical relationship between the reader and the world of the novel is not a direct one. Rather, it is fundamentally determined by the intervening presence of the narrator as mediator of the novelistic world, in the same way that the dialectic between the character and the object of his desire is fundamentally determined by the presence of the mediator of that desire.

Girard goes on to establish the difference between "external" and "internal" mediation: "We shall speak of external mediation when the distance is sufficient to eliminate any contact between the two spheres of possibilities of which the mediator and the subject occupy the respective centers. We shall speak of internal mediation when this same distance is sufficiently reduced to allow these two spheres to penetrate each other more or less profoundly."[48] In other words, in Cervantes the mediator "is enthroned in an inaccessible heaven and transmits to his faithful follower a little of his serenity. In Stendhal, this same mediator has come down to earth."[49] This difference between external and internal mediation corresponds to the difference between the impersonal narrator of the epic (and of Cervantes' novel), existing above and beyond his novelistic world; and the personal narrator characteristic of the modern novel.

Equally suggestive is Girard's observation that as the modern novel develops, the single mediator of desire is replaced by the multiple mediator: the character lives, not in imitation of one Other, but of any other. The hero's self is fragmented into a series of monadic selves in a process of disintegration of the personality. This fragmentation of the character's self is clearly parallel to the fragmentation of the narrator, the loss of the single unified narrator and the growth of multiple narration and multiple point of view which characterizes the novel at the beginning of the twentieth cenutry.

The Hegelian model in its purest form is found in Georg Lukács' theory of the novel. As Paul de Man points out in his article "Lukács' Theory of the Novel,"[50] Lukács sees the emergence of the novel as the major modern genre as the result of a change in the structure of human consciousness. For Lukács, the development of the novel reflects modifications in man's way of defining himself in relation to all categories of existence. Lukács' theory, then, is neither sociological, nor psychological, but almost metaphysical in character. The distinction between the epic and the novel is founded on a distinction between the Hellenic and the Western mind. This distinction is stated in terms of the category of alienation, seen as the intrinsic characteristic of the reflective consciousness.

Lukács' theory of the novel emerges in a cogent and coherent way out of the dialectic between the urge for totality and man's alienated situation. The novel becomes "the epic of a world from which God has departed."[51] As a result of the separation between our actual experience and our desire, any attempt at a total understanding of our being will stand in contrast to actual experience. The novel, in effect, describes the separation between life (*Leben*) and being (*Wesen*). Because the novel describes life, and not being, it remains rooted in the particularity of experience. The theme of the novel is thus necessarily limited to the individual, and to this individual's frustrating experience of his own inability to acquire universal dimensions. For Lukács, as for Harry Levin and for Ortega y Gassett, the novel originates in the Quixotic tension between the world of romance and that of reality.

As Paul de Man points out, this thematic duality, the "tension between an earth-bound destiny and a consciousness that tries to transcend this condition, leads (in Lukács' theory) to structural discontinuities in the form of the novel."[52] Lukács believes that the novel displays a "heterogeneous and contingent discontinuity"[53] in the form of irony. Lukács raises irony to the level of a structural category, for it becomes "the determining and organizing principle of the novel's form."[54] As Paul de Man explains, "Lukács can state that irony actually provides the means by which the novelist transcends, within the form of the work, the avowed contingency of his condition. In the novel, irony is the freedom of the poet in relation to the divine . . . for it is by means of irony that, in an intuitively ambiguous vision, we can perceive divine presence in a world forsaken by the gods."[55] The ironic language of the novel mediates between experience and desire, and unites ideal and real within the complex paradox of the form.

For Paul de Man, Lukács, in his concept of irony as the determining and organizing principle of the novel, has succeeded in "freeing himself from preconceived notions about the novel as an imitation of reality. Irony steadily undermines this claim at imitation and substitutes for it a conscious, interpreted awareness of the distance that separates an actual experience from the understanding of this experience."[56] In Lukács' theory, the novel "is founded on an act of consciousness, not on the imitation of a natural object."[57]

Many of Lukács' ideas about the nature of the novel and the difference between the epic and the novel are echoed in Wolfgang Kayser's article, "Origen y crisis de la novela."[58] Kayser believes the presence of a personal narrator is the distinguishing characteristic of the modern novel. The appearance of a personal narrator in whose consciousness alone the world is reflected, says Kayser, signalled the birth of the modern novel in the words of such authors as Fielding and Sterne.[59] This is the personal, indeed often personified, narrator who directs his narrative to the reader and who accompanies him as a guide through the novel. It is this narrator who appears to give form and meaning to the novelistic world, commenting upon and interpreting events and characters, directing the reader's attention to significant events by drawing closer to them, passing over others with a quick summary. His narration has a familiar tone, for he speaks not with the voice of distant authority, but from within the realm of human experience. Because he is subject to the limitations of human knowledge, he must consciously use the language of irony, says Kayser, for if there is no longer any absolute truth, if the only truth we have is that which is filtered through the consciousness of the narrator, a fellow human being, there can no longer be faith in the capacity of language to reveal the world of reality. All is relative and dependent upon the perspective of the narrator.[60]

For Kayser, the personal narrator contrasts sharply with the anonymous narrator of the epic who remains distant and impersonal, never adopting a personal point of view, always speaking with the cold voice of anonymity and authority, limiting himself only to relating what is already known. Kayser suggests that the difference corresponds to the difference in the worlds of which they are a part. The world of the epic is a world of pure essence, of absolute truth, where there is no disparity between intention and action, being and appearance, where language unequivocally communicates the truth. The world of the novel, on the other hand, is a world of existence, a world known intimately by man, where consequently all is relative, equivocal, a world whose essence is the conflict between reality and appearance. Only a personal narrator, limited as a human being to a particular point of view, is suited to reflect a world where all is relative and dependent on perspective. This implicit perspectivism reflects a world where reality is stratified, a world where there are levels of reality, where appearance is not reality.

Kayser, like Ian Watt, believes that the appearance of the modern novel and its most salient characteristic, the personal narrator, reflected the growing philosophical emphasis on the individual which had begun in the Renaissance and reached its peak in the eighteenth century, "la afirmación de que el individuo que siente y presiente es el sentido de la existencia."[61] The reflection of the world in the soul of one individual, the narrator: this constituted the greatest potential of the novel as a new literary form.

All of these theories of realism in the novel are, to some extent, concerned with the literal concept of mimesis as the representation of reality. They all deal with the basic epistemological problem of the relationship of art to life, for as René Wellek says, "Art cannot help dealing with reality, however much we narrow down its meaning or emphasize the transforming or creative power of an artist. 'Reality,' like 'truth,' 'nature,' or 'life,' is, in art, in philosophy, and in everyday usage a value-charged word. All art in the past aimed at a reality even if it spoke of a higher reality: a reality of essences or a reality of dreams and symbols."[62] Of the four concepts of reality which George Becker discusses in his survey of realism: 1) that of absolute essence (as in Plato or the transcendentalists); 2) that which is unique in individual experience and has its being outside of time (as in Proust); 3) that which inheres in external phenomena; and 4) that which has its being in some kind of relation between external phenomena and perceiving consciousness,[63] it is the last variety which seems to conform most closely to the concepts of historical realism we have been discussing. Yet, as Becker says, "Whatever reality is . . . it is not identical with a work of art and is anterior to it. Realism, then, is a formula of art, which conceiving of reality in a certain way, undertakes to present a simulacrum of it on the basis of more or less fixed rules."[64]

Realism as a "Formula of Art"

What clues are there among these various theories of realism and the novel which might give us the key to its "formula of art?" Ortega y Gasset believes the key lies within the novel itself and not in any relationship between the novel and the world outside. According to Ortega, it is because the novel is a realistic genre, that is, because the world of the novel is the world of existence as it is known by man in his daily life, that it can never stand comparison with the real world. In Ortega's words: "Precisely because it is a preeminently realistic genre it is incompatible with outer reality. In order to establish its own inner world it must dislodge and abolish the surrounding one."[65] For this reason, the novelist must ideally create a closed world, a hermetically sealed universe. He must see to it that the reader is cut off from his real horizon and imprisoned in the inner realm of the novel. "For were we allowed to compare the inner world of the book with outer reality and invited to 'live'," says Ortega, "the conflicts, problems and emotions the book has to offer would seem so small and futile that all their significance would be lost. It would be like looking in a garden at a picture representing a garden."[66]

This particular characteristic of the novel Ortega calls imperviousness (*hermetismo*), which is simply the generic equivalent of the autonomous character of all art. Were the novel to fail to carry out this imperative, it could no longer be considered a work of art. Thus a definition of realism based on a relationship between the novel and exterior reality denies the imperviousness of the novel and its status as a work of art.

Hazel Barnes, in her article on "Modes of Aesthetic Consciousness in Fiction," puts forth essentially the same argument. The aesthetic consciousness, she says, is one which engages itself to believe. Such a belief is an "imaginary" belief, for the aesthetic consciousness is an image-making one. Of the three modes of consciousness—emotion, perception, and imagination—the first two are very different from the third. In perception, the external or "real" world is the determinant, for perception without an outside object is unthinkable. Imagination, on the other hand, "cancels out the real world, sets it aside in favor of the mental image. It is incidental, not essential, that this image may have an object correlate outside."[67] The reader enters this imaginary world, embracing it by temporarily putting aside the real world.

To comply with the aesthetic imperative of autonomy, the generic imperative of imperviousness, the novel, says Ortega, "is destined to be perceived from within itself—the same as the real world in which, by inexorable metaphysical order, each man forms, in each moment of his life, the center of his own universe."[68] The reader then must be placed in an imaginary world, impervious to external reality, existing at its very center, as he himself is the center of his own real world. Hazel Barnes suggests that it is a question of "shared consciousness," an identification of reader and character in which the psychological distance which usually exists between self and other in real life is eliminated: "The reader's consciousness exists in a world centered in character. The reader is in that center, and so the world is the same for both."[69] The reader perceives the world of the novel as the character knows it, as it is reflected in his consciousness.

Miss Barnes' concept of a shared consciousness which enables the reader to perceive the novel from within is based on the identification of the reader with the other characters of the novel. It does seem to reflect Lukács' concept that the novel is founded on an act of consciousness, not on the imitation of a natural object. Also, it seems to provide a "formula of art" which corresponds to the conception of reality as some sort of dialectic between perceiving consciousness and external reality which realists share. But I would suggest that identification of reader and character alone is insufficient to describe the complexity of relationships inherent in the modern novel. Following Wolfgang Kayser's dictum that the genius of the modern novel lies in its reflection of reality in the soul of a single individual, the personal narrator, I would suggest that the reader identifies instead with another figure of paramount importance in determining the reality of the novel: the narrator himself. It is this shared consciousness between the reader and the narrator as mediator of novelistic reality which constitutes the psychological basis of the novel's realism. The reader, through the changing psychological relationship of the narrator with the other characters, can enter into the shared consciousness with the characters themselves which Miss Barnes describes. Together, narrator and reader enter into a complex and shifting web of relationships with other elements of the novel which recreates within the fictional realm the experience of reality as the reader has known it in the real world—he, himself, as the center of his own universe. Thus is created the "circumstantial view of life" of which Ian Watt spoke.

If the narrator is seen to be the key of the novel's realism, there are certain concepts about the nature of the narrator of the modern novel which should be made clear. First of all, it should be pointed out that the narrator is not the author. He is as much a part of the fictional world as are the characters themselves. The typical narrator of the nineteenth-century novel is a personal narrator, who identifies himself, explicitly or implicitly, as "I" or "we" and directs his interpretive comments toward the reader. Often he develops as a character in his own right and enters, if only marginally, into the action of the novel itself. He may make many different kinds of comments about the characters and their actions: psychological interpretations of the characters' behavior, moral judgments which he passes on their actions, or generalizations about human behavior and life itself which he extracts from the concrete situations of the novel. This commentary usually reveals his omniscience, in the sense of "complete privilege,"[70] or "unlimited point of view."[71]

The narrator's importance in determining the novel's realism (based on the dialectic of perceiving consciousness and external reality) is best revealed in his relationship to the other elements of the narrative situation. Wayne Booth, in *The Rhetoric of Fiction*, explains that "in any novel there is an implied dialogue between the narrator, the implied author, the other characters in the novel, and the reader. Any of the four can range, in relation to any of the others, from complete identification to complete opposition, measured on any axis of value: moral, intellectual, aesthetic and even physical."[72] The relationship of the narrator to these other elements of the narrative situation is clearly what determines the narrative structure of the novel: the point of view manifest at any point in the course of the novel, and the number and nature of narrative planes, which in turn determine such things as modes of narration, narrative pace, time, space, focus, tone, etc.—those elements traditionally considered to constitute a novel's style.

All of this leads me to suggest that realism as a literary style can be defined structurally: that is, it results from the basic narrative structure of the novel as it is determined by the narrator in his relationship with his narration. It is easier to comprehend how the style of any one novel might result from its narrative structure than it is to comprehend how the literary style of an author or of a whole literary period can be defined structurally. To make such a structural definition we must assume that there are structural elements which are common to all novels considered realistic: patterns of relationships between the narrator and his narration which are repeated in many different novels to such an extent that they may be considered typical. If such patterns of relationships can indeed be found to exist, a definition of realism as a literary style could be formulated which would be aesthetically valid and which would explain how realism's "formula of art" is created.

Realism and the Novels of Pérez Galdós

The study of the novels of Benito Pérez Galdós which follows is an attempt to find those patterns of relationships, to discover how realism's "formula of art" is implemented by the greatest of nineteenth-century Spanish novelists. The choice of Galdós' work is an obvious one. All of his works, but especially the *novelas contemporáneas*, exhibit to an extraordinary degree the characteristics of literary realism we have just described. Galdós' own announced aesthetic creed, described in his essay *Observaciones sobre la novela contemporánea en España* (1870) and the speech he gave on the occasion of his entrance into the Royal Academy in 1897 parallel exactly René Wellek's working definition of realism as the objective representation of contemporary social reality.

Galdós, like any good realist, wrote about the world he knew best—middle-class Spanish society of the last three decades of the nineteenth century. The world he creates is one he knew intimately, from first-hand experience. Galdós was a keen observer of the world in which he lived. Many anecdotes are told of this shy, retiring man who travelled by train throughout Spain in third-class compartments, who wandered through the lower and middle class districts of Madrid, who sat for hours at the edge of café *tertulias,* always with notebook in hand, carefully recording the human drama unfolding before him.

For the most part, Galdós rejects the fantastic, the allegorical, the symbolic, the highly stylized, the purely abstract and decorative, the world of extraordinary event. His world is made up of the humble events of everyday existence. His characters, leading a life of humdrum mediocrity and routine, fade in and out of the social mass of which they are a part. His stories are told in a simple, direct and colloquial language which contrasts sharply with the rhetorical, bombastic prose of his predecessors and the consciously stylized prose of his modernist successors. To be sure, the fantastic elements critics have noted in Galdós' work: his interest in dreams, the subconscious, his characters' fantasies; the growing tendency toward symbol and allegory in his later works, are present, but they are not central, and do not represent the characteristic tone of the *novelas contemporáneas.* Indeed, this very tonality has led Galdós' critics to accuse him of vulgarity and to nickname him "don Benito el garbancero."

Galdós' novels are essentially bourgeois in character. In spite of occasional incursions into the world of the decadent lower aristocracy (*La familia de Leon Roch, Lo prohibido*) or into the world of the miserable urban poor (*Fortunata y Jacinta, La desheredada, Misericordia*) Galdós, for the most part, limits himself to a portrayal of the middle-class experience. For this reason, all of the *novelas contemporáneas* have an urban setting—Madrid. The *novelas contemporáneas* recount the formation of the bourgeoisie, "class amorfa, sin conciencia propia: pequeños tenderos, abogados, vividores, sablistas y sobre todo, empleados y cesantes, siempre esperando del Estado, del favor o del milagro la solución de su existencia,"[73] through a fusion of a suddenly impoverished and powerless aristocracy, and a proletariat which had managed to acquire a modest amount of wealth. Galdós chronicles the middle class' struggle for economic security and dominance, social acceptance and political stability. He recounts the victimization of the middle class in the hands of the state, an arbitrary and absurd bureaucracy. Galdós, like other realists, reveals a slow but sure loss of faith in the values propounded by the middle class, the positivist-capitalist ethic. His criticism of Restoration society created by the new middle class becomes increasingly severe.

Galdós' own announced purpose in writing the *Novelas contemporáneas* is the representation of the whole of contemporary Spanish society. To that end he becomes a social historian, recounting the relationship among the various social classes and the economic, political and historical factors affecting this relationship. He portrays a whole gallery of social types representing the total configuration of Madrid society, anxious to fix them in society's memory before they disappear in the social levelling process inherent in the rise of the middle class. As a kind of social geographer, he pictures the changing face of Madrid itself, neighborhoods changing character and appearance overnight as the economic fortunes of their inhabitants change.

If Galdós is a sociologist, he is at the same time an historian. His novels are deeply historical in character, not only because the society he portrays is carefully fixed in a particular moment in time; but, more importantly, because in the *novelas contemporáneas,* as in the *episodios nacionales,* he is interested in the portrayal of the historical process itself: the ideological forces at work in Spain throughout the nineteenth century, the historical process described by Angel del Río as "el intento siempre fracasado de salvar la esencia tradicional, haciéndola compatible con una civilización moderna de signo opuesto, de unir dentro de la comunidad europea el pasado y el presente de la nación."[74] Galdós' habit, noted by many critics, of paralleling private and public event, of carefully interweaving the story of his fictional characters and the history of the nation, reinforces his strong historical character.

Yet, as Sherman Eoff has pointed out,[75] Galdós is not so much a social historian or sociologist, as a social psychologist: what interested him most was not society in itself and the abstract forces at work therein, but the individual human being and his relationship to that society. As Del Río says, Galdós "tiene el presentimiento de la peculiaridad de la sociedad española, y sobre todo, de que para entender los factores en pugna había que estudiar la conciencia individual al mismo tiempo que el ambiente histórico donde esa conciencia se había creado."[76] Conversely, Galdós felt that the individual could only be understood in relationship to the society in which he lived. In Ricardo Gullón's words: "El interés de Galdós por la sociedad de su tiempo se debía a su convicción de que solamente en ella y vinculado a ella podía entenderse al hombre."[77] And so we find again and again the portrayal of the individual's encounter with the society in which he lives: the formation of his values in that society, the definition of his own needs, the conflict between society's values and his own needs, his acceptance or rejection of society's dictates, his re-integration into society or eventual destruction by that society.

The conflict between the individual and the world in which he lives portrayed in Galdós' novels is not merely a social one, nor even merely a psychological one. Ultimately, in the *novelas contemporáneas,* as in all realist novels, it becomes a metaphysical one. The characters in Galdós' novels also "suffer from the discrepancy between dream and reality and are the victim of the conflict between their illusions and practical, common-place middle class life."[78] As Angel del Río describes them, "los personajes de Galdós, son espíritus inquietos, sometidos a la tortura de encontrar dentro de sí mismos la verdad y la finalidad última de su existencia. En la mayoría de los casos no lo consiguen, se estrellan contra la muerte y el fracaso, . . . pero todos luchan por superar la mezquina realidad que les rodea y aun la mezquina realidad de sus pasiones."[79] Galdós' novels, too, are novels of disillusionment portraying the hero's sentimental education.

Galdós' novels reveal, as well, the innovations in technique which the realist doctrine required. They are characterized by their objectivity, in the sense that objectivity means a rejection of lyricism, of the personal mood. Galdós was interested in the portrayal of the objective world, the world outside himself, and not the world within his own mind. His works generally subordinate plot and action to the portrayal of atmosphere and character. Characters are thoroughly individuated and are placed in a particular moment in space and time. His novels are characterized by extraordinary physical density and temporal particularity. The language is colloquial and anti-rhetorical.[80]

All of the theories which attempt to explain the nature of literary realism: Hauser's theory of the novel as a reflection of the individual's conflict with society; Watt's theory of the novel as the circumstantial view of life which presents a world apprehensible through the senses of the individual; Levin's theory of the realist novel as systematic disillusionment; or Ortega's theory of the novel as "el desmoronamiento de una poesía" in a process of demythification—can all be applied equally well to Galdós' novels. Perhaps the importance of all these theories to the understanding of Galdós' novels is that they all exhibit the same theoretical model, the Hegelian dialectical process.

Sherman Eoff's important study, *The Novels of Pérez Galdós,* shows Hegelian thought to be central to Galdós' view of the world. Galdós is not essentially a philosophical novelist, but as Eoff explains, "Though he soon plunges into the portrayal of life so thoroughly that the reader almost loses sight of any philosophical purpose, such a purpose gradually assumes form as if it were growing out of life itself. It is a philosophy grounded upon an interpretation of the 'self and others' relationship, which is the subject of greatest magnitude in Galdós, whether regarded from a psychological, moral or metaphysical viewpoint."[81]

Other critics (Del Río, Casalduero) have noted the essentially synthetic character of Galdós' art, and have vaguely suggested the Hegelian influence. Eoff sees this search for synthesis in Galdós' adherence to Krausism: "The idealism of Galdós reveals a general similarity to the Krausism of Sanz del Río in the belief in the unity of God with all things in a relationship where the parts, though they may be in opposition to each other, form a whole whose totality is superior to any particular being or to any particular relationship."[82] As Eoff goes on to explain, Galdós sought a solider theory, and found it in Hegel's theory of self-consciousness: "the process of self-realization by which individual consciousness passes laboriously from materiality to spirituality, slipping back upon its lower self in the process, but ever acquiring new awareness that leads to a realization of unity with the Absolute Spirit."[83] Whether this Hegelian dialectic is found in the individual's growth to self-consciousness through his relationship to others; in the conflict between and eventual integration of social classes; the opposition, integration and consequent expansion of elements within the Self; or the final fusion of Truth and Reality, or of multiple realities into Reality—the Hegelian dialectic, says Eoff, underlies all of Galdós' work.

The implications of Eoff's observations for this study are obvious. The relationship of Self and Other basic to Galdós' view of the world on the psychological, social, moral and metaphysical level is the exact parallel of the dialectic of perceiving consciousness and external reality created by the narrator on the stylistic level. To demonstrate the creation of this dialectic of perceiving consciousness and external reality is to demonstrate the creation of the dialectic of Self and Other.

The study which follows examines the creation and elaboration of the dialectic through the words themselves (Chapter III) and through the narrator's always shifting distance from his narrative (Chapter IV). Chapter V examines the problems present in the maintenance of the dialectic in so-called "unreliable narration." This in-depth examination is prefaced by a review of critical commentaries on the nature of Galdós' realism.

FOOTNOTES

[1] Erich Auerbach, *Mimesis,* Trans. by Willard Trask, (New York, Doubleday and Co., 1957), p. 491.

[2] René Wellek, "The Concept of Realism in Literary Scholarship," in *Concepts of Criticism,* ed. Stephen G. Nichols, Jr. (New Haven and London: Yale University Press, 1963), p. 236.

[3] *Ibid.,* p. 236.

[4] C. S. Lewis, *An Experiment in Criticism* (Cambridge: Cambridge University Press. 1965), pp. 57, 59.

[5] *Ibid.,* p. 57.

[6] *Ibid.,* p. 58.

[7] *Ibid.,* p. 59.

[8] *Ibid.,* pp. 59-60.

[9] Wellek, p. 225.

[10] *Ibid.,* pp. 240-241.

[11] *Ibid.,* p. 241.

[12] *Ibid.,* p. 241.

[13] George Becker, "Modern Realism as a Literary Movement," Introduction to *Documents of Modern Literary Realism,* ed. George Becker (Princeton: Princeton University Press, 1963), p. 23.

[14] Auerbach, pp. 433-34.

[15] Arnold Hauser, *The Social History of Art,* vol. 4, Trans. by Stanley Godman, (New York: Vintage Books, 1951), p. 31.

[16] *Ibid.,* p. 28.

[17] *Ibid.,* p. 29.

[18] *Ibid.,* p. 45.

[19] Becker, p. 30.

[20] Wellek, p. 242.

[21] Hauser, vol. 3, p. 76.

[22] Harry Levin, *The Gates of Horn: A Study of Five French Realists* (New York: Oxford University Press, 1966), pp. 39ff.

[23] Wellek, p. 242.

[24] *Ibid.,* p. 246.

[25] Ian Watt, *The Rise of the Novel: Studies of Defoe, Richardson and Fielding* (Berkely and Los Angeles: University of California Press, 1967), p. 32.

[26] Becker, p. 31.

[27] Watt, p. 22.

[28] Becker, p. 27.

[29] Hauser, vol. 3, pp. 38-84.

[30] *Ibid.,* p. 68.

[31] *Ibid.*, p. 63.
[32] *Ibid.*, p. 63.
[33] *Ibid.*, p. 61.
[34] *Ibid.*, p. 61.
[35] *Ibid.*, p. 72.
[36] *Ibid.*, p. 72.
[37] Watt, p. 11.
[38] *Ibid.*, p. 12.
[39] *Ibid.*, p. 12.
[40] *Ibid.*, p. 32.
[41] Levin, pp. 32-33.
[42] *Ibid.*, p. 48.
[43] *Ibid.*, p. 54.
[44] *Ibid.*, p. 55.
[45] José Ortega y Gasset, *Meditaciones del Quijote* (Madrid: Revista de Occidente, 1966), p. 151.
[46] *Ibid.*, pp. 154-55.
[47] René Girard, Deceit, *Desire and the Novel, Self and Other in Literary Structure*, Trans. by Yvonne Freccero, (Baltimore, Johns Hopkins Press, 1965), p. 1.
[48] *Ibid.*, p. 9.
[49] *Ibid.*, p. 8.
[50] Paul de Man, "Georg Lukàcs' *Theory of the Novel.*" *Modern Language Notes*, vol. 81 (1966), p. 529.
[51] *Ibid.*, p. 530.
[52] *Ibid.*, p. 531.
[53] *Ibid.*, p. 531.
[54] *Ibid.*, p. 531.
[55] *Ibid.*, p. 532.
[56] *Ibid.*, p. 532.
[57] *Ibid.*, p. 532.
[58] Wolfgang Kayser, "Origen y crisis de la novela moderna," *Cultura universitaria*, no. 47 (enero-febrero de 1955), pp. 5-50.
[59] *Ibid.*, pp. 14-15.
[60] *Ibid.*, p. 18.
[61] *Ibid.*, p. 25.
[62] Wellek, p. 224.
[63] Becker, p. 36.
[64] *Ibid.*, p. 36.
[65] José Ortega y Gasset, "Notes on the Novel" in *The Dehumanization of Art and Other Writings on Art and Culture*, (Garden City, N. Y.; Doubleday Anchor Books, 1956), p. 89.
[66] *Ibid.*, p. 85.
[67] Hazel Barnes, "Modes of Aesthetic Consciousness in Fiction," *Bucknell Review*, 12 (March, 1964), p. 82.
[68] Ortega, "Notes on the Novel," p. 89.
[69] Barnes, p. 91.
[70] Wayne Booth, *The Rhetoric of Fiction* (Chicago: University of Chicago Press, 1961), p. 160.

A narrator may often appear to know what could not be learned by strictly natural means or what is limited by realistic vision and inference. Booth calls such knowledge "privilege," and defines omniscience as "complete privilege."

[71]Norman Friedman, "Point of View in Fiction: The Development of a Critical Concept," PMLA, 70 (December, 1955), p. 1171.

Friedman defines omniscience as meaning literally "a completely unlimited . . . point of view. The story may be seen from any or all angles at will: from a godlike vantage point beyond time and place, from the center, periphery, or front. There is nothing to stop the author from choosing any of them or from shifting from one to the other as often or as rarely as he pleases."

[72]Booth, p. 155.

[73]Angel del Río, "Galdós: el hombre y el novelista," Introduction to *Torquemada en la hoguera*, (New York: Las Americas, 1962), p. xxiii.

[74]*Ibid.*, p xv.

[75]Sherman Eoff, *The Novels of Pérez Galdós* (St. Louis: Washington University Studies, 1954), p. 3.

[76]Del Río, p. xvi.

[77]Ricardo Gullón, *Galdós, novelista moderno* (Madrid, Gredos, 1966), p. 131.

[78]Hauser, vol. 3, p. 76.

[79]Del Río, p. xxviii.

[80]This description of Galdós style is necessarily brief, for in fact the way in which Galdós' style is created through the relationship of the narrator with the other elements of the narrative situation is the subject of this study, and is studied at length in chapters three and four.

[81]Eoff, p. 136.

[82]*Ibid.*, p. 138.

[83]*Ibid.*, p. 138.

Chapter II

GALDÓS AND THE CRITICS

Benito Pérez Galdós is the traditionally acknowledged master of nineteenth-century Spanish realism. From the beginning, critics who have commented on Galdós' realism explain that his novels offer a virtual reproduction of Spanish society in the last third of the nineteenth century. The great literary scholar and contemporary of Galdós', Menéndez y Pelayo, for example, saw the *novelas contemporáneas* as "pinturas fidelísimas de la realidad,"[1] rich in almost microscopically detailed observation and faithful rendering of popular language, which together formed a kind of "gran almacén de documentos sociales."[2] Subsequent criticism persisted in the same interpretation of realism as the representation of contemporary social reality. The English critic Walton, whose book on Galdós and the nineteenth-century novel was the first major study to be written,[3] proclaims Galdós the creator of the realistic novel in Spain. Although he does not bother to offer an explicit definition of what he means by "realistic," his historical approach, which traces the development of the realistic novel from the earlier *cuadros de costumbres* and the regional novel, implies a similar view of realism. His designation of the *novelas contemporáneas* as novels of customs comes closest to an explicit definition, and clearly reflects that view of realism which supposes a close relationship between novelistic reality and the external reality of contemporary society.

Leopoldo Alas, or "Clarín," the greatest naturalist novelist in Spain of the late nineteenth century, offers the most penetrating observations on Galdós' style of any of his contemporaries. For Clarín, Galdós, like Pereda and Emilia Pardo Bazán, is a "naturalist." Clarín uses the word "naturalist" interchangeably with the word "realist" in describing Galdós' novels, each of which, he says, "es parte de un gran conjunto en que ha de quedar retratada nuestra sociedad según es en el día, retratada a lo menos en todo aquello a que alcancen la observación y las fuerzas del autor, que no será poco."[4]

Clarín accepts Stendhal's definition of realism as "the mirror in the roadway." The novel offers a faithful imitation of real life ("la novela, si quiere ser imitación de la vida real, en lo que todos convenimos")[5] and is thus what Clarín calls "la novela de observación" or "la novela de costumbres"[6] which offers an imitation of the customs of contemporary life.

Clarín identifies Galdós with Balzac, and praises both for their extraordinary powers of observation. He compares Galdós' *novelas contemporáneas* to Balzac's *Comédie humaine.* Both Galdós and Balzac attempt to portray the whole of society, of man's relationship with other men. Clarín thus identifies the nature of Galdós' realism as a kind of social realism, interested in "toda la verdad de los fenómenos sociales."[7]

Yet, at the same time, Clarín was aware that realism went beyond mere observation and servile imitation of reality. He is aware of the role of creative genius in the creation of any work of art, even a realistic novel. He wonders at length, for example, about Galdós' depiction of the life of the nuns in the convent of the Micaelas in *Fortunata y Jacinta,* something about which Galdós could have had no direct knowledge. For Clarín, there must have been an element of "adivinación" of reality in the creation of the scene. He admits that for Galdós, as for Balzac, realism is a mixture of observation and "adivinación," creative genius and artistic purpose.[8]

Clarín is also aware of the transformation in Galdós' style from the social realism of the *novelas contemporáneas* (what Clarín calls Galdós' *novelas de costumbres*) to the psychological realism of his later works, beginning with *Realidad* (what Clarín calls Galdós' *novelas de carácter*). In the later works, Galdós is less interested in the presentation of the external world of man in society than in the exploration of his characters' inner, spiritual reality.

Literary histories of the period (1920-1940) offer essentially the same observations. The early Hurtado-Palencia history speaks of Galdós' extraordinary powers of observation, the richness of detail, and faithful reproduction of the language of the lower classes. Almost all of the *novelas contemporáneas,* they say, are "novelas de costumbres madrileñas (clase media y baja)"[9] and are of great sociological value. They go on to quote the critic Maura, who says Galdós' work is "la historia íntima de los españoles que vivieron durante la centuria decimonona."[10] Time and again, individual works are said to reflect the life of a particular group, or social class. Madariaga, in his essay on Galdós in 1924, says that the *novelas contemporáneas* consist of a series of "treinta obras que describen la vida del pueblo español durante el postrer cuarto del siglo XIX."[11] Romera-Navarro, in his history (1928), speaks of Galdós' novels of contemporary customs and praises his skill in "la poesía del pormenor externo, el arte de la minuciosidad descriptiva."[12] He also expresses the view of those who see the realistic novel as an instrument of social reform, or propaganda, when he comments that "En las novelas en que pinta las desastrosas condiciones de la sociedad se ve que las enfoca con la luz del arte para que la sociedad se beneficie con la enseñanza."[13] Even a more recent critic like Serrano Poncela expresses the same view when he excuses the "unpoetic" nature of Galdós' style by stating that "en su época la novela era sobre todo un documento social que observaba y corregía."[14]

The critics' real attitudes toward realism are perhaps best revealed, not in explicit statements, but in the use of the term in the course of their commentary on a particular novel. Serrano Poncela, for example, speaks of the "excesiva crudeza realista"[15] of *Misericordia*. Even so recent a critic as James Stamm in his 1967 history of Spanish literature explains that Galdós, in *Misericordia*, "investigates, with shattering touches of realism, a squalid world of physical and spiritual poverty."[16] Then, there are those critics who praise Galdós as one who continues in the tradition of Spanish realism observable in Cervantes and the picaresque novel, a realism consistent with the "traditional realism" of the Spanish people. For them, the realist is one who deals with the lower levels of society, who describes the more unpleasant aspects of human existence. Those who would call Galdós a realist in the tradition of the Spanish people obviously confuse literary realism with a philosophical or ethical acceptance of the painful realities of existence which "realists" describe.

Traditional Hispanic criticism thus makes one or more of four assumptions about the basis of realism: 1) that a novel is realistic to the extent that the interior reality of the novelistic world approximates external reality (generally, a well-defined sociological, historical, cultural world); 2) that a novel is realistic because of the nature of the reality described: either a) a material reality composed of phenomena apprehensible through the senses: objects, places, sights, sounds or b) the "lower levels of reality" which reflect the harsher aspects of the human condition: a world of physical and moral poverty which reduces man to animal and reality to materiality; and more marginally 3) that a novel is realistic because of its social or moral utility: that is, that the reality it describes serves a didactic or propagandistic purpose in helping to show the defects in society and in urging needed changes; 4) that a novel is realistic because it reflects the philosophical or moral realism of a people: that is, that a novel which describes certain harsher aspects of life shows a philosophical acceptance of or resignation to those realities.

It would be in error to infer from what has been said so far that these critics saw Galdós as a mere recorder of the surfaces of reality. From the beginning, the more perceptive among them recognized the complex nature of Galdós' work and the difficulty in labelling him a realist in any narrow sense. Menéndez y Pelayo, for example, first points out Galdós' mastery in the presentation of character and the depths of his insight into their psychology ("tan ingeniosa y amena la psicología, o como quiera llamarse aquel entrar y salir por los subterráneos del alma").[17] Other critics, too, were aware of Galdós' interest in those areas of experience beyond the realm of the material, and describe Galdós' development from the materialism (which some call naturalism) of the early *novelas contemporáneas* to the spirituality and symbolism of the later works. This led them to qualify Galdós' realism in some way: as psychological realism, for example. Yet their adherence to a very literal definition of realism as the reproduction of reality kept them from any serious or in-depth consideration of these extraneous elements they describe. Because of an essentially historical orientation, they are confined to thematic and ideological studies of Galdós' novels or their sociological, historical, and political background. Basically, they look at the novel from the outside, an inevitable result of a view of realism which sees the novel as no more than a reproduction of that exterior reality.

It was only with Angel del Río's *Estudios galdosianos* (1932) and later with Joaquín Casalduero's *Vida y obra de Galdós* (1943) and Ricardo Gullón's *Galdós, novelista moderno* (1960) that the complex character of Galdós' novelistic world began to be studied in depth. Casalduero carefully follows Galdós' stylistic and philosophical development from his early period of historical abstraction, through naturalism, to symbolism. Del Río claims that Galdós is the real creator of what we understand by modern realism, having freed the Spanish novel of the period from its limitations—regionalism, superficial realism and dogmatism—by taking the best elements from contemporary literary movements, adapting them to his own work, and integrating them into a unified whole. For del Río, "así adquiere el realismo su gran trascendencia como una de las formas fundamentales del arte occidental."[18] For Gullón, Galdosian realism is "el realismo trascendente,"[19] which explores those areas of human experience which lie beyond the material and thus transcends realism, narrowly defined. He studies in depths those dark regions ("los ámbitos oscuros") of Galdós' novelistic world which earlier criticism, obsessed with a literal view of realism, had largely ignored. More importantly, Gullón goes on to study the literary techniques which Galdós employs to illuminate those darker regions, techniques which show him to be far ahead of his time. The importance of this study cannot be overemphasized, for it for the first time considers Galdós, the realist, as an artist rather than fundamentally a social historian. It approaches Galdós' novelistic world from within, as an entity in and of itself. These later studies reveal the inadequacies of the traditional approaches to realism in the description of the complexity of Galdós' novelistic world and the need for an approach based on aesthetically valid criteria, criteria which would admit the author of a realistic novel as an authentic, conscious literary artist.

Francisco Ayala's "Sobre el realismo en literatura con referencia a Galdós,"[20] stands as a kind of summary of everything which had been said or implied about Galdós' realism up to that time. Ayala attempts to fit Galdós into the framework of French realism or naturalism of the nineteenth century and of "traditional" Spanish realism of the Golden Age and of the first half of the nineteenth century. In so doing he examines the statements which Galdós himself made on the question of realism in various prologues, speeches and letters.

Ayala links the realism of the nineteenth-century French novelists directly to the naturalism of Zola, with its materialistic, deterministic view of the world. Although he recognizes that there are traces of some naturalist themes (the influence of heredity and environment, for example) in Galdós' novels, particularly those written around 1884-85, Ayala refuses to consider Galdós a naturalist in any real sense of the word. Galdós own comments on naturalism, says Ayala, reveal that "su actitud frente a este movimiento fue más bien de reticencia."[21]

Ayala maintains that Galdós' relationship to the *costumbrista* movement in Spain in the early nineteenth century is not as direct as most would have it. He points out that although there are many *costumbrista* elements in Galdós' novels, the basis of *costumbrismo* and that of realism are very different. *Costumbrismo,* he says, is an essentially romantic phenomenon, "resultado del descubrimiento valorativo que el romanticismo hace del 'pueblo' (que) se complace en lo típico, espontáneo, natural y peculiar de las costumbres, hallando en descubrirlas o pintarlas la completa safisfacción de sus objetivos estéticos."[22] In contrast, the intent of realism in describing contemporary social customs and mores is essentially moralizing and critical.

Galdós himself, as Ayala shows, feels a closer allegiance to traditional Spanish realism, specifically the picaresque. Ayala appears to believe that the basis of this traditional Spanish realism was "el empleo de aquellos materiales de experiencia pertenecientes a las categorías negativas de lo innoble, de lo cruel, de lo torpe. . . ."[23] Galdós, too, says Ayala, "reconoce tácitamente que el realismo consiste, ante todo, en aceptar dentro de la obra literaria crudezas de toda laya."[24] At one point in his article, Ayala seems to say that a direct line can be traced from the "realistic" novel of the Spanish tradition to the "naturalist" novel of the nineteenth century—a fundamental tendency to stylize reality in a certain way: "una iluminación del aspecto negativo de la condición humana mediante el recurso de seleccionar y acumular deliberadamente los detalles más penosos e ingratos, para expresar así una determinada concepción del mundo y de la vida: la que subyace en la metafísica materialista."[25]

Throughout most of the article, however, Ayala openly contradicts this statement by pointing out that the impression of realism in art depends not so much on the inclusion of those repulsive elements as on the manner in which the artist treats them, his artistic intention. Ayala analyses two very similar passages, one from Quevedo's *El buscón,* the other from Galdós' *Misericordia,* to show that realism does not consist in reflecting a particular social reality, but in the manner of its presentation. Quevedo's description of the miserable but haughty nobles attempts to annihilate, while Galdós' description of the *protocursi* Frasquito Ponte aims to present reality *whole* to the reader. Ayala's rather confusing article ends with a description of Galdós' "transcendent" realism which treats both matter and spirit. Despite its confusion, however, the article is valuable precisely for what it shows about the need for an aesthetically valid concept of realism.

The first study to approach the problem of Galdós' realism from an exclusively aesthetic point of view is one by S. Bacarisse, who re-opens the question of realism, "approaching it, as it were, from its visible side, language."[26] Bacarisse rejects the "latent circularity" of the traditional approach which sees realism as "the faithful representation of reality," because it only tends "to define reality by means of the novel and the novel by means of reality."[27] The purpose of his article is to suggest that "realism can be defined in terms of the medium used to create the illusion, rather than in terms of the impression of *verosimilitud* it produces on readers."[28] Bacarisse's careful analysis of the language of a passage from Galdós' *Fortunata y Jacinta* leads him to conclude that "writing is realistic to the extent that the conceptual and logical properties of language are neutralized, giving the illusion of perceptual acquaintance with content."[29] The realist gives to his world the impression of "immediacy" which permits the reader to perceive the world simultaneously with the character, free from any interference, in the form of abstraction of conceptualization, from the author.

Bacarisse insists that the passage he has chosen is in no way extraordinary and that any page chosen at random would do quite as well. He is surely correct when he says that the passage is not extraordinary. There are hundreds of others like it in Galdós' novels. But, as we shall see, to say that this kind of passage represents all the complexities of Galdós' realism is indeed a great oversimplification. Also, Bacarisse's insistence on perceptual immediacy and simultaneity as the basis of realism leads one to the strange conclusion that contemporary stream-of-consciousness novels represent the ultimate of literary realism. This idea parallels that expressed by the German critic Brinkmann in *Wirklichkeit und Illusion,* who comes to the conclusion that realism is found ultimately in "the stream of consciousness technique, in the attempt to 'dramatize the mind,' a technique which actually achieved the most radical dissolution of ordinary reality."[30] Brinkmann's conclusion "that 'the subjective experience ... is the only objective experience' identifies impressionism, the exact notation of mental states of mind, with realism and proclaims it the only true realism. The accepted nineteenth-century meaning of realism is turned upside down."[31] In spite of his conclusions, however, Bacarisse should be commended for undertaking the approach he did. Surely this kind of linguistic approach is the only adequate basis for a study of style, of the realistic "formula of art."

The major study of recent date which attempts to deal with the question of Galdós' literary realism in a systematic way is Gustavo Correa's *Realidad, ficción y símbolo en las novelas de Pérez Galdós* (1967). Correa's study shows that Galdós was a conscious literary artist who was aware of the problems inherent in the realist aesthetic and who expressed his awareness of these problems explicitly, in various prologues, letters, and speeches, and implicitly in the novels themselves. Correa's careful study of individual novels also shows how Galdós' concept of reality and his manner of expressing that concept changes and grows as his style matures.

Correa begins by placing Galdós within the context of literary realism. He sees in Galdós' work the convergence of three literary traditions: the traditional Spanish realism of the Golden Age, the systematic cultivation of objectivity of the nineteenth-century French realists, and the powerful interest in the subconscious manifest in the nineteenth-century Russian novelists. Writing at the end of the nineteenth century, Galdós, says Correa, successfully integrates these various currents of European literary realism in a style "que trasciende el mundo de la descripción material para explorar zonas de significación espiritual y de hondura multifaria y de diversidad de perspectivas."[32] The fusion of these currents allows Galdós to investigate diverse planes of reality, but, as Correa says, the direction of Galdós' realism is always toward an exploration of the individual as "el centro irradiante de comunicación con el mundo exterior, la inevitable interacción entre personaje y medio ambiente."[33] Correa's concept of the nature of Galdós' realism thus coincides with the theories of realism as the portrayal of the circumstantial view of life discussed in the first chapter.

Correa examines in some detail Galdós' own aesthetic creed, primarily as evidenced in his *Observaciones sobre la novela contemporánea en España* (1870) and the speech he made on his entrance into the Real Academia Española in 1897. Both of these statements reveal the dual basis of Galdós' realist aesthetic: the novel as the product of observation, as the representation of reality and as a world of fiction. As Galdós declares in his famous speech to the academy:[34]

> Imagen de la vida es la Novela, y el Arte de componerla estriba en reproducir los caracteres humanos, las pasiones, las debilidades, lo grande y lo pequeño, las almas y las fisonomías, todo lo espiritual y lo físico que nos constituye y nos rodea, y el lenguaje, que es la marca de raza, y las viviendas, que son el signo de familia, y la vestidura, que diseña los últimos trazos externos de la personalidad: todo esto sin olvidar que debe existir perfecto fiel de balanza entre la exactitud y la belleza de la reproducción.

The novel, then, for Galdós, ceases to be merely "una construcción imitativa de la realidad a fin de ser una creación específica de arte con sus propias características internas."[35]

This dual quality of Galdós' aesthetic creed, as expressed in the last sentence of the speech quoted above, becomes the basis of

Correa's systematic study of Galdós' realism. The bulk of his study traces the development of Galdós' realism, his representation of reality, from the early *novelas de la primera época,* which treat reality abstractly or problematically; through the middle period of the *novelas contemporáneas,* which first portray reality in all its materiality; through the mature *novelas contemporáneas,* where reality takes on a dynamic quality; to the last novels, which evidence a growing interiorization of reality and an increasing interest in the religious and the spiritual. In subsequent chapters Correa discusses those novels in which Galdós addresses himself directly to the question of the nature of fiction, the nature of reality, and the relationship between fiction and reality.

That part of Correa's book which deals with Galdós' representation of reality shows little originality in its inception. It is, for the most part, only an elaboration of earlier studies by Casalduero and Del Río which traced Galdós' stylistic and philosophical development from his early period of historical abstraction, through naturalism, to symbolism. Although Correa's study is perhaps more systematic, and his approach more stylistic than the earlier studies, it does not alter their basic conclusions. Its value, rather, lies precisely in the fact that it shows how each of Galdós' novels constitutes an implicit statement of his dual aesthetic creed. Each novel presents again the question of reality, fiction, and the relationship between reality and fiction.

As Correa points out, the central theme of Galdós' novels, like those of all realists, is the individual man's encounter with the world of reality. Like the typical heroes of Balzac, Dickens and Flaubert, many of Galdós' characters live in a world of illusions, of dreams, which they insist on imposing on the world of reality. They refuse to accept the world as it is, living in a world of fantasy, attempting to transform the real world so that it corresponds to their dreams. Galdós' novels chronicle the individual's efforts to resolve this conflict between his inner world of illusion and the real world without.

Correa explains that a related theme of continuing interest to Galdós throughout his novelistic career is the theme of the world of fiction, of books, novels, or illusion versus the world of history, reality or truth. In true quixotic fashion, many of the deluded characters of Galdós' novels owe their illusions to the influence of books. The lives which these characters, like Isidora Rufete or Agustín Miquis, choose to lead take on a peculiarly fictional, novelesque, even farcical quality in contrast to the prosaic reality which surrounds them. Their inevitable defeat at the hands of reality reveals Galdós' belief, at an early stage of his novelistic career, in the superiority of the world of reality over the world of fiction as a source for his work. Galdós' disdain for the kind of literature these characters represented is clearly evidenced in the absurd figure of José Ido del Sagrario, through whom Galdós satirizes the ridiculous style of the *novelas de entregas,* with their false concept of reality and what is legitimately the subject of art.

Correa goes on to demonstrate how, in spite of this early announced preference for reality over fiction as the subject of his art, Galdós discovers and continues to investigate the intricate and complex relationship between the world of fiction and the world of reality. In *Tormento,* for example, Galdós explores the "fictional" nature of reality, of life itself which invents its own novels which the novelist merely observes and to which he gives final form. In *El amigo Manso* and *Lo prohibido* Galdós presents two characters, Máximo Manso and José María Bueno de Guzmán, who lead double lives as both real and fictional beings. In *Fortunata y Jacinta,* Galdós again contrasts the world of fiction (José Ido's novel of el Pitusín) with the world of reality (the "dos historias de casadas"). More importantly, in this novel, with its interweaving of public history and private event, he formulates a new concept of the novel as both history and fiction which is the basis of his realistic aesthetic. As Correa explains it, "La novela es, así, historia, en cuanto es verídica representación de biografías singularizadas, dentro de la textura de la vida social y del dinamismo característico del fluir histórico, pero es también una creación hecha más allá del mundo de la historia, en la esfera exclusiva de las criaturas de ficción. Este doble plano, el ser la novela historia (realidad) y ficción al mismo tiempo constituye, dentro de su significación ambivalente, la esencia misma del realismo galdosiano."[36] In subsequent novels (*Realidad* and *La incógnita*) Galdós shows that reality itself is subject to various interpretaciones, and goes beyond the surface to investigate the inner reality of the individual mind and subconscious. In novels like *Nazarín* and *Halma,* this interiorization of reality is followed by a new evaluation of the religious and moral sphere. Finally, in *Misericordia,* Galdós shows that a fiction, maintained by faith, the strength of the spirit, can create a reality where none previously existed.

The threefold basis of Correa's theory of Galdós' realism: 1) that it transcends objective description of the material world and enters into an exploration of the world of the spirit; 2) that it is always directed toward an exploration of the individual as the center of communication with the exterior world; and 3) that it follows from Galdós' concept of the novel as a world of both reality and fiction, corresponds directly to the Heleglian dialectical model found to underlie all the theories of realism and the novel presented in the first chapter. Correa's theory of a progression and development in Galdós' realism, a growing emphasis on things spiritual and on the triumph of spirit over matter, and a growing depth of understanding of the nature of fiction, reality, and the relationship between them clearly parallels earlier theories advanced by Casalduero and others. Correa's theory, however, is largely based on observations more thematic than stylistic in nature: on the kinds of characters which inhabit Galdós' novelistic world, on the nature of the conflicts they face and the manner in which these conflicts are resolved, on the way Galdós presents the characters' conflicts (problematically, historically, or symbolically), on the presentation of the background world and the characters' relationship with that world. Only in the broadest sense can it be said that Correa takes a stylistic approach, for he does not deal at all with such basic matters of style as rhetoric (use of language), modes of narration, description, and characterization, tone, narrative pace, etc. However valid the theoretical model of Correa's theory of Galdós' realism, however correct his thematic observations, it cannot be said that his study offers and adequate examination of the "formula of art" which is the basis of Galdós' realism.

Anyone who has read all, or even most, of Galdós' novels, is aware of a certain stylistic continuity evident throughout. Even if one takes into consideration Galdós' refinement of his novelistic technique, the obvious maturation of his style, it seems obvious to even the most casual reader that the author of *Gloria, Miau* and *Misericordia* is the same man. Evidence of that stylistic continuity which runs throughout Galdós novels is certainly best sought at the level of language, rhetoric, and narrative and descriptive technique. It is here that the basic configuration of the "formula of art" which constitutes Galdós' realism will surely be found.

In the light of Correa's study, it remains to be seen whether that stylistic continuity, that formula of art basic to Galdós' realism in fact operates completely independently of the obvious thematic shift toward spirituality evident in Galdós' novels, or whether this shift is reflected, in some way not obvious to the casual reader, in the style itself.

The chapters which follow attempt to substantiate, at the most basic stylistic level, the theories about the nature of literary realism which have been formulated in these first chapters, both in a general sense, and more particularly, in reference to the works of Benito Pérez Gáldós. These chapters investigate in detail the key role of the narrator in the establishment and the elaboration of the dialectic of perceiving consciousness and external reality, the "circumstantial view of life" which is the basis of realism's formula of art.

FOOTNOTES

[1] Marcelino Menéndez y Pelayo. *Estudios de crítica literaria* (Madrid, 1908), v. p. 116.

[2] *Ibid.*, p. 115.

[3] L. B. Walton, *Pérez Galdós and the Spanish Novel of the Nineteenth Century*. (London: J. M. Dent and Sons, Ltd., 1927).

[4] Leopoldo Alas, *Galdós* in *Obras completas*, (Madrid: Renacimiento, 1912), I, p. 165.

[5] *Ibid.*, p. 110.

[6] *Ibid.*, p. 124.

[7] *Ibid.*, p. 169.

[8] *Ibid.*, p. 159.

[9] Juan Hurtado y Palencia, *Historia de la literature española*, (Madrid: 1932), p. 957.

[10] *Ibid.*, p. 959.

[11] Salvador de Madariaga, *Semblanzas literarias contemporáneas* (Barcelona: Ediciones Cervantas, 1924), p. 71.

[12] Miguel Romera Navarro, *Historia de la literatura española*, (Boston: D. C. Heath, 1928), p. 585.

[13] *Ibid.*, p. 269.

[14] Segundo Serrano Poncela, *Introducción a la literatura española* (Caracas: Universidad Central de Venezuela, 1969), p. 271.

[15] *Ibid.*, p. 269.

[16] James Stamm, *A Short History of Spanish Literature* (Garden City, N. Y.: Doubleday, 1967), p. 158.

[17] Menéndez y Pelayo, p. 122.

[18] Angel del Río, *Historia de la literatura española* (New York: Holt, Rinehart & Winston: 1963), II, p. 207.

[19] Ricardo Gullón, *Galdós, novelista moderno* (Madrid: Editorial Gredos, 1966), p. 133.

[20] Francisco Ayala, "Sobre el realismo en literatura con referencia a Galdós," *La Torre*, num. 26, San Juan de Puerto Rico (abril-junio), 1959.

[21] *Ibid.*, p. 95.

[22] *Ibid.*, p. 99.

[23] *Ibid.*, p. 100.

[24] *Ibid.*, p. 101.

[25] *Ibid.*, p. 104.

[26] S. Bacarisse, "The Realism of Galdós: Some Reflections on Language and the Perception of Reality," *Bulletin of Hispanic Studies*, 42 (1965), p. 239.

[27]*Ibid.*, p. 240.
[28]*Ibid.*, p. 241.
[29]*Ibid.*, p. 248.
[30]Quoted by René Wellek, "The Concept of Realism in Literary Scholarship," in *Concepts of Criticism*, ed. Stephen G. Nichols, Jr. (New Haven and London: Yale University Press, 1963), p. 237.
[31]*Ibid.*, p. 237.
[32]Gustavo Correa. *Realidad, ficción y símbolo en las novelas* de *Pérez Galdós*, (Bogotá: Instituto Caro y Cuervo, 1967), p. 8.
[33]*Ibid*, p. 9.
[34]*Ibid.*, p. 19.
[35]*Ibid.*, p. 11.
[36]*Ibid.*, p. 143.

Chapter III

POINT OF VIEW

A Theoretical Basis

The basic tool of the novelist in the creation of his fictional world is language, the words themselves as they are used to make that world come alive, and to give it order and meaning. The German linguist Karl Bühler's traditional model of language established three functions of language: emotive, conative and referential, corresponding to the three basic elements of any linguistic situation: the speaker, the listener, and the thing spoken about.[1] The emotive function is focused on the speaker: language here aims to express the speaker's attitude toward what he is speaking about. The conative function of language focuses on the listener, and gramatically it is expressed by the vocative or imperative. The referential function focuses on the thing being spoken about: the context of the linguistic situation.

The Chilean critic Félix Martínez-Bonati, in his *Estructura de la obra literaria,* applies Bühler's model to the language of fiction. In his theory, the language of fiction, like the language of actual discourse, has three basic functions:[2] a mimetic or representational function when it creates an image of the world through narration of events ("representación puramente lingüística de las alteraciones de determinadas personas, situaciones y circunstancias en el curso del tiempo")[3] and through description ("representación de aspectos inalterados de las cosas permanentes, momentáneas o recurrentes, o de hechos sin mayor duración")[4]; an expressive or interpretive function when it reveals the character of the speaker (narrator); and a dramatic function when it incites the listener to action; or in fiction, when it advances the action of the novel. The fictional narrative ideally consists of 1) the words of the narrator as conveyor of the fictional world: those purely mimetic passages which serve as the basis for the reader's conception of the novelistic world; 2) the words of the characters, which may have any of the functions just described; and 3) the words of the narrator as interpreter of the novelistic world: that is, passages in which the narrator reveals his own character by commenting on and interpreting the actions of the other inhabitants of the novelistic world.

In Martínez-Bonati's theory, the referential function of the language of actual discourse becomes the mimetic function of the language of fiction; the emotive function of actual discourse, the expressive function of fictional language; and the conative function of actual discourse becomes the dramatic function of fictional language.

Martínez-Bonati believes that mimetic or representational passages constitute the bulk of the modern novel, and qualitatively represent the core of novelistic reality. They are the basis for the reader's knowledge of that reality. He theorizes that, in mimetic discourse, the reader turns his attention toward the world whose particular dimensions the mimetic sentences narrate or describe, and becomes unaware of the language itself as language. Mimetic language is as if transparent and does not come between the reader and the things it speaks of. In other words, the language becomes the world. The word becomes the thing.

Martínez-Bonati's theory implies that there is something unique about mimetic language, characteristics which enable us to identify and label it clearly. From the example he gives,[5] we may infer that he conceives of mimetic language as extraordinarily concrete, words whose referents are individual, concrete, objective phenomena. It avoids conceptualization, abstraction or interpretation. It tends to appeal more directly to the senses, allowing immediate, unmediated perception of the world. Psychologically, Martínez-Bonati's theory implies that mimetic language allows the reader direct access to the world, uninhibited by an awareness of the perceiving consciousness which organizes, conceptualizes, abstracts, or interprets. Unaware of the perceiving consciousness of the narrator, the reader himself perceives that world as independent of the perceiving consciousness. Narrator and reader together (as one consciousness) perceive the world as independent of both of them. To say that the mimetic language of fiction does not come between the reader and the world it speaks of is to say that, in mimetic discourse, the narrator doesn't come between the reader and the world of the novel.[6] The reader's attention is turned toward the world itself and away from the narrator. Unaware of the personality of the narrator as an entity distinct from himself, the reader's distance from the narrator is nil.

According to Martínez-Bonati's theory, then, the mimetic passages thus make up the basic stratum of the novelistic world, the *sine qua non* of its existence. The non-representational passages in the novel (the narrator's comments and observations, the dialogues and monologues of the other characters) are meaningful only in relation to the world created by the narrator's mimesis and now independent of him. The non-representational passages which, according to Martínez-

Bonati's theory, draw the reader's attention away from the world and toward the speaker (be he character or narrator) are possible only in the context of the basic mimetic plane ("plano mimético"). The psychological implication is that perceiving consciousness only operates in the presence of a stimulus, something outside of itself to be perceived. The mimetic passages create a reality whose image is mirrored in the mind of the narrator, there to be given meaning and form.

Martínez-Bonati's theory implies that non-mimetic language, as well, has certain unique characteristics which allow us to identify and label it easily. His example suggests that while mimetic language is concrete, particular and objective (has as its referent something outside of the speaker), non-mimetic language is more abstract, general and subjective (has as its object something within the speaker). Language as it is used to reason, to generalize, to analyze and interpret reveals as much or more about the speaker as it does about the world, as much or more about the perceiving consciousness as about the reality perceived. It refers only indirectly to the external world. These expressive or interpretive passages soon make the reader explicitly aware of an intelligence other than his own, one seeking to interpret, to give meaning and order to the novelistic world. He is made aware of the point from which reality is viewed (the consciousness which perceives reality), whereas in mimetic passages he is aware of a reality seemingly independent of point of view.

Martínez-Bonati's theory implies that most passages in a novel can be clearly identified and labeled according to their linguistic function: a given sentence, accordingly, is either mimetic or non-mimetic. It refers the reader either to the world it represents or to the character it expresses. Yet an examination of any actual text from Galdós' novels reveals the inadequacy of Martínez-Bonati's theory to describe a very complex phenomenon.

More contemporary linguists like Roman Jakobson have revised Bühler's model, expanding the number of linguistic functions from three to six. Jakobson adds to the model of the communication situation three important elements:[7] the message itself, the code used to convey that message, and the element of contact essential to assure the message's transmission. He observes three additional corresponding functions of language: a phatic function, in which language merely serves to establish contact; a metalingual function in which language is used to talk about language itself (the code); and a poetic function, in which the focus is on the message for its own sake.

Clearly the most important of these additional functions in analyzing the language of fiction is the poetic function. In fiction, an art form, the dominant function of language is, of course, poetic. The theories of the Russian formalist Victor Schlovsky shed some light on the exact nature of the poetic function of language. According to Schlovsky,[8] the purpose of art is to force us to notice, to make us newly aware of the world around us, to see it for the first time. The artist, through language, "defamiliarizes" the object. Schlovsky explains that defamiliarization is not so much a device as a result obtainable by any number of poetic devices. These poetic devices (language in its poetic function, in Jakobson's terms) focus our attention on the message itself. As language focuses our attention on that message, the reality it conveys is revealed to us in a new unfamiliar light.

Although the poetic function dominates the language of fiction, it is of course not the only one present. As Jakobson says, "Although we distinguish six basic aspects of language, we could, however, hardly find verbal messages that would fulfill only one function. The diversity lies not in a monopoly of some one of these several functions but in a different hierarchical order of functions. The verbal structure of a message depends primarily on the predominant function."[9]

The following passage from *La desheredada* exhibits clearly the kind of multiple linguistic function typical of the language of Galdós' fiction. The passage is from the opening chapter of the novel, and describes the manner of speaking of Tomás Rufete, Isidora's poor, mad father:[10]

> El que de tal modo habla—si merece nombre de lenguaje esta expresión atropellada y difusa, en la cual los retazos de oraciones corresponden al espantoso fraccionamiento de ideas—es uno de esos hombres que han llegado a perder la normalidad de la fisonomía, y con ella, la inscripción aproximada de la edad.
>
> ¿Hállase en el punto de la vida, o en miserable decrepitud? La movilidad de sus facciones y el llamear de sus ojos, ¿anuncian exaltado ingenio, o desconsoladora imbecilidad? No es fácil decirlo, ni el espectador, oyéndole y viéndole, sabe decidirse entre la compasión y la risa. Tiene la cabeza casi totalmente exhausta de pelo, la barba escasa, entrecana y afeitada a trozos, como un prado a medio segar. El labio superior, demasiado largo y colgante, parece haber crecido y ablandádose recientemente, y no cesa de agitarse con ner-

viosos temblores, que dan a su boca cierta semejanza con el hocico gracioso del conejo royendo berzas. Es pálido su rostro, la piel papirácea, las piernas flacas, la estatura corta, ligeramente corva la espalda. Su voz sonora regalaría el oído si su palabra no fuera un compendio de todas las maneras posibles de reir, de todas las maneras posibles de increpar, de los tonos del enfático discurso y del plañidero sermón.

The first words of the passage make the reader aware of the presence of someone speaking in a way which the narrator finds difficult to explain or classify. The rest of the passage serves to make more vivid and precise Rufete's manner and appearance and the confusion of the narrator in trying to interpret it. Language in its mimetic function creates the image of a pale, thin, nearly bald man of mobile features and flashing eyes, with an over-hanging upper lip which trembles as he speaks. The man's poorly shaven face is compared to a half-mown meadow; his trembling upper lip to the funny face of a rabbit eating cabbage. Here the language is primarily mimetic (it describes a concrete, external reality), but it is also expressive in that it reveals the image of that reality in the mind of the narrator. The reader's attention is drawn simultaneously toward the external world and toward the consciousness which perceives the scene. The narrator describes Tomás Rufete as a man whose physical appearance is so abnormal as to make it impossible to determine his true age. He wonders whether Rufete is still in the prime of life or whether he is truly as ancient as he appears. The language here reveals the narrator's attempt to classify Rufete in terms of his (the narrator's) previous experience, which has shown that some men, because of their mental anguish or suffering, appear to be much older than they actually are. The narrator sees the mobile features of Rufete's face, yet does not know whether to interpret them as genius or madness. Here the language is primarily expressive of the narrator's attempt to classify and interpret, and only indirectly mimetic or representational (of Tomás Rufete). The narrator then expresses his own difficulty (as observer of the scene) in interpretation of this external reality ("no es fácil decirlo"), and even of his own emotional reaction to that reality ("no sabe decidirse entre la compasión y la risa"). Here the language is almost exclusively expressive of the narrator, referring only in the most indirect way to the world of the novel.

The multiplicity of linguistic function which characterizes the language of Galdós' novels thus establishes the interrelationship of external reality and perceiving consciousness which is the psychological basis of those novels. The interrelationship basic to these novels is, of course, that between the narrator and the world of the novel. The interrelationship of that external reality and the perceiving consciousness of the narrator provides the basic framework of the novel. Yet within that framework there exists a multiplicity of other relationships between external reality and perceiving consciousness: the characters' language exhibits the same functions as that of the narrator, and so there is repeated with each of the characters the relationship of reality and perceiving consciousness characteristic of the narrator. These relationships add new dimensions to the reality of the novel and infinitely complicate its basic structure.

This relationship between perceiving consciousness and external reality of the novel is what has been traditionally called point of view. The point from which the reader views the reality of the novel depends upon whose consciousness serves as the reflector of that reality, the figure through whose consciousness the reader perceives the world of the novel. To say that the relationship of perceiving consciousness to external reality is established linguistically is to say that point of view is determined linguistically. The point of view manifest at any given moment in the novel is determined by language itself.

Because in Galdós' novels the basic framework is determined by the relationship of the narrator to the novelistic world, and the relationship of the characters to the novelistic world is dependent upon that relationship, the question of point of view ultimately involves the relationship of the language of the narrator (as it determines his relationship to the world) to the language of the characters (as it determines their relationship to that world). But an examination of the nature of that relationship necessitates a prior examination of the means by which the narrator defines his own place in the novelistic scheme: an examination of how, once having created the illusion of a reality within the novel independent of him, he establishes his own presence (point of view) in the novel.

The Narrator: Creation of an Autonomous Reality

The illusion of an autonomous external reality is created by the language of the narrator in its mimetic or referential function. Any of the narrator's words which have even the slightest referential function contribute to the creation of that external reality, but the basis of the illusion are those passages whose function is predominantly mimetic. Mimetic language, as discussed above and in Martínez-Bonati's theory, is defined by its referents: particular objects or events; by its direction: the world outside the consciousness of the narrator; by its appeal: to the senses more than to the intellect; by its nominative function: the "naming" and thus the creation of reality rather than its understanding; by its effect: immediacy rather than mediation. The very nature of mimetic language (the kinds of words used) precludes the presence of the narrator. Mimetic language is language at its most perceptual and least conceptual, referring to the "perceived" and not the "perceiver."

The characteristics of the language of mimesis are very similar to those used by Friedman in his discussion of "scene" and "summary." Scene, of course, includes dialogues, but is not exclusively dialogue. It also includes those passages characterized by their "particularity." According to Friedman, "Scene emerges as soon as the specific, continuous and successive details of time, place, action, character and dialogue begin to appear."[11] Scenes are in fact those passages where the presence of the narrator is least evident. In Friedman's words, "The event itself rather than the attitude of the narrator dominates."[12] Because the language of the passage is mimetic, ("concrete detail in a specific time-space scheme is the *sine qua non* of scene")[13] it, in Martínez-Bonati's terms, refers the reader to the world outside and not to the narrator. The narrator's presence is not evident because the very nature of mimetic language precludes it. The "scene" appears independent of the point of view of the narrator simply because he is not present, he has "disappeared" linguistically.[14]

In Galdós' novels, these scenes of pure mimetic language, although they do not dominate the novel, provide the basis of the illusion of a reality independent of the narrator. They may be descriptions of the physical dimensions of the novelistic world (people and places), the narration of particular events or actions, or statements about particular emotional or psychological states. But they all directly evoke the world of the novel, making it immediately available to the reader.

In *La desheredada* there is a delightful passage in which the narrator describes Isidora and Miquis' excursion in the park:

> Luego se iban a otro sitio. Isidora, sentada junto a un tronco, se quedaba meditabunda, mirando por un hueco del ramaje las blancas masas de nubes que avanzaban sobre lo azul del cielo con soberana lentitud. Miquis cogía una rama seca, y

> acercándose cautelosamente por detrás de la joven, se la pasaba por la cara y decía con voz lúgubre: "¡La mano del muerto!" Isidora daba un chillido; después reían los dos, Miquis cantaba trozos de ópera, corrían un poco. . . .
> (IV, 988)

The narrator directs the reader's attention directly to the interaction between the two young people in the scene and their reactions to each other. Isidora and Miquis are both a part of the scene, and the reader's attention is drawn alternately to both. The scene is presented directly, independent of either character's or of the narrator's perception of it.

In *Miau* there is a description of the entrance to the house where Luis lives with his family:

> En el portal de la casa en que Cadalso habitaba había un memorialista. El biombo o bastidor forrado de papel, imitando jaspes de variadas vetas y colores, ocultaba el hueco del escritorio o agencia donde asuntos de tanta monta se despachaban de continuo. La multitud de ellos se declaraba en manuscrito papel que en la puerta de la casa colgaba. Tenía forma de índice, y decía de esta manera: . . . . (V, 552)

The passage evokes clearly the physical dimensions of the scene: the window covered with a screen of colored paper, hiding the desk where the amanuensis conducts his daily business, the humorous sign advertising the multiplicity of services offered. But Luis, who is the center of the narration at the moment, is absorbed in his own thoughts, and surely, having passed by there daily, takes no notice of the particularities of the scene. So the point of view is not his, nor is it the narrator's, for there is no linguistic evidence of his presence. The scene is simply there, created by the language of mimesis.

Passages like these which describe a reality apparently independent of any point of view are rare. Because "scene" is particular it is usually centered on one character, and the reality surrounding him may appear to be seen from his point of view. (The full implications of this will be examined later in the discussion of point of view of characters). But to the extent that the reality "belongs" to the character and his world, it appears to be independent of the narrator.

Examples are legion. They appear on almost every page of every novel. Often mimetic passages, either descriptive or narrative, are not extensive, but they appear consistently throughout the novels, constantly referring the reader to the world of those novels. From *Fortunata y Jacinta*:

> "Los partícipes iban llegando a la casa . . ." (V, 126)
> "Un noche que hacía mucho frío entró el Delfín en casa muy tarde . . ." (V, 157)
> "Maximiliano la sujetó por el vestido y la obligó a sentarse . . ." (V, 201)
> "Miraba el hueso de dátil que se acaba ba de comer . . ." (V, 276)
> "Doña Lupe la invitó dos días después de la tarde del choque con Jacinta a volver a visitar a Mauricia." (V, 371)

From *La desheredada*:

> "Doña Laura se levantó, y las niñas dejaron la costura. La criada tomó el dinero de la compra. Isidora desapareció . . ." (IV, 1017)
> "Las niñas de Pez apenas se fijaban en la muchacha que entraba . . ." (IV, 1039)
> "Isidora y el escribano entraban en un vestíbulo nada espacioso." (IV, 1128)

From *Miau*:

> "Doña Pura durmió, al fin, profundamente toda la madrugada y parte de la mañana. Villaamil se levantó a las ocho sin haber pegado los ojos . . . Cuando salió de su alcoba, entre ocho y nueve, después de haberse refregado el hocico con un poco de agua fría y de pasarse el peine por la rala cabellera, nadie se había levantado aún." (V, 566)
> "Luisito salió a paseo aquella tarde con Paca, y al volver se puso a estudiar en la mesa del comedor." (V, 663)
> "Vagaba por aquellos andurriales, sombrero en manos, recibiendo en el cráneo los rayos del sol." (V, 679)

If the illusion of a reality independent of the narrator is created by the narrator's language in its referential function, that illusion is sustained, indeed, is made flesh, in the linguistic presence of the characters of the novel. The words of the characters confirm their autonomous existence. Characters act, speak and perceive the world independently of the narrator. The world of the novel is just as much theirs as it is the narrator's. The fact that in most of Galdós' novels the narrator appears, if only marginally, as a character in the novel on equal footing with the others, makes the narrator also a part of that world, rather than vice versa. The appearance of a character like doña Cándida in *La de Bringas,* who guides the narrator (physically and linguistically) through the world of the novel, momentarily personifying the narrator's role, clearly indicates the independent status of that world. In fact, in much of the language of Galdós' novels, the narrator (and his explicit point of view), seem to have disappeared. Many scenes consist almost entirely of dialogue, or are couched in language which is either purely mimetic, or expressive of one of the characters. To the extent that the narrator disappears linguistically (i.e. to the extent that language is expressive of others and not of the narrator) the illusion of the autonomy of novelistic reality is maintained.

Selection and Summary

Anyone familiar with Galdós' novels is aware, however, that they are not pure "scene," in the sense that some of Ernest Hemingway's short stories may be pure "scene." Galdós' novels, like most, are what Friedman calls "a judicious mixture of scene and summary." Friedman describes summary as "a generalized account or report of a series of events covering some extended period and a variety of scales."[15] It is here that the presence of the narrator, as one who organizes and gives form to that reality, becomes evident.

The presence of the narrator first becomes evident when his language becomes more general, more abstract, and less concrete and particular. The language may still be mimetic, in that it refers the reader to the world of the novel and does not reflect the narrator's character, but the reader is now aware of an intelligence other than his own in the process of organizing and giving form to that reality: relating present to past in giving the history of a character or his family; relating the particular to the general; presenting something as a customary or habitual practice rather than as a particular event; summarizing the nature of a relationship rather than showing or even narrating a particular event characteristic of that relationship. Note, for example, the description of the Christmas season in Madrid, from *La desheredada:*

Las confiterías y tiendas de comidas ofrecen en sus vitrinas una abundancia eructante y pesada, que por la vista, ataruga el estómago. No bastan las tiendas, y en esquinas y rincones se alzan montañas de mazapán, canteras de turrón, donde el hacha del alicantino corta y recorta, sin agotarlas nunca. Las pescaderías inundan de cuanto Dios crió en mares del Norte y del Sur. Sobre un fondo de esteras coloca Valencia sus naranjas, cidras y granadas rojas, llenas de apretados rubíes. En los barrios pobres, las instalaciones son igualmente abundantes. . . . (IV, 1042)

The passage evokes vividly the physical dimensions of the scene: crowded streets, restaurants and bars, store windows bursting with merchandise, vendors selling the delicacies of the season—oranges, marzipan, olives, fresh fish. Yet this is not a particular scene of a particular Christmas, but of any Christmas, written as a background to the narration of José Relimpio's efforts to provide his family a "traditional" Christmas at all cost. In contrast, note the scene in *Fortunata y Jacinta* (V, pp. 133-134) where, on Christmas eve, Jacinta and Guillermina carry el Pitusín, whom Jacinta believes to be Juan's son, to her sister's house. Here the scene is a particular one—the crowded streets and vendor's stands of a particular Christmas eve.

Typical of summary are those histories of upper middle-class families of Madrid in the first book of *Fortunata y Jacinta,* the narrator's sketchy account of what happened to Isidora in the time intervening between the first and second part of *La desheredada,* the narrator's account of the past life of Villaamil and his family in *Miau.* In contrast, see the account of his past as Villaamil remembered it. (V, pp. 562-563)

In *Miau* there is a passage which describes what the three "Miaus" would do the evening they did not go to the theater. The narrator describes the play the *tertuliantes* were presenting, the *tertuliantes* themselves, and their roles. But we do not see them as they rehearse their roles, as they present the play. The narrator only tells us what they usually did. The language is mimetic; it refers to the world outside the narrator, but its referents have been placed in the realm of the general, taken out of the context of the particular, perceptible situation.

Contrast the passage from the same novel where the three "Miaus" have gone to the theater on a particular evening. It is an event that the reader experiences directly, as does Abelarda, as a particular experience, and not as a customary one:

> Todo se redujo a ir a delantera de paraíso una noche que dieron La Africana, y al punto de sentarse las tres cundió por la concurrencia de aquellas alturas el comentario propio de tan desusado acontecimiento: "¡Las Miaus en delantera!" ... Desde su delantera, las Miaus saludaron con sonrisas a los amigos que en la banda de la derecha y en el centro tenían, y de una y otra parte las asaetearon con miradas y frasecitas ...
>
> Abelarda ... fijó su atención en la concurrencia, recorriendo con su ansiosa mirada palcos y butacas, reparando en todas las señoras que entraban por la calle del centro con lujosos abrigos, arrastrando la cola e introduciéndose después con todo aquel falderío por las filas ya ocupadas. ... (V, 631)

When mimetic language is used in the presence of its referent in a concrete situation in time and space, the result is immediate perception, with little hint of the presence of the perceiving consciousness. On the contrary, when mimetic language is used in the absence of its referent, that is, when its referent is taken out of the context of a particular, concrete, perceptible situation in the novel, the result is mediation: the reader is first made aware of a consciousness other than his own organizing and giving form to that reality. Note the difference, for example, between those passages which describe a character in the context of a particular, perceptible situation and those which describe a character in his absence: those long, organized summary definitions of a character. In the former, the reader receives the information about the character in a rather haphazard fashion as he himself perceives the scene directly. In the latter, he receives what in fact may be the same information, but in the context of an ordered presentation.

Examine the difference between a scene where mimetic language is used to describe a character in the context of a particular situation and one where it is used to describe a character in the context of summary: The reader (and Juanito Santa Cruz) first catches a glimpse of Fortunata as Santa Cruz ascends the stairway to visit Estupiñá. A tall, beautiful young woman with a bright blue kerchief on her head stands in a doorway, eating a raw egg (V, 41). We see her again, at the beginning of the second book of the novel, having returned to Madrid and begun her "honorable" life. The narrator is describing, in summary fashion, Fortunata's new relationship with Maxi. (V, 179) Maxi would attempt to teach her the proper ways of speaking and acting, and would sit for hours fascinated as Fortunata worked about the house, washing, cleaning and ironing. The language is largely mimetic, evoking a picture of a strong healthy young woman, totally unashamed of her natural beauty, walking about the house half-dressed as she goes about her household chores. The language here is no less vivid nor are the referents less specific than in the first example. Yet clearly, the narrator is present here in describing a customary scene as he was not present before, in narrating a particular one.

In *Miau* we find good examples of how the effect of mimetic language changes according to context, even from one paragraph to the next. In the opening scene of the novel the narrator describes a noisy crowd of children leaving school and among them the smallest boy, who appears to be the brunt of their jokes. (V, 551) Then in the following paragraph, the words "bastante mezquino de talla" again evoke the presence of the small boy, but now he is seen in the context of the narrator's generalizations about the frequency of such scenes. The narrator's presence is here evident in his efforts to identify "el pobre chico de este modo burlado," to generalize, to relate present to past: "Siempre fue el más arrojado . . ."

On the following page we find a sentence describing Mendizábal's wife: "acercóse el muchacho, y una mujerona muy grandona echó los brazos fuera del biombo para cogerle en ellos y acariciarle." (V, 552) The language simply evokes the picture of a big, fat, kind woman who is extraordinarily fond of Luis. Then, two paragraphs later, we read the narrator's words: "La señora de Mendizábal era de tal corpulencia . . ." The referent is the same, but the language is more abstract, and even before the narrator goes on to describe the image of Mendizábal's wife in his mind, and to explain her affection for Luis, his presence is evident.

In an earlier novel like *La desheredada,* most characters are introduced by those long summary definitions which clearly evidence the narrator's presence. Cases in point are the near chapter-length introduction to Juan Bou, the introduction to José Relimpio and his family, and the description of the innumerable "peces." Much of the language in these passages is mimetic, but because it is used in the course of an ordered exposition, it reveals, if only minimally, the presence of the narrator as an organizing intelligence. In contrast, and rather an exception in *La desheredada,* we find that a character like Sánchez Botín appears only fleetingly at first, as Isidora catches a glimpse of him in the interlude in the church. The narrator never offers a summary definition of Sánchez Botín's character or appearance. The nearest thing to such a summary emerges in the course of Isidora's conversation with Joaquín Pez.

The Narrator: Language as Image

The narrator's presence is also made evident throughout Galdós' novels to the extent that language is used as image or metaphor. Here language is still mimetic, in that its referent is a concrete object or phenomenon of the novelistic world outside of the narrator, but it is also expressive in that it reveals the image which that reality reflects in the narrator's mind. (The primary function of such language is, of course, poetic or "revelatory" in Schlovsky's terms, in that it "reveals" or "defamiliarizes" the object or phenomenon described. But considering the question of point of view, it is important to point out its expressive function in revealing the presence of the narrator.) In other words, language used as image has a dual function, and refers the reader simultaneously to the world of the novel and to the consciousness which perceives that world.

The image may be merely a passing one, as in the passage from *La desheredada* cited above, where Tomás Rufete's beard appears to be a half-mown meadow; as in the opening passage of *Miau,* where children let out of school are seen as birds escaping from a cage; as in the scene from *Fortunata y Jacinta* in which Maxi appears as a poor, thin bird which has had nothing to eat:

> Maximiliano se desnudaba para acostarse. Al quitarse el chaleco, salían de las bocamangas los hombros, como alones de un ave flaca que no tiene nada que comer. Luego los pantalones echaron de sí aquellas piernas como bastones que se desenfundan. (V, 387)

More frequently the image is an extended one, dominating a whole scene, a whole chapter, or even a whole novel. The best known example is that famous scene from *El amigo Manso* in which Máximo Manso goes to find a wet-nurse for his nephew. The central image is the animal-like nature of the women who work as wet-nurses. Their prospective employers examine them as prospective buyers would examine a milch cow or a horse, comparing the size of their udders and the condition of their teeth. In *La desheredada* the narrator describes a fight between street gangs as a battle which foreshadows more civil war in Spain. The gangs are "armies," each with its own "general," playing at civil war:

> Era una página de la historia contemporánea, puesta en aleluyas en un olvidado rincón de la capital. Fueron los niños hombres y las calles provincias, y la aleluya habría sido una página seria, demasiado seria. Y era digno de verse como se coordinaba poco a poco el menudo ejército; como, sin prodigar órdenes, se formaban columnas; como se eliminaban a las hembras ... (IV, 1001)

We see the boys marching to the music of their own loud laughter and raucous shouting, arming themselves with brooms and sticks. Their leader, el *Majito,* dreams of being General Prim. In *Fortunata y Jacinta* the nuns in the convent where Fortunata goes to be "reformed" appear as the tamers of wild beasts. The nuns work to bring back into society those who have broken its rules. Mauricia's outbursts give her the appearance of an enraged animal: "A Mauricia le temblaba la quijada, y sus ojos tomaban esa opacidad siniestra de los ojos de los gatos cuando van a atacar." (V, 237) But the nuns have long dealt with such creatures: "Habían domado fieras tan espantables, que ya las injurias no les hacían efecto." (V, 237) The women are subjected to a harsh regiment of physical labor and deprivation of pleasures which will make them once again socially adaptable, as animals are made to obey the commands of the tamer, and deprived of pleasure and punished if they do not obey.

Miau provides examples of images which extend throughout the novel. The cat-like appearance of the three women, Pura, Milagros and Abelarda, is associated with Villaamil as well. He is seen as "el tigre inválido," a noble animal now weakened by endless battles, imprisoned by an absurd world and domesticated by the women around him. The feline nature of Villaamil and his family is most evident in the passages describing their physical appearance, but is also found throughout the novel in the descriptions of their actions. Note the narrator's description of Villaamil's appearance:

> Era un hombre alto y seco; los ojos grandes y terroríficos; la piel, amarilla, toda ella surcada por pliegues enormes, en los cuales las rayas de sombra parecían manchas; las orejas, trans-

> parentes, largas y pegadas al cráneo; la barba, corta, rala y cerdosa, con las canas distribuidas caprichosamente, formando ráfagas blancas entre los negros; el cráneo, liso y de color de hueso desenterrado como si acabara de recogerlo de un osario para taparse con él los sesos. La robustez de la mandíbula, el grandor de la boca, la combinación de los tres colores: negro, blanco y amarillo, dispuestos en rayas; la ferocidad de los ojos negros, inducían a comparar tal cara con la de un tigre viejo y tísico que después de haberse lucido en las exhibiciones ambulantes de fieras, no conserva ya de su antigua belleza más que la pintorreada piel. (V, 554)

Later, the narrator describes Pura's action in accepting money from Victor as that of a cat grabbing its prey: ". . . echando la zarpa al billete como si éste fuera un ratón." (V, 585) Villaamil's restless pacing of the house is that of a caged beast.

The narrator of *Miau* presents Victor's malicious and diabolical dishonesty in his relationship with Abelarda in the image of Victor as the actor. Soon after Victor appears, the narrator identifies his basic dishonesty: "A ratos se ponía ceñudo y receloso, pero a la manera de un actor que recobra su papel. . . ." (V, 580) Relating the history of Victor's relationship with the family, he recounts how Victor first became involved with them in a small provincial town, and describes Victor as "un artista social digno de teatro mayor." (V, 589) The narrator continues to make evident Victor's image as an actor in a play of his own invention. The dialogues in which Victor perpetrates his cruel deception of Abelarda are interspersed with comments like: "variando de registro," "afectando una confusión bonita y muy al caso," "Lo dijo con tal acento de verdad que Abelarda lo creyó. . . ." (V, 597) He describes how Victor maintains his deception: "Pero al instante compuso la fisonomía, que para cada situación tenía una hermosa máscara en el variado repertorio de su histrionismo moral. . . ." (V, 646)

In *La desheredada,* the narrator describes Juan Bou's formidable physique and ferocious appearance in the image of a bear. He first creates the reality which is the basis of the image:

> Juan Bou era un barcelonés duro y atlético, de más de cuarenta años, dotado de esa avidez de trabajar y de esa potenta iniciativa que distinguen al pueblo catalán; saludable como un toro, según su propia expresión; de humor festivo y

palabra trabajosa. Su cara, enfundada en copiosa barba negra y revuelta, mostraba por entre tanto áspero pelo dos ojos desiguales; el uno vivísimo, dotado de un ligero movimiento rotatorio; el otro, fijo y sin brillo; más abajo y puesta como al acaso, una nariz ciclópea; más arriba, una frente lobulosa que estaba pidiendo algunos golpes de escoplo para ser como las demás frentes humanas . . . Respiraba como el fuelle de una fragua, y siempre tenía tos; pero una tos tan bronca y sofocante, que cuando le daba el acceso, se quedaba mi hombre cabeceando y todo encendido . . . (IV, 1078)

A few pages later we find the narrator again using the image of Juan Bou as a clumsy bear as the central image of a whole chapter. Juan Bou has fallen in love with Isidora, and his love and the openness and generosity of his heart lead him to offer to marry Isidora, to give her a solid, respectable economically sound, stable way of life. His offer takes place in the course of a visit the two make to the palace of the Aransis family, the very family in which Isidora's claims to nobility rest. To Isidora the palace is her "patria perdida" (IV, 1103), a place sacred to her ideals. But to Juan Bou, "el obrero-sol," the outspoken champion of the rights of the people, the working class, the palace represents only the blood and sweat of the people who suffered and labored all their lives, only to see the fruits of their labor taken away from them by people like the Aransis, the "sanguijuelas del pueblo." Juan Bou is unaware of the effects of his words, and that his generous offer of marriage represents to Isidora, at that moment, the profanation of all her ideals. As the narrator explains, "Las galanterías de Bou con Isidora semejaban a las del oso que quiso mostrar el cariño a su amo matándole una mosca sobre la frente." (IV, 1103) So the central image, and the title, of the chapter is "la caricia del oso." The narrator emphasizes Juan Bou's bear-like qualities, his heaviness, clumsiness, and heavy breathing. Isidora is horrified by "el bestial lenjuaje de su amigo;" Juan Bou is unaware of the effect of his words: "tan inocente del efecto que producían sus ladridos." (IV, 1105)

So in all these examples we see how the central image (Victor as an actor, Juan Bou as a bear, the Miaus as cats) is manifested linguistically throughout the work in words which keep the central image alive.

The narrator's presence is even more evident in his use of epithets. Epithets offer a clear example of the multiple function of language:

they are both representational and interpretive, drawing the reader simultaneously toward the world of the novel and toward the consciousness which perceives that world. (Epithets too, like images and metaphors, have a poetic function which serves to "reveal" or "defamiliarize" the person described.) Epithets name reality; they evoke its presence. At the same time, epithets interpret reality; they offer in a single phrase a synthesis of that reality reflected in the narrator's mind. They may reflect the character's physical appearance, but more often the language is more abstract, and so the epithet serves to synthesize the character's personality or the role he plays in the novel. Sometimes the epithet seems to reflect solely the narrator's point of view, as when he calls the scribe Canencia "el bebedor de aire;" José Relimpio, "un ramillete de confitería" or "el libertino platónico." Epithets which reflect only the narrator's point of view are often literary, historical or artistic allusions, used ironically: Mauricia is seen as Napoleón, José Izquierdo as Plato, Estupiñá as Polichinela or "el gran Rossini;" Doctor Quevedo and his wife as Othello and Desdemona; Villaamil and his fellow bureaucrat wandering through government offices as Dante and Virgil wandering through hell. More often the epithet reflects the point of view of society as a whole, adopted momentarily by the narrator: doña Lupe as "la de los Pavos;" Mauricia as "la dura;" Maxi as "el sietemesino;" Gullermina as "la fundadora" or "la rata ecesiástica;" Juanito Santa Cruz as "el Delfín;" José Ido as "el hombre eléctrico;" Villaamil's wife and sister-in-law as "los Miaus;" Milagros as "la pudorosa Ofelia;" Pura as "la figura arrancada a un cuadro de Fra Angélico"; Mariano as "Pecado;" Villaamil himself as "Ramses II."

Complex characters may be referred to by several epithets in the course of the novel.[16] The particular epithet used by the narrator at any given moment reflects the role the character is playing at that point in the novel. In *Fortunata y Jacinta,* Maxi, in his moments of weakness, is "el sietemesino;" at the height of his ability to "reason," he becomes "el iluminado." Fortunata, in the context of her relationship with Juan, is "la Pitusa;" in the context of her redemption in las Micaelas, she becomes "la pecadora." Abelarda, in her relationship with Victor in *Miau,* is "la insignificante."

The Language of Irony

The presence of the narrator is no less evident in the tone that dominates the narrative at any given moment. Anyone familiar with Galdós' novels (indeed, with any typical realistic novel) is aware that the dominant tone of these novels is clearly that of irony. The distinctively ironic tone of Galdós' *novelas contemporáneas* is primarily the result of verbal irony, which as Nimetz says,[17] "may be compared to a glaze whose sheen keeps the reader at a distance from the surface details so as to give him an unobstructed view of the entire panorama." As Kayser explained in his definitive "Origen y crisis de la novela moderna,"[18] the modern novelist has learned that language and appearance may lie, as well as tell the truth; so he often consciously uses language ironically (in a kind of mirror effect) to reveal the truth behind the illusion.

The nature and function of irony in Galdós' novels is indeed complex, as revealed in Nimetz' excellent study, for irony extends beyond language to character, theme and structure. But as Nimetz correctly points out, its basis is verbal. Verbal irony may be found in dialogues and monologues: "More often, though, it is the peculiar nuance which the narrator gives to people and events he describes."[19] In other words, verbal irony is controlled by the narrator. Or, put another way, verbal irony effectively if sometimes subtly expresses the narrator's point of view. Language in these passages is not solely referential, but is also expressive (of the narrator's point of view) and poetic (revealing, or defamiliarizing reality).

Nimetz established four different kinds of verbal irony:[20] denotative irony, connotative irony, irony of tone, and irony of reference. Denotative irony results from an author's use of a word to describe its exact opposite. He cites the example from *La de Bringas* in which the narrator calls Bringas' cenotaph "esta bella obra de arte"[21] when it is perfectly clear from the preceding description that the work in question is not beautiful at all, but a morbid monstrosity. The early novel *Doña Perfecta* is full of this kind of denotative irony: the protagonist doña Perfecta is anything but perfect; the priest and doña Perfecta's mentor don Inocencio, anything but innocent; Orbajosa (*urbs augusta*), the small town, is anything but an august city. In *Miau*, the narrator's insistent use of the adjective "ínclito" to describe Abelarda's official suitor Ponce, only reinforces the disdain the reader and the other characters feel for him.

The more subtle connotative irony results when "the literal meaning of a word is maintained but is qualified by contextual overtones. Here the reader must be aware of the tone of the work as a whole in order to catch the ambiguity of a specific word in context."[22] Nimetz cites as an example a passage from *Torquemada en la hoguera* in which José Bailón, who lives with a very rich widow and also keeps a herd of milch burras, is described as leading a very "biblical" life. "Biblical" accurately describes his pastoral life, but the use of the word referring to his life with the widow is clearly ironic.

Irony of tone results, rather, from "phraseology, punctuation and word order,"[23] or often from parenthetical tongue-in-cheek remarks on the part of the narrator.

But the most extensive kind of verbal irony found in these novels is "irony of reference," which Nimetz defines as "an outrageously inappropriate comparison, either explicit or implicit, of one subject with another, and its aim is to give the original subject an air of dignity, method, reason or importance which does not belong to it and thereby emphasize its lack of the quality suggested."[24] A classic example cited by Nimetz is the description in *Miau* of a fight among school-boys as "una lucha homérica" (V, 575) when the epic sounding word "homérica" is used to describe what is in reality a very trivial thing. Nimetz also analyzes in detail a scene from *Tormento* in which Bringas' and Rosalías's installing themselves in a new apartment is described as an heroic action. Bringas, on all fours, covered with dust and ridiculously attired is called a "dignísimo personaje" whose "persona respetabilísima" is engaged in "funciones augustas." At one point in the scene Bringas is absurdly compared to Napoleón, which only "underlines the unheroic, mediocre nature of Bringas and his activities."[25]

Nimetz points out the very thin line of difference between referential irony and a technique he chooses to call "metaphor." In fact, the former is often a function of the latter. In these cases, both involve the sort of absurd and outrageous comparisons previously described. Both involve the process of inflation and subsequent deflation characteristic of what Harry Levin called the "romantic realism" of the nineteenth-century novel. Levin sees realism as a synthesis: "the imposition of reality upon romance, the transposition of reality into romance,"[26] for although the realistic novel was born in opposition to the so-called novel of fantasy, it (in Ortega's terms) "carries adventure enclosed within its body."[27] So however gray and monochromatic and ordinary the world of the novel, the characters who inhabit that world still carry with them in their illusions the legacy of the world of romance. A realist like Galdós uses the technique Nimetz calls "metaphor" to reveal the often pathetic nature of his characters' illusions and the often unbridgeable gap between their illusions and reality.

Nowhere is the ironic function of metaphor and the technique of inflation-deflation more obvious than in the narrator's use of epithets to describe the other characters of the novel. The narrator uses epithets which allude to historical, literary or biblical figures with clearly ironic intent. The narrow-minded bureaucrat Bringas is the eminent French historian Thiers, or Napoleón himself; Rosalía Bringas is Josephine Bonaparte. In *La desheredada,* Isidora Rufete, imprisoned for falsifying papers, is Marie Antoinette imprisoned by the aristocracy. In *Miau,* the would-be opera singer Milagros becomes "la pudorosa Ofelia;" her sister Pura, "una figura arrancada de un cuadro de Fra Angélico." In *Fortunata y Jacinta,* Juan, the one and only heir to the bourgeois Santa Cruz family, is el *Delfín*; his wife Jacinta la *Delfina*; Estupiñá, the family jester and historian, is Rossini; the would-be revolutionary philosopher José Izquierdo is Plato; the jealous old doctor Quevedo and his obese wife are Othello and Desdemona; poor Villaamil, now a specter of spiritual death haunting café *tertulias,* is Ramses II.

Nowhere is the ironic use of metaphor clearer than in *Lo prohibido,* the memoirs of the cynical aristocrat José María Bueno de Guzmán. In fact, in this novel, the process of inflation-deflation characteristic of romantic realism is the essence of the novel, thematically and structurally. The narrator consciously adopts an ironic stance in order to "deflate" those around him, to reveal their illusions for what they are: pitiful, pathetic imitations of the ideal.

Much of the description of José María's relationship with his cousin Eloísa, for example, is couched in clearly ironic literary allusions. Eloísa appears to José María "una obra maestra;" but, of course, "obra maestra de carne mortal." (IV, 1682) When he helps Eloísa establish her salon, she is "la Musa del Buen Gusto." (IV, 1695) Eloísa's taste for luxury is represented as the temptation of Eve (IV, p. 1721). When Eloísa returns from the theater to find her husband dying she, in her feigned sorrow, appears to José María as "una elegante pastora del pequeño Trianón llorando ausencia de algún pastor de peluca." (IV, 1740) Eloísa's complicity in the death of her husband Carillo allows the narrator to compare her to Lady Macbeth. The ironic nature of his literary allusions extends to entire scenes, which become, in José María's own words "parodias grotescas" of famous scenes from literary tradition. The most obvious example is the love scene between Eloísa and José María, which is a parody of the balcony scene from *Romeo and Juliet.* (IV, 1750)

A similar effect is gained by the technique of ironic reprise,[28] when the irony of reference results from a comparison to something within, rather than outside of, the novel. A classic case in point is the description in *La desheredada* of the aristocratic Aransis family and their palace, followed by an ironic reprise of the same scene in the following chapter. The motif of the music of Beethoven played by the aristocratic marquess's talented grandson (a motif symbolic of the serious tone of the chapter's narration) is repeated in "Sigue Beethoven," where with good-natured buffoonery Miquis clumsily attempts to play the same romantic music, an appropriate accompaniment to the bourgeois Miquis' and the revolutionary Juan Bou's wandering through the old palace. Here, too, the motif of the music of Beethoven (played by a bourgeois clown) is symbolic of the ironic tone of the chapter.

The Language of Familiarity

If irony is the dominant tone of Galdós' novels, that ironic tone is always carefully balanced by a tone of familiarity. Galdós' irony is never cold, cruel or bitter; it is always tempered by the compassion Galdós felt for the creatures who inhabit his novelistic world. This tone of familiarity results primarily from the convention of the personal narrator characteristic of the modern novel—a narrator who is not the distant voice of authority but the voice of a fellow human being. The narrator establishes himself as a fellow resident of the novelistic world, and subsequently establishes his tone of familiarity through his language. The language of most of the narrators of the *novelas contemporáneas* differs little from the language of the other inhabitants of the novelistic world he is describing. This is especially true of those passages where a familiar tone is most evident (as opposed to the often stilted language of passages of documentary tone). The more familiar the tone, the more colloquial is the language (that is, the more the language approximates that of characters who might have witnessed the scene the narrator is describing.)

In his article "Vulgaridad y genio de Galdós," Antonio Sánchez-Barbudo describes in detail the nature and purpose of this kind of language (which many have attributed to Galdós' supposed "vulgaridad"). He cites as examples several passages from *Miau*. In the opening pages of *Miau,* the child Luis Cadalso returns home, and his grandmother opens the door for him. There follows a description of Pura:

> Abrióle la puerta una señora cuya cara podía dar motivo a controversias numismáticas, como la antigüedad de ciertas monedas que tienen borrada la inscripción, pues unas veces, mirada de perfil y a cierta luz, daban ganas de echarle los

sesenta, y otras el observador entendido se contenía en la apreciación de los cuarenta y ocho o los cincuenta, bien conservaditos. (V, 553)

Sánchez-Barbudo explains:

> El párrafo es expresivo, aunque bien pudiera irritar a algún purista eso de que una cara dé lugar a "controversias numismáticas"; o el tener gana de "echarle los sesenta" a alguién, o el contenerse "en la apreciación" de los cuarenta y ocho. Pero lo que a nosotros más nos interesa es el "bien conservaditos". No agrada esto mucho, en verdad, a la descripción de la cara de doña Pura, pero nos proporciona como un punto de vista, precisamente, de quienes la solían contemplar, y emplearían esa expresión; "bien conservaditos". Al usarla Galdós, nos hace sentir como si estuviéramos allí, entre quienes podían contemplarla en verdad, y eso contribuye a dar realidad a la escena, realidad a doña Pura y a su cara de edad imprecisa. Pero fijémonos por otro lado en la vulgaridad de ese mismo "bien conservaditos". Muy frecuentemente usa Galdós diminutivos de sabor coloquial al describir un personaje; y en gran parte debido a ellos, cuando imaginamos a quien él describe, parece que le vemos con los ojos y con el espíritu de alguna señora madrileña de la clase media.[29]

Later we find another passage where the description includes phrases which might be used by the same "señora madrileña." Here Galdós describes the Miaus' preoccupations with appearance, here manifest in their manner of dress:

> La capota de doña Pura había pasado por una serie de vidas diferentes, que al modo de las encarnaciones la hacían siempre nueva y siempre vieja. La martirizada armadura del sombrero de Abelarda había tomado ya, durante la época de la cesantía, formas y estilos diferentes, según las pragmáticas de la moda, y con este exquisito arte de disimular la indigencia, salían las Villaamil a la calle hechas unos brazos de mar. (V, 601)

Most of the description and the humor which results is the narrator's, but the expression "hechas unos brazos de mar" is rather that of some woman friend of the Miaus, although it is the narrator who is speaking. As Sánchez-Barbudo says: "Galdós, en suma, ve a esas mujeres, cuando las ve por fuera, como las vería cualquier Virginia Pantoja, y como todos, se burla un poco de ellas."[30]

The narrator also often uses the diminutive and the dative of interest to convey the same tone of familiarity and affection. Sánchez-Barbudo cites as an example a passage from the second part of *Fortunata y Jacinta,* when the narrator, describing how weak poor Maxi had always been, says "Como que había nacido de siete meses y luego *me* le criaron con biberón y con una cabra . . ." (V, 291) Here the "me" clearly indicates the affection and familiarity the narrator feels for Maxi.

Nimetz, too, attributes the tone of familiarity evident in the *novelas contemporáneas* to Galdós' "oral style." *Torquemada en la hoguera,* he states, is written with "a breezy informality."[31] Much of the narrative of these novels is liberally sprinkled with colloquial expressions taken from popular speech. Certainly these expressions aid in the creation of a familiar tone which, again, manifests the narrator's presence.

Interpretation

The language of those passages where the narrator interprets and analyzes the characters and their behavior and proceeds to generalize about the situations of the novel, is primarily expressive. It refers the reader first to the narrator, and only indirectly to the external world, although, because it is based on the concrete situations of the novel, it is never independent of that world. The narrator's interpretive commentary ranges from the most particular to the most general, from the perceptual to the conceptual, from the emotional to the aesthetic. As his commentary moves away from the particular context of the scene (the perceptual) to the general nature of things (the conceptual), the narrator's presence becomes increasingly evident.

The most particular of his comments are those which interpret the behavior of a certain character in a particular scene. For example, in *La desheredada,* the narrator explains Isidora's terror of the rope factory where her brother Mariano works: "Isidora lo sentía de esta manera, porque era muy nerviosa, y solía ver en las formas y movimientos objetivos acciones y estremecimientos de su propia persona . . ." (IV, 981). In *Miau,* the narrator explains Abelarda's confusion in the face of Victor's glibness and sophistication. Victor plays a cruel game of deception with Abelarda, pretending to love her, alternately encouraging or discouraging the girl's interest by declaring his love in phrases taken from bad romantic novels, and by withdrawing his love, declaring it impossible. Victor has just told Abelarda that, as fate would have it, he must suffer from unrequited love, for he "knows" that Abelarda loves another:

> Abelarda sintió tan viva aflicción al oír esto, que no pudo encubrirla. No tenía ella en su pobre caletre armas de razonamiento para combatir con aquel monstruo de infinitos recursos e ingenio inagotable, avezado a jugar con todos los sentimientos serios y profundos. (V, 609)

In *Fortunata y Jacinta* the narrator explains Fortunata's reaction to seeing Jacinta for the first time. Fortunata is undergoing her "reformation" in the convent of the Micaelas, and Jacinta, together with other women of the upper middle class, visits the convent on a charitable mission. The whole atmosphere encourages Fortunata's desire to be an "honorable" woman: "La impresión moral que recibió la samaritana era tan compleja, que ella misma no se daba cuenta de lo que sentía. Indudablemente, su natural rudo y apasionado la llevó en el primer momento a la envidia. Aquella mujer le había quitado lo suyo . . ." (V, 244) In *Miau,* the narrator explains Villaamil's desire to be left alone in the house:

> El buen Villaamil sintió gran alivio en su alma cuando las vió salir. Mejor que su familia le acompañaba su propia pena, y se entretenía y consolaba con ella mejor que con las palabras de su mujer, porque su pena, si le oprimía el corazón, no le arañaba la cara, y doña Pura, al cuestionar con él, era todo pico y uñas toda. (V, 562)

Sometimes the narrator's comments interpret a character's behavior during a period of time in the course of the novel, and not simply in a particular scene. In *Fortunata y Jacinta,* the narrator explains Fortunata's state of mind in the period when she lives under Feijóo's tutelage: "Fortunata, preciso es decirlo, no estaba contenta, ni aun medianamente. Hallábase más bien resignada y se consolaba con la idea de que dentro de la desgracia no había solución mejor que aquélla . . ." (V, 332) In the same novel, he explains the "restoration," Juanito's abandonment of Fortunata and return to Jacinta:

> El Delfín había entrado, desde los últimos días del 74, en aquel período sedante que seguía infaliblemente a sus desvaríos. En realidad, no era aquella virtud, sino cansancio del pecado, no era el sentimiento puro y regulador del orden, sino el hastío de la revolución . . ." (V, 311)

Sometimes his commentary serves to define the relationship between two characters, either as seen in a particular moment in the novel, or throughout the novel. In *Fortunata y Jacinta,* he explains Juanito's relationship with Jacinta:

> En honor de la verdad, se ha de decir que Santa Cruz amaba a su mujer. Ni aún en los días en que más viva estaba la marea de la infidelidad dejó de haber para Jacinta un hueco de preferencia en aquel corazón que tenía tantos rincones y callejuelas. Ni la variedad de aficiones y caprichos excluía un sentimiento inamovible hacia su compañera por la ley y la religión. Conociendo perfectamente su valor moral, admiraba en ella las virtudes que él no tenía y que según su criterio, tampoco le hacían mucha falta . . . Vicioso y discreto, sibarita y hombre de talento, aspirando a la erudición de todos los goces y con bastante buen gusto para espiritualizar las cosas materiales, no podía contenerse con gustar de la belleza comprada o conquistada, la gracia, el donaire, la extravagancia; quería gustar también la virtud, no precisamente la vencida, que deja de serlo, sino la pura, que en su pureza misma tenía para él su picante. (V, 84-85)

In *La desheredada,* the narrator explains don José's faithful service to Isidora:

> Don José era el que parecía menos feliz. Estaba triste, según decía, por la falta de ocupación. Castaño, que no necesitaba tenedurías, le empleó en llevar recados y cobrar cuentas; pero aunque el buen señor desempeñaba estos encargos con docilidad, bien se le conocía que su principal gusto era no hacer nada, contemplar a Isidora, pasear con ella y prestarle cuántos servicios hubiese menester. (IV, 1112)

In a step toward conceptualization, the narrator often comments on a character's behavior in a particular scene by relating it to what he knows of human behavior in general. In *Miau*, the narrator explains Luis' fascination with the stamp albums his father gave him as a present: "Luis estaba en la edad en que empieza a desarrollarse el sentido de la clasificación." (V, 607) In the same novel he explains Luis' intuitive understanding of the reasons for his grandfather's suffering. Luis, in his innocence, understands better than the adults the true nature of the situation. That morning Luis had overheard his grandmother saying that Villaamil had not been given a government position, and when he saw his grandfather's face he immediately understood his suffering:

> Estas palabras, impresas en la mente del chiquillo, las relacionó luego con la cara de adjusticiado del abuelo cuando entró a verle. Luis, como niño, asociaba las ideas imperfectamente, pero las asociaba poniendo siempre entre ellas afinidades extrañas sugeridas por su inocencia. Si no hubiera conocido a su abuelo como le conocía, le habría tenido miedo en aquella ocasión, porque en verdad su cara era cual la de los ogros que se zampan a las criaturas . . . "No le colocan", pensó Luisito, y al decirlo juntaba otras dos ideas en su mente, aun turbada por la mal extinguida calentura. La dialéctica infantil es a veces de una precisión aterradora, y lo prueba este razonamiento de Cadalsito: "Pues si no le quiere colocar, no sé por qué se enfada Dios conmigo y no me enseña la cara. Más bien debiera yo estar enfadado con Él."
> (V, 599)

In *La desheredada*, the narrator comments that Isidora's stopping to look in the store windows as she walks through the streets indicates her vain desire to look at her reflection in the glass panes, then goes on to explain that "es costumbre de las mujeres, y aún de los hombres, echarse una ojeada en las vitrinas para ver si van tan bien como suponen o pretenden." (IV, 987) In the same novel, he explains why Isidora could forgive Joaquín Pez for offending her honor, but not for having called her "cursilona:" "Tal es la condición humana, que a veces el rasguño hecho al amor propio le duele más que la puñalada asestada contra la honra." (IV, 1041) In *Fortunata y Jacinta*, the narrator explains Fortunata's sudden change of intentions. Fortunata had just been abandoned by Juanito and, in a fury of hurt and rage and disappointment, had impulsively run off to Santa Cruz' house to find Jacinta and vent all her pain and frustration on the one who she felt had taken away from her what was rightfully hers. She ran precipitously through the streets until she came face to face with the house and suddenly stopped, unsure of herself. As the narrator comments:

> Ver el portal fue para la prójima, como para el pájaro que ciego y disparado vuela, topar violentamente contra un muro. Los que obran bajo la acción de impulsos cerebrales irresistibles y mecánicos, como los instintos que atañen a la conservación, van muy bien en su carrera mientras no ven el fin más que en la representación falsa que de él les da su deseo; pero cuando la realidad de aquel fin se les pone delante, ofreciéndoseles como acción sometida a las leyes generales, no hay velocidad que no tenga su rechazo.
> (V, 324)

The narrator's presence is even more evident in those comments which appear the most independent of any particular context: for example, those comments about the characters, mostly in the form of summary definitions, which are not based on scene (on behavior just observed or about to be perceived by the narrator), and in those comments on history or social phenomena which, to many, may appear extraneous to the novel.

In the discussion of mimetic language it was pointed out that in the course of one of those summary definitions, such language takes on a different character. Mimetic language, no matter how vivid and concrete, reveals the presence of the narrator (perceiving consciousness) simply because it is used in the context of an ordered presentation. By the same token, expressive language in the context of an ordered presentation (taken out of the context of the particular) reveals the presence of the narrator (the perceiving consciousness and ordering intelligence) even more clearly than it does when used in the course of the narration and when it arises from a concrete situation in the novel. Examples of these summary definitions are legion: Juan Bou and José Relimpio in *La desheredada*; Maxi, doña Lupe, Guillermina in *Fortunata y Jacinta*. These long introductions consist of physical descriptions of the character, a biographical sketch of his past history, a compilation of other characters' opinions of the character, and the narrator's opinion of him. Note, for example, the narrator's description of Guillermina Pacheco in *Fortunata y Jacinta* (in the course of a long introduction):

> Tenía un carácter inflexible y un tesoro de dotes de mando y de facultades de organización que ya quisieran para sí algunos de los hombres que dirigen los destinos del mundo. Era mujer que cuando se proponía algo iba a su fin, derecha como una bala, con perseverancia grandiosa, sin torcerse nunca ni desmayar un momento, inflexible y serena. Si en este camino recto encontraba espinas, las pisaba y adelante, con los pies ensangrentados. (V, 76)

Another example is his description of José Relimpio in *La desheredada*: "Era el hombre mejor del mundo. Era un hombre que no servía para nada." (IV, 1014) Because they are not linked to any particular context (scene) in the novel, and are included in an ordered presentation, they appear only indirectly as the result of perception, more directly as the result of conception or abstraction. That is, they could be removed from the context of the novel and would still be meaningful, although of course they are even more meaningful in the context of the novel.

This is even more true of those passages in which the narrator comments on the social, historical or political situation which is the background of the novel. These passages are related to the novel in only a very indirect way, and could be read out of the context of the novel with little or no loss of meaning. These are the passages which the modern reader finds most objectionable, for he sees them somehow as an intrusion in the novel, unnecessary interruptions in the flow of the narrative. As an example, note how, in *La desheredada*, the narrator moves from a description of Tomás Rufete to a description (based on perception) of Leganés, to a discussion of society's treatment of the insane, and finally to a discussion of the nature of madness and sanity. In the same novel, he moves from a description of Mariano's character as a rebel and vagabond, to a discussion of the necessity for studying the reasons for such behavior. In *Fortunata y Jacinta*, he discusses the history of commerce in nineteenth-century Madrid, the nature of the relationship between social classes and the nature of Spanish democracy.

We have seen that as the narrator's commentary becomes more abstract and less dependent on the concrete situations of the novel, his presence becomes more and more evident. In other words, his presence becomes more evident as the language becomes less mimetic (loses its neutrality) and more expressive of the narrator. The nature of that presence, revealed in the sorts of commentary we have just described, is essentially intellectual. We are aware of the narrator as the consciousness which perceives the world of the novel, organizes and interprets it, that is, gives it form and meaning. But this commentary reveals little of the narrator as an individual, reacting personally and sometimes emotionally to the world of the novel. This personal reaction is implicit in some novels (in tone or style) but is rarely expressed explicitly. An exception is found in those passages in *La desheredada* in which the narrator pretends to speak directly to a particular character, as he explains the character's behavior to him and directly expresses his own opinion of that behavior and gives advice. The narrator addresses Isidora not as character but as narrator and suggests that perhaps he is the voice of her own conscience: "Voz de la conciencia de Isidora o interrogatorio indiscreto del autor, lo escrito vale." (IV, 1069) He advises Isidora to try to control her fantastic imagination, to abandon her pretense to nobility:

> Sostienes que ese vicio, aberración o como quiera llamarle Miquis, es una fuente de consuelos para tí. Ya, ya se conoce tu sistema. Después de un día de penas, apuros, celos y disputas, llega la noche, y para consolarte . . . das un baile. ¡qué gracioso! Safisfaces tu orgullo y tus apetitos determinando en tí una gran excitación cerebral, de la cual irradian sensaciones y goces. Sabes vestir con tal arte la mentira, que tú misma llegas a tenerla por verdad . . . Enseñas a tus nervios a falsificar las sensaciones y a obrar por sí mismos, no como receptores de la impresión, sino como iniciadores de ella. ¡Bonito juego! ¡Violación de los órganos de la Naturaleza! . . .
> (IV, 1068)

Later in the same novel, the narrator directs himself to José Relimpio in language which clearly expresses his own personal emotional reaction. When Isidora finds her second "benefactor" Sánchez Botín, don José is politely but firmly dismissed from further serving her. The narrator exclaims:

> ¡Pobrecito don José! Ahora sí que eres el más infeliz de los hombres. No sólo te han quitado tus venerandos libros, sino que te han puesto de patitas en la calle con orden expresa de no volver a presentarte en la casa de tu ahijada. ¡Crueldad sin ejemplo! Hay hombres que parecen fieras . . . José, eres un mártir.
> (IV, 1077)

Finally, there are those expressive passages in which the narrator comments upon himself as narrator and the problems he encounters and those passages in which he directly addresses the reader. Both serve to remind the reader of the fictional nature of the narrative and refer to the narrator as an aesthetic entity rather than as a perceiving consciousness or as a thinking, ordering intelligence.

Then phenomenon of the narrator's presence in the narrative may be explained in terms of the narrator's distance from his narrative. The greater the narrator's distance (aesthetic, temporal, spatial, psychological) from his narrative the more evident his presence and his point of view. Distance, as we have seen, is expressed linguistically in terms of the nature and function of the language used: the more abstract and conceptual the language, the more expressive its function, the greater the distance of the narrator from the narrative and the more evident his presence. In order to abstract, to conceptualize, to order, to interpret, the narrator must stand at a certain distance from his narrative.

The narrator likewise enters into a relationship with each of the characters of the novel and may stand at any distance from them on any axis of value: psychological, aesthetic, intellectual, or moral. This changing distance between the narrator and the other characters results in multiple point of view. As the distance between the narrator and character becomes smaller the narrator adopts the character's point of view. This distance can be measured linguistically. The extent to which the narrator disappears linguistically in favor of the linguistic presence of the characters determines the point of view manifest at any one moment in the novel.

The Characters: The Language of Perception

The first perceptible change in point of view occurs when a particular character becomes the center of the narration and the reader sees the world of the novel as the character sees it. This new center of perception is identified by the use of certain verbs of perception—seeing, hearing, observing, noticing—which are associated with a certain character. Consider, for example, the scene in *Fortunata y Jacinta* when Juanito goes to visit Estupiñá at home and there meets Fortunata for the first time, standing in a doorway of the house where his friend lives. Notice the number of verbs throughout the passage which refer to the perception of the scene, Juanito's perception of the scene: *reconoció, vió, vió;* le *parecía; miró; pensó no ver nada y al ver, al observar, advirtió* . . . etc. (V, 41) The language of the scene is still mimetic or representational, extraordinarily concrete and vivid, referring the reader directly toward the world of the novel, but the use of those verbs of perception is the first clear indication that the point from which that very concrete reality is perceived has changed.

The same is true of the passage in *Fortunata y Jacinta* where the narrator describes the visit of Guillermina and Jacinta to the fourth estate. The narrator follows them as they enter this world of the poor and makes clear through use of verbs of perception that what the reader sees of the fourth estate is what Guillermina and Jacinta see. Again, the language is mimetic, and its referents particular and concrete, but the reader is quite aware of the point from which the scene is viewed. Verbs describe the women's movement through the scene and follow their perception: "Veían las cocinas." (V, 101); "Guillermina se paró, mirando . . ." (V, 101); "Echaron una mirada a lo alto . . ." (V, 102); "Vió la Delfina que por cima . . ." (V, 102); "(les) parecían moras . . ." (V, 102); "Vió Jacinta . . ." (V, 103).

In *Miau*, the child Luis Cadalso is often the center of perception. Luis' innocence permits him to perceive the truth in a way impossible for an adult. Luis is his grandfather's loyal messenger, faithfully making the rounds of bureaucrats and minor government officials, patiently awaiting an answer to his grandfather's pleas for help. In a scene near the beginning of the novel (V, 557), we find Luis sitting on a bench in the hallway of Curcúrbitas' house, waiting for his grandfather's indefatigable protector. The verbs of the passage identify the center of perception, but we are made even more aware of the point from which the scene is viewed by the nature of the things perceived: Luis' legs are so short that his feet don't reach the ground; Curcúrbitas' little girls, with whom he would like to play, look at him only in pity or disdain; Curcúrbitas' fat and imposing wife looks like Pizarro, the trained elephant then popular in Madrid. Clearly the point of view is that of a child. Luis feels overwhelmed by a world too big for him and is increasingly aware of the world's indifference and disdain for him and his family. Luis is the first to learn that his grandfather's indefatigable protector has at last grown weary of helping him.

In the same novel, we find that Victor's shrewd and calculating nature allows him to see through his mother-in-law's vain pretensions of elegance. Through Victor's eyes we can see the real shabbiness of the Miau's house:

... en el cerebro insomne y febril de Victor esta penumbra y el olor a comida fiambre que flotaba en la atmósfera se confundían en una sola impresión desagradable. Examinó punto por punto el comedor, las paredes vestidas de papel, a trozos desgarrado, a trozos sucio. En algunos sitios, particularmente junto a las puertas, la crasitud marcaba el roce de las personas; en otros se veían impresas la mano de Luisito y aún los trazos de su artístico lápiz. El techo, ahumado en la proyección de la lámpara, tenía dos o tres grietas, dibujando una inmensa M y quizá otras letras menos claras. En la pared, agujeros de clavos, de los cuales colgaron en otro tiempo láminas. Victor recordaba haber visto ahí un reloj ...; también hubo antaño bodegones al cromo como sandías y melones despanzurrados. Láminas y reloj habían desaparecido ... El aparador subsistía; ¡pero qué viejo y qué aburrido estaba, con vivos negros despintados, un cristal roto, caído el copete! (V, 583)

In the last pages of the novel, the narrative focuses on Villaamil himself, and follows him as he wanders aimlessly through the streets of Madrid in the hours before his suicide, free at last from the oppressive burden of his belief in the absurd world of bureaucracy, seeing the world around him as it really is for the first time. The reader sees the world as Villaamil sees it, directly (in passages where the point of view is indicated by verbs of perception) or indirectly (as reflected in Villaamil's interior monologues). Villaamil nervously watches Mendizábal, fearing that the "hombre-gorila" will drag him back to the world he so recently escaped:

Al decir esto, vió a Mendizábal en la puerta y éste, por desgracia, le vió también a él. Grandes fueron la alarma y turbación del anciano al notar que el memorialista le observaba con ademán sospechoso. "Ese animal me ha conocido y viene tras de mí", pensó Villaamil, deslizándose pegado al muro de las Comendadoras. Antes de volver la esquina, miró, y, en efecto, Mendizábal le seguía paso a paso, como cazador que anda quedito tras la res, procurando no espantarla. (V, 681)

In *La desheredada* we see (as Isidora saw it) the poor *barrio* where Isidora's aunt Encarnación lives:

> Al ver, pues, las miserables tiendas, las fachadas mezquinas y desconchadas, los letreros innobles, los rótulos de torcidas letras, los faroles de aceite amenazando caerse; . . . al oír el estrépito de machacar sartenes, los berridos de pregonas ininteligibles, el pisar fatigoso de bestias tirando de carros atascados y el susurro de los transeuntes . . . creyó que estaba en la caricatura de una ciudad hecha de cartón podrido . . .
> (IV, 978)

In the same novel, the scene which describes Isidora's long hoped for reunion with her supposed grandmother Aransis is seen through Isidora's eyes. Isidora is the center of the narrative, which follows her as she takes leave of José Relimpio, enters the Aransis' palace, awaits the arrival of the marquess and finally as she sees her "grandmother" for the first time. The verbs of perception make clear the point from which the scene is viewed: "Al fin vió en al extremo de una callejuela un esquinazo de revoco, un balcón, el primero de una larga fila de balcones y se detuvo mirándolo." (IV, 1053) "Isidora vió entrar una dama de cabello casi blanco, grave, hermosa. . . . Entonces vió que la marquesa sacó unos lentes de oro. . . ." (IV, 1053) "Al oír a la marquesa. . . ." (IV, 1054)

In all of these passages the reader perceives the details of the external world which the character perceives but is nevertheless kept at a certain distance, in that he perceives as well the character himself in the act of perception. So the point of view here is a kind of intermediate one. The narrator has taken only a first step from the neutrality of mimesis toward the particular view of the character. The language is purely mimetic, and only the verbs of perception indicate the point from which reality is viewed.

The Characters: Language as Image

As the language of a passage becomes increasingly expressive, the shift in point of view from narrator to character becomes more obvious. Perhaps the next step in shift of point of view is evidenced in those passages in which language is used as image or metaphor. The language of these passages is still mimetic, in that it refers to a reality outside the speaker, but it is primarily expressive and "revelatory," in that it reveals the image or reality reflected in the consciousness of the character.

The best example of this is the famous scene from *Fortunata y*

Jacinta in which Maxi, in order to be able to help Fortunata, breaks the bank which contains his life savings. Maxi is so overwhelmed by fear and guilt at having disobeyed his aunt, doña Lupe, that the act seems to him a "crime," the bank a "victim," and he himself a "criminal." The very words of the passage: *atentado, premeditación, delito, víctima, febril mano, el cacharro herido, el asesino* (V, 169-171) clearly indicate the point of view from which the scene is perceived. The reader perceives the scene from a point closer to the character's point of view and for the first time begins to experience the scene as does the character: to feel with him. At least in this passage, the images used to convey the character's point of view are emotionally charged, so that the emotional and psychological distance between character and reader is considerably lessened.

Language used as epithet serves a similar function. The epithet used to refer to a particular character often reveals as much about the character's opinion of himself as it does about society's or another character's opinion of him. In *Miau*, Abelarda is referred to throughout the novel as "la insignificante," a term which reveals her own inherent sense of inferiority rather than others' opinion of her, although Victor doesn't hesitate to take advantage of this inherent sense of inferiority in his cruel games with her. In fact, Abelarda feels most insignificant—common, ordinary, foolish and ignorant of the ways of the world—in the context of her relationship with Victor. It follows that the epithet "insignificante" is used most often to refer to Abelarda in those scenes which describe her encounters with Victor.

Epithets in fact serve a variety of functions in the novel. As was noted previously, complex characters may be referred to by several epithets in the course of the novel. It was observed at that point that the particular epithet given a character at any one moment in the novel reflects the role the character is playing at that point in the novel. It may also be said that if this same epithet reflects the character's opinion of himself, the narrative at that moment has moved closer to the character's point of view. Surely the epithet "el iluminado" accurately reflects the "enlightened" Maxi's new-found faith in himself and the strength of his "reason," just as the epithet "el sietemesino" accurately reflects Maxi's own sense of inferiority, even if it has been reinforced by society. When Fortunata is called "la pecadora" during her stay in the convent of the Micaelas, it is because she has been placed in that role by society; but, nevertheless, because Fortunata has momentarily accepted the role society has given her, the epithet accurately reflects Fortunata's opinion of herself. So epithets clearly function as clues to the discovery of the point of view manifest at any one point in the novel.

Indirect Free Style

The narrator further identifies the center of consciousness, and moves closer to the character, by use of indirect discourse, the so-called "indirect free style," using words appropriate to the expression of the character's emotional reaction to what he is perceiving. Stephen Ullman, in "Reported Speech in Flaubert," from his book *Style in the French Novel,* defines indirect free style as "reported speech masquerading as narrative."[32] Because it attempts to represent the speech or thought patterns of the character, "it has certain obvious affinities with the spoken language: it avoids explicit subordination, retains the expressive elements of speech, and tries to imitate the inflexions and intonations of the speaking voice."[33] These linguistic clues of indirect style identify a point of view other than the narrator's, but the fact that passages written in free indirect style are not set off in quotes and that they are written in third rather than in first person gives them the appearance of being a part of the narrative itself. It may be said that passages written in indirect free style represent the intermediate point between the neutrality of mimesis and the particularity of expression: the ultimate shift of point of view to the character himself, when the character's language assumes the mimetic and expressive function once exclusive of the narrator.

Ullman, in his study of Flaubert's novels, establishes two broad categories of indirect free style:[34] one which attempts the reproduction of speech; the other, which attempts the reproduction of thought. The first category includes those passages in which Flaubert (primarily for the sake of objectivity and of removing himself from the novel) merely reports indirectly what a character said, without the use of quotes or the intrusive introductory clause (i.e. "he said"). The second category Ullman equates with what others have traditionally called interior monologue, an attempt to transcribe the character's "inner speech" indirectly, by imitating the looser syntactical patterns of mental processes in dreams, reveries, or hallucinatory states. According to Ullman, passages written in indirect style may only briefly interrupt the flow of the narrative, or they may encompass many paragraphs, even pages.

The Spanish novelist perhaps best known for his use of indirect free style is Vicente Blasco Ibañez. It is often said that Blasco Ibañez' use of indirect free style, particularly in his Valencian novels, results from the necessity of reporting his characters' words and thoughts in Castilian rather than in Valencian, a dialect unintelligible to many of his readers. However true this may be, it seems more likely that Blasco Ibañez' use of free indirect style corresponds more to intrinsic rather than extrinsic necessities. As in Flaubert's works, there are passages in Blasco Ibañez' novels which depict both reported speech[35] and reported thought.[36] In both cases, however, the use of free indirect style corresponds to a desire to create a sympathy between reader and character, an emotional overtone which draws the reader closer to the character.

The distinction made by Ullman between reported speech and thought does not appear to be a particularly useful one for describing the function of free indirect style in Galdós' novels, either. The primary function of indirect free style in Galdós' novels is the creation of an emotional overtone which draws the reader closer to a particular character and thus facilitates a shift in point of view. The speech patterns imitated are those most characteristic of emotive speech, the spoken language at its most expressive: interjections, exclamations, questions, incomplete sentences, or colloquialisms. As such the passages reflect clearly the character whose consciousness is the center of perception at the moment. Regardless of the content expressed, the linguistic clues are often sufficient to identify the point of view manifest in the passage, although generally the identity of the point of view is reinforced by the content of the passage.

There are passages in Galdós' novels written in indirect free style which transcribe indirectly what a character said, as in the scene from *Fortunata y Jacinta* where Maxi listens sympathetically to Fortunata's sad tale of her experiences with Juan. The narrator explains: "Cuando parte de esta historia fue contada, al joven le faltó poco para que le saltaran las lágrimas . . ." The narrator continues, clearly giving Maxi's opinion: "La tierna criatura, sin más amparo que su madre pobre, y la aflicción de ésta al verse abandonada, eran, en verdad, un cuadro tristísimo que partía el corazón," and goes on to transcribe indirectly what Maxi must have said to Fortunata at that point:

> ¿Por qué no le citó ante los tribunales? Es lo que debía haber hecho. A estos tunantes hay que tratarlos a la baqueta. Otra cosa. ¿Por qué no se le ocurrió darle un escándalo, ir a la casa con el crío en brazos y presentarse a doña Bárbara y don Baldomero y contarles allí bien clarito la gracia que había hecho su hijo? . . . Pero no; esto no hubiera sido muy conforme con la dignidad. Más valía despreciarle, dejándole

> entregado a su conciencia, sí, a su conciencia, que buen jaleo
> le había de armar tarde o temprano.   (V, 175)

Likewise, there are passages written in indirect free style which represent indirectly what a character thought, or might have thought, in a particular situation, as for example this passage from *Fortunata y Jacinta* which describes Jacinta's confusion on hearing for the first time José Ido's story of el Pitusín:

> Quería llorar: pero ¿qué diría la familia al verla hecha un mar de lágrimas? Habría que decir el motivo . . . ¡Si todo era un embuste, si aquel hombre estaba loco! Era autor de novelas de brocha gorda, y no pudiendo ya escribirlas para el público, intentaba llevar a la vida real los productos de su imaginación llena de tuberculosis. Sí, sí, sí: no podía ser otra cosa: tisis de la fantasía. . . .   (V, 95)

Some passages accurately reflect a character's speech patterns, as does this passage describing doña Lupe's reaction when she first learns of Maxi's interest in Fortunata:

> Después dió a entender que algo barruntaba ella por la conducta anómala de su sobrino. ¡Casarse con una que ha tenido que ver con muchos hombres! ¡Bah! No sería cierto, quizá. Y si lo era pronto se había de saber; porque, eso sí, a doña Lupe no se le apagaría en el cuerpo la bomba, y aquella misma noche o al día siguiente por la mañana Maximiliano y ella se verían las caras . . . ¡Como estuviera en casa el muy hipocritón su tía le iba a poner verde! Pero no estaría, seguramente, porque eran las once de la noche y el señoritingo no entraba ya nunca antes de las doce o la una . . . ¡Quién lo había de decir! . . . Aquel cuitado, aquella calamidad de chico, aquella inutilidad, tan fulastre y para poco, que no tenía talento para apagar una vela y que a los dieciocho años, sí, bien lo podía asegurar doña Lupe, no sabía lo que son mujeres . . .; aquel hombre fallido enamorarse así, ¿y de quién?, de una mujer perdida . . . , pero perdida . . . en toda la extensión de la palabra.   (V, 190-191)

Doña Lupe's presence is clearly evidenced in such characteristic expressions as "en toda la extensión de la palabra" and in the words used to describe Maxi: "el muy hipocritón," "el señoritingo," "aquella calamidad de chico," which only doña Lupe would have used. The reader is only too aware of doña Lupe's self-righteous indignation at the thought that Maxi not only has rebelled against her, but has done so without her knowledge.

Perhaps a more useful description of the nature of indirect free style in Galdós is that there appear to be three basic kinds of passages. In the first, language is basically expressive, but also has clear mimetic function as well. These passages simultaneously describe something outside of the character, and the character's inner reaction to that exterior reality. The reader perceives exterior reality only indirectly through the filter of the character's emotions. In the second type, language is almost exclusively expressive, referring the reader to the character whose consciousness is the center of perception at the moment. These passages describe the character's inner state of mind and body. And finally there are passages which simultaneously describe reality within and outside of the character. In every case, the expressive function of language is primary; its mimetic function, secondary.

In *La desheredada,* there are many examples of the first type of passage. Isidora is the center of consciousness throughout much of the novel. But as was previously noted, Isidora's primary mode of consciousness is not perception but imagination. So much of what the reader perceives of exterior reality in the novel he sees only through the filter of Isidora's imagination. Consider, for example, this description of the spectacle of upper middle-class society parading in full dress on a Sunday afternoon:

> ¡Qué gente aquélla tan feliz! ¡Qué envidiable cosa aquel ir y venir en carruaje, viéndose, saludándose y comentándose! . . . ¡Qué bonito mareo el que producían las dos filas encontradas, y el cruzamiento de perfiles marchando en dirección distinta! Los jinetes y las amazonas alegraban con su rápida aparición el hermoso tumulto! . . . (IV, 994)

The language is still mimetic in describing the spectacle itself, but is at the same time clearly expressive of the emotions of the character, Isidora, as she witnesses the scene.

In the same novel we also find an example of the second kind of passage. Here Isidora reacts to Juan Bou's proposal of marriage:

> Isidora, estupefacta, no sabía en qué términos responder . . .
> ¡En qué vacilación tan grande estaba! En su alma el asco era
> inseparable del agradecimiento. ¿Cómo contestarle y expresar
> en una frase el desprecio y la consideración? . . . ¡Qué un
> ganso semejante se atreviese a poner sus ojos en persona tan
> selecta! Pero al mismo tiempo . . . ¡cuán sencillo y generoso!
> . . .   (IV, 1106)

In *Fortunata y Jacinta* we find an example of the third type in the passage describing Maxi's fascination in watching the young cadets from the military academy and his subsequent reflections on his own sense of inferiority:

> Maximiliano veía desde la ventana de su tercer piso a los
> alumnos de Estado Mayor . . . y no hay idea de la admira-
> ción que le causaban aquellos jóvenes, ni del arrobamiento
> que le producía la franja azul en el pantalón, el ros, la levita
> con las hojas de roble bordadas en el cuello y la espalda . . . ,
> ¡tan chicos algunos y ya con espada! . . . ¡Qué suerte tan
> negra! Si él no fuera tan desgarbado de cuerpo y le hubieran
> puesto a estudiar aquella carrera, ¡cuánto se habría aplicado!
> Seguramente, a fuerza de sobar los libros, le habría salido el
> talento, como se saca lumbre a la madera frotándola mucho.
>   (V, 161-162)

The important factor seems to be not whether the passage written in indirect free style represents the character's speech or his thought (generally one tends to reflect the other), but rather, that through the expressive function of language itself, a linguistic presence other than that of the narrator is established. Because passages written in indirect free style appear to be an integral part of the primary narration (that of the narrator), the narrator's presence is still maintained, if only minimally, and a complete shift in point of view is prevented.

The Characters Speak

The most obvious shift in point of view occurs when the character's words, clearly identified as such (written in quotes) assume the mimetic and interpretive functions once held by the narrator. The language of these passages is sometimes mimetic, when it refers to a reality outside of the character who is speaking, but it is simultaneously expressive, constantly revealing the character's emotions as he speaks. The distance here between narrator and character is nil, for the narrator has disappeared linguistically as the narrative adopts the character's language and his point of view.

Most characters, both major and minor, assume the role of narrator at some point in the novel: as they tell their own past history, describe a scene they witnessed or participated in, interpret and analyze their own behavior and that of others, or express their own desires, beliefs, hopes and fears. Often the character's narration is in direct contrast with a reality already established by the narrator's mimesis or that of another character. At other times the character's narration serves as the only source of information the reader has about a particular event. But in any case a character's words are always to be judged in the context of the novel as a whole and of the reality established by the narrator's mimesis. The character's narration is always colored by his own personality. Whatever mimetic or interpretive value his narration has is secondary to its value as an expression of his own personality.

In *La desheredada,* for example, Isidora tells the story of her early experiences with Tomás Rufete, "el que llamo mi padre." Isidor's self-pity and sense of injustice at being deprived of her "rightful heritage" is encouraged by a sympathetic listener, the scribe Canencia, who comments: "Todo sea por Dios . . . Noble criatura, su juventud de usted ha sido muy triste: ha nacido usted en un páramo . . ." (V, 973) Isidora, of course, believes that she is not the daughter of Tomás Rufete, but the illegitimate granddaughter of the marquess of Aransis. So, to her, all that she "suffered" as Tomás Rufete's "daughter" was unjust. Unconsciously Isidora reveals in her story just how like her own madness was Tomás Rufete's. Her narration makes very clear that she is, indeed, Tomás Rufete's daughter. The irony which results from contrasting Isidora's story with what we know of her from reading the whole novel is that Isidora does indeed suffer all her life from being Tomás Rufete's daughter but in a way Isidora herself could never have understood.

In the same novel, we find that it is José Relimpio who tells of Isidora's relationship with Sánchez Botín. Don José's affection for Isidora colors his narration, and his sympathy for her is obvious:

> Si al menos la dejara salir a la calle siempre que ella quisiera . . . Pero quiá, quiá. Tiene que valerse de mil tretas de esta

vida y no sé cómo aguanta . . . Los domingos le hace ir a misa, y aquí paz . . . Dicen que ese señor es mojigato.
(IV, 1085)

In the first book of *Fortunata y Jacinta,* we find Juanito Santa Cruz' story of his relationship with Fortunata. Relentlessly prodded by his curious, and at that point rather gullible, wife Jacinta, Juanito reluctantly, bit by bit, reveals the details of his story. Juanito, the vain and spoiled only son, takes great pains to make sure that the image Jacinta has of him remains as untarnished as possible. Juanito is weak, immature, self-centered and has little sense of moral responsibility to himself or others, but he does have a great sense of the role he must play in society. In the story he tells Jacinta, he appears as one momentarily tempted, fascinated by the *pueblo.* As Juanito explains: "Parece mentira que yo me divirtiera con tales escándalos. ¡Lo que es el hombre! Pero yo estaba ciego; tenía entonces la manía de lo popular." (V, 52) He takes no responsibility for having become involved with Fortunata, but once having admitted that he was involved, he tries to make himself appear as noble as possible in his actions toward her. Only his confessions made under the influence of liquor seem completely sincere. Never again is Juan's genuine affection for Fortunata so obvious, nor does he ever again so freely admit his mistreatment of her:

¡Si la hubieras visto! . . . Fortunata tenía los ojos como dos estrellas, muy semejantes a los de la Virgen del Carmen que antes estaba en Santo Tomás y ahora está en San Ginés . . . Fortunata tenía las manos bastas de tanto trabajar, el corazón lleno de inocencia . . . ¡Pobre Fortunata!, ¡pobre Pitusa! ¿Te he dicho que la llamaban la Pitusa? ¿No? Pues te lo digo ahora. Que conste . . . Yo la perdí . . . , sí . . . ; que conste también; yo la perdí, la engané, la dije mil mentiras, la hice creer que me iba a casar con ella . . . Los hombres, digo, los señoritos, somos unos miserables; creemos que el honor de las hijas del pueblo es cosa de juego. (V, 60)

In contrast, we find that Fortunata's narratives always have the ring of truth about them. This of course reflects Fortunata's character; the simple, honest, uneducated woman of the *pueblo,* who ultimately must be true only to that identity. By the third book of the novel it is clear that not even Juan can make her pretend to be what she is not. As Fortunata explains to Feijóo, telling of her life with Juan at that period of time:

> Juan me decía que no sirvo para nada, y que no merezco el palmito que tengo. El se empeñaba en que yo fuera de otro modo; pero la cabra siempre tira al monte. Pueblo nací y pueblo soy; quiero decir, ordinariota y salvaje . . . ¡Ah, si viera usted lo furioso que se ponía cuando le decía yo que me gustaba un guisado del falda y pecho como los que se comen en los bodegones! Pero nada, que tenía que esconderme para comer a mi gusto. (V, 329)

In the third book of *Fortunata y Jacinta,* we are surprised to find it is doña Lupe who relates the events surrounding the death of Mauricia la dura. When Fortunata asks if Mauricia has died, Lupe replies:

> —Sí, a las nueve y media. Parecía que estaba esperando a que llegara yo para morirse . . . , ¡pobrecilla! Vengo horrorizada. Si yo lo sé, no parezco por allá. Estos cuadros no son para mí. Cuando llegué estaba en su sano juicio. ¡Preguntóme por tí con un interés! . . . Dijo que te quería más que a nadie, y que en cuantito que entrara en el Cielo, le iba a pedir al Señor que te hiciera feliz. Yo, francamente, al oír esto, ví que estaba fatal. . . . (V, 393)

What interests doña Lupe throughout the scene is the behavior of Guillermina, whom she greatly admires, in the face of the behavior of Mauricia, who still cries for liquor on her deathbed. Doña Lupe continues:

> La santa tuvo una idea feliz. Le dió a beber una copa de jerez, llena hasta los bordes. Mauricia apretaba los dientes: pero al fin debió darle en la nariz el olorcillo, porque abriendo la bocaza, se lo atizó de un trago. ¡Cómo se relamía la infeliz! Se calmó y ¡pum!, la cabeza en la almohada. (V, 393)

The reader's knowledge of the event comes through doña Lupe, who, because of her attitude toward Mauricia, must turn the scene into a degrading experience.

The shift in point of view is perhaps more obvious when the character speaks, assuming the interpretive function once held by the narrator. Here the character expresses explicitly the view of the world implicit in his other words and actions. Because it is formulated more abstractly and expressed more explicitly, the reader is more aware of the character's point of view. In Galdós' novels all the characters share this function to some extent. Very often there is one character whose words explicitly represent the point of view of the narrator implicit in the novel. In *La desheredada,* for example, the narrator consistently relies on Miquis to express or reinforce his own vision of the characters and their world. From the beginning, Miquis correctly diagnoses Isidora's illness and prescribes the antidote; a strong dose of "truth," which he often provides. In the following passage, for example, Miquis' commentary on the spectacle of upper middle class society on parade, in contrast to Isidora's fascination with the spectacle, clearly represents the narrator's opinion:

> Aquí, en días de fiesta, verás a todas las clases sociales. Vienen a observarse, a medirse, y a ver las respectivas distancias que hay entre cada una, para asaltarse. El caso es subir al escalón inmediato. (IV, 995)

To Isidora's question, on hearing the noise of the carriages, "¿Hay torrente?" Miquis answers: "Si, torrente hay . . . de vanidad." (IV, 994) Likewise the words of Isidora's aunt Encarnación, Juan Bou and Mariano offer a vision clearly in contrast to Isidora's point of view.

In *Fortunata y Jacinta,* it is Feijóo who most clearly and explicitly represents the narrator's point of view. He fulfills the narrator's function of interpreting, analyzing and generalizing based on the concrete situations of the novel. His observations on Fortunata's predicament are a theoretical synthesis of the same conflicts presented dramatically in the first two books and psychologically in the last book of the novel. Feijóo's perspective offers the most comprehensive and all-inclusive vision of reality. Only his interpretation allows for the accommodation of passion and reason, instinct and decorum, spirit and flesh, individual and society. He correctly views Fortunata's conflict as one between the needs of the individual and the needs of society, which in Fortunata's case has been internalized as a conflict between the two aspects of her self: her passion for Juan and her desire to be a "decent" woman, accepted by society. His solution is that

Fortunata try to control her heart, but if she must give free rein to her passion, that she maintain the appearance of decency at all cost:

> Tonta, tontaína, si todo en este mundo depende del modo, del estilo . . . Nada es bueno ni malo por sí. ¿Me entiendes? Ojo al corazón; es lo primero que te digo. No permitas que te domine. Eso de echar todo por la ventana en cuanto el señor carazón se atufe es un disparate que se paga caro. Hay que dar al corazón sus miajitas de carne; es fiera y las hambres largas le ponen furioso; pero también hay que dar a la fiera de la sociedad la parte que le corresponde, para que no alborote. Si no, lo echas todo a rodar, y no hay vida posible. (V, 341)

In *Miau,* it is possibly the child Luis Cadalso, more than any other character, who represents the narrator's point of view. Luis' innocence permits him the freedom to discover the essential absurdity of the world which others never question. In fact it is Luisito who finally shows Villaamil the truth that gives him his final freedom:

> —¿Tú? Te diré. Ya no te colocan . . . ¿entiendes? Ya no te colocan, ni ahora ni nunca . . . Veo a Dios . . . Me da así como un sueño y entonces se me pone delante y me habla . . . Me dice todo lo que pasa . . . Y anoche me dijo que no te colocarán, y que este mundo es muy malo, y que tú no tienes nada que hacer en él, y que cuanto más pronto te vayas al cielo, mejor. (V, 674)

Other characters offer more limited views which are more radical, yet which often go much deeper psychologically and emotionally. In *Fortunata y Jacinta,* minor characters like José Ido del Sagrario and Mauricia la dura are themselves extreme manifestations of the conflicts which characterize Maxi and Fortunata. Their words shed a sometimes irrational but always psychologically valid light on the conflicts of the main characters. It is Mauricia who senses the strength of Fortunata's passion for Juan and out of her own rebelliousness encourages Fortunata to seek the fulfillment of that passion at the first opportunity:

> —Arrepiéntete, chica, y no lo dejes para luego. Vete arrepintiendo de todo menos de querer a quien te sale de

> *entre tí,* que esto no es, como quien dice, pecado. No robar, no *ajumarse,* no decir mentiras: pero en el querer, ¡aire, aire! y caiga el que caiga. Siempre y cuando lo hagas así, tu miajita de cielo no te la quita nadie. (V, 370)

In contrast, Guillermina, recognizing Fortunata's basic goodness and her desire to be an "honorable" woman, encourages Fortunata to suppress her "sinful" (i.e. anti-social) desires and live again in accord with society:

> —Es que usted, como si lo viera, conserva resentimientos y quizá pretensiones que son un gran pecado; es que usted no está curada de su enfermedad del ánimo; es que usted, si no tiene ahora trato con aquel sujeto, se halla dispuesta a volverlo a tener . . . Bien sé que es difícil mandar al corazón. Pero eso mismo le da a usted motivo para dejar de ser mala, como dice, y adquirir méritos inmensos . . . Cumplir ciertos deberes, cuando el amor no facilita el cumplimiento, es la mayor hermosura del alma. Hacer esto bastaría para que todas las culpas de usted fueran lavadas . . .
> (V, 396, 397, 398)

In all cases, but especially in the latter, the commentaries reveal as much or more about the person who makes them as they do about the subject of the commentary.

Interior Monologue

The final step in the shift of point of view is the complete "interiorization" of language in interior monologue. Robert Humphreys, in *Stream of Consciousness in the Modern Novel,* defines interior monologue as "the technique used in fiction for representing the psychic content and processes of character, partly or entirely unuttered, just as these processes exist at various levels of conscious control before they are formulated for deliberate speech."[37] Therefore, in interior monologue, language has no communicative function. In Humphreys' words, "no auditor (is) assumed."[38] Its function is exclusively expressive of the character's inner state of mind and body. The reader perceives the external world of the novel only as it is reflected in the character's mind.

The kind of interior monologue found in Galdós' novels corresponds most closely to what Humphreys calls "indirect" interior monologue: "that type of interior monologue in which an omniscient author presents unspoken material as if it were directly from the unconsciousness of a character and, with commentary and description, guides the reader through it. It differs from direct interior monologue basically in that the author intervenes between the character's psyche and the reader. The author is an on-the-scene guide for the reader."[39] Nevertheless, indirect interior monologue "retains the fundamental quality of interior monologue in that what it presents of consciousness is direct: that is, it is in the idiom and with the pecularities of the character's psychic processes."[40]

The important point in the distinction of direct and indirect interior monologue is the role of the author (narrator). In Galdós' novels, the narrator never disappears for long, he is always in control of his narration. But certainly, within the interior monologue itself, which appears set off by quotation marks in the text, the narrator has abnegated both his representational and interpretive function. Linguistically he has disappeared completely. Identification of character and narrator is complete. Any of the forms of narrative itself can be found in interior monologue: narration of events (memories of the past or fantasies of the future), descriptions of scenes witnessed or participated in, mimetic realization of the physical world, analysis of self or others, etc. One of the most surprising features of interior monologue in Galdós' novels is their referential function in describing exterior space in the inner space of the character's mind. In *Fortunata y Jacinta,* Moreno-Isla's monologue is an interesting example of how movement through exterior space is shown only as it is reflected in the character's mind. Moreno, tired and suffering the effects of a bad heart, is returning home from a walk in the Retiro. The things he notices as he walks are reflected in the monologue, and thus is made explicit the nature of his journey:

> Muy mal debe de andar la máquina, cuando a la mitad de la calle de Alcalá ya estoy rendido. Y no he hecho más que dar la vuelta al estanque. ¡Demonio de neurosis o lo que sea! . . . Esta es la capital de las setecientas colinas. ¡Ah!, ya están regando estos brutos, y tengo que pasarme a la otra acera para que no me atice una ducha este salvaje con su manga de riego . . . Ya poco me falta. Francamente, es cosa de tomar un coche; pero no, aguántate, que pronto llegarás . . . Vamos, ya entro por mi calle de Correos . . .   (V, 445)

In the last pages of *Miau,* we find a similar phenomenon in Villaamil's monologue, which reveals the course of his wanderings through Madrid in the hours before his suicide and describes the people he meets:

> Allá sale el ínclito Ponce de estampía. De seguro ha ido a casa de Pantoja, al café, a todos los sitios que acostumbro frecuentar . . . Esa que llega echando los bofes me parece que es Federico Ruiz. De fijo viene de la Prevención o del Juzgado de guardia . . . Habrá salido a averiguar . . . ¡As! Alguien sale y viene hacia acá . . . Me parece que es Ponce otra vez . . . (V, 680)

Some interior monologues reveal episodes of a character's past history. In *Fortunata y Jacinta,* doña Lupe sits reminiscing about Feijóo's onetime courtship of her:

> Y, aunque el señor de Feijóo lo niegue hoy, es tan verdad que me rondaba la calle al año de perder a mi Jáuregui . . . tan verdad como que nos hemos de morir. Y si no, ¿qué hacía plantado en aquella dichosa esquina de la calle de Tintoreros? Esto fue poco antes de la guerra de Africa, bien me acuerdo; y si el tal no se va a matar moros, sabe Dios si . . . (V, 358)

Fortunata's interior monologue in the fourth book of *Fortunata y Jacinta* also demonstrates how external reality of the past is revealed only in the internal reality of the present (the character's mind) and altered by it. Such is the confusion that the narrator feels obliged to interrupt the monologue with comments designed to aid the reader in deciphering it and in distinguishing past from present. The narrator explains fully before the monologue begins the process it will follow:

> Sin que se interrumpiera la acción mecánica, el espíritu de la pobre mujer reproducía fielmente la escena aquella, con las palabras, los gestos y las inflexiones más insignificantes del diálogo. En medio de la reproducción iban colocándose, como anotaciones puestas al acaso, los comentarios que se le ocurrían. El trabajo de su cerebro era una calenturienta y dolorosa mezcla de las funciones del juicio y de la memoria,

revolviéndose con desorden y alumbrándose unas tras otras con aquella claridad de relámpago que a cada instante despedían. (V, 463)

In this monologue, in which Fortunata re-lives the scene in which Juanito tells her she can never equal Jacinta, the narrator clearly labels each fragment as "reproducción" or "comentario:"

> Reproducción de algo que ella le había contestado: "Mira, no lo tomes tan a pechos. Podría ser mentira. ¿Yo qué sé? No creerás que lo he inventado yo. Para que veas que no me gustan farsas contigo, eso que te incomoda tanto es cosa de Aurora..."
> Y él: "Como yo la coja, la arranco la lengua. Es una víbora esa mujer..."
> Comentario: "De veras que estuve muy imprudente. No se debe hablar mal de nadie sin tener seguridad de lo que se dice..." (V, 464)

Most interior monologues, however, consist primarily of the character's reflections on himself and his relationships with other people. This confirms the statement that interior monologues have a primarily expressive function: that of revealing character through the individual's reflections on himself. These interior monologues provide the reader the greatest depth of knowledge of the character at a conscious level. Here the character reveals truths about himself that he would have revealed to no one else.

In *La desheredada,* Isidora spends a sleepless night reliving her first visit to the Aransis' palace. Her monologue reveals the strength of her belief in the identity she has created for herself:

> ¡Qué hermoso palacio, Dios de mi vida! ¡Cuánto habrá costado todo aquello! ¡Pensar que es mío por la Naturaleza, por la ley, por Dios y por los hombres, y que no puedo poseerlo!... Esto me vuelve loca. Dios no quiere protegerme, o quiere atormentarme para que aprecie después mejor el bien que me destina... El corazón no puede engañarme, el corazón me dice que cuando yo me presente a ella, cuando me vea... No, no quiero pleitos; quiero entrar en mi nueva, en mi verdadera familia con paz, no con guerra, recibiendo

un beso de mi abuela y sintiendo que la cara se me moja con sus lágrimas. ¡Es tan buena mi abuelita! (IV, 1030)

In *Miau,* Abelarda's monologue reveals the depth of her sense of inferiority and her incapacity for ever dealing with Víctor as an equal:

¡Qué fea soy! ¡Dios mío; qué poco valgo! Más que fea, sosa, insignificante; no tengo ni un grano de sal. ¡Si al menos tuviera talento! Pero ni eso . . . ¿Cómo me ha de querer a mí, habiendo en el mundo tanta mujer hermosa y siendo él un hombre de mérito superior, de porvenir, elegante, guapo y con muchísimo entendimiento, digan lo que quieran? . . .
(V, 602)

Villaamil's monologue reveals for the first time his awareness of the psychologically emasculating effects of thirty years of life with a woman like Pura:

. . . ¡Treinta años así, Dios mío! Y a eso llaman vivir. "Ramón, ¿qué haces que no te diriges a tal o cual amigo? . . . Ramón, ¿en qué piensas? ¿Crees que somos camaleones? . . . Ramón, determínate a empeñar tu reloj, que la niña necesita botas . . . Ramón . . ." ¡Y que yo no haya sido hombre para trincar a mi mujer y ponerle una mordaza en aquella boca, que debió de hacérsela un fraile, según es de pedigüeña! ¡Cuidado que soportar esto treinta años! . . . (V, 678)

In *Fortunata y Jacinta,* Fortunata's monologue after her first encounter with Jacinta expresses the depth of her desire to be, like Jacinta, an honorable woman, and the depth of her frustration at society's refusal to recognize her as such:

¡Si creerá esta señora que no hay en el mundo más mujeres honradas que ella! . . . Que se le quite a usted eso de la cabeza. ¡Vaya con el modelo! . . . ¡A buena parte viene usted! . . . ¿Sabe usted, niña, que como a mí se me meta en la cabeza, le doy a usted honradez y virtudes por los hocicos hasta que no quiera más? Porque eso es cuestión de decir: ¡Ea! . . . Sí, y si me atufo, no hay quien me tosa. Pues, ¿qué cree usted, que a mi me costaría trabajo cuidar enfermos y dármelas de muy católica? . . . ¡Vaya con *la mona del Cielo!* ¡Ea! . . . , no vengas acá vendiendo mérito . . . ¡Y ángel me soy! Pues para que lo sepa, también yo, si me da la gana de ser ángel, lo seré, y más que usted, mucho más. Todas tenemos nuestro ángel en el cuerpo . . . (V, 386)

Her thoughts lead her to reverse roles, thinking that society's view of reality is false, for in reality *she* is Juanito's wife, and it was Jacinta who stole him from her:

Tu marido es mío y te lo tengo que quitar . . . Pinturera . . . , santurrona; ya te diré yo si eres ángel o lo que eres . . . Tu marido es mío; me lo has robado . . . como se puede robar un pañuelo . . . (V, 386)

At the height of her fury and rage against society (represented by Jacinta) and what it has denied her, Fortunata constructs a world turned upside down where she is Juan's wife, where Mauricia's and Guillermina's traditional devil and angel roles are reversed: Mauricia, the profoundly anti-social one, is the saint; Guillermina, the devil:

Pero, ¿yo qué he hecho? . . . ¡Oh! Bien hecho está . . . ¡Llamarme a mi *ladrona* ella, que me ha robado lo mío! . . . Tú me llamarás lo que quieras . . . Llámame tal o cual y tendrás razón . . . Tú serás un ángel . . . pero tú no has tenido hijos. Los ángeles no los tienen. Y yo sí . . . Es mi idea, una idea mía. Rabia, rabia, rabia . . . Y no los tendrás nunca, y yo sí . . .

. . . ¡Lo mismo que la otra, la señora del Espíritu Santo! Doña Mauricia, digo, Guillermina la Dura . . . Quiere hacernos creer que es santa . . . ¡Buen peine está! . . . Púa de sacristía, amancebada con todos los clérigos . . . (V, 408)

These passages are almost pure emotion, and reveal realities which rightly belong to the subconscious, beyond the capacity of the character's language (i.e. his conscious mental processes) to express. Language is exclusively expressive of the character's inner reality. At this point psychological and emotional distance between character and narrator is nil. Identification of character and narrator (and reader) is complete. The shift of point of view in the narrative is complete.

The Language of Dreams

The only reality left untouched is that of the subconscious. Galdós, unlike later novelists like Joyce (in stream of consciousness), does not trust the spoken language to reveal adequately the realities of that region of the human spirit, and turns instead to the symbolic language of dreams. Thus, although dreams in Galdós' novels offer the deepest psychological insight into a character and his view of reality, the verbal language of these dreams is not expressive of the character, but rather seems the neutral language of reference or representation. In dreams, it is not the words themselves but the images and symbols of the dream which are expressive of the character and his inner realities.

Consider, for example, Mauricia's dream from *Fortunata y Jacinta* in which she enters the chapel in the convent of the Micaelas in an attempt to steal the child Jesus from the altar and return him to his mother. The passage clearly describes Mauricia's state of mind, the excitement and awe she feels as she approaches the altar, opens the ciborium, takes out the monstrance and holds it up. The passage is narrated in third person, and at first glance appears to be indirect free style. But it is clear that the language itself is not Mauricia's (it is not representative of her thought or speech patterns):

> Por fin, gracias a Dios, pudo abrir la puerta que sólo tocan las manos ungidas del sacerdote. Levantando la cortinilla buscó un momento en el misterioso, santo y venerando hueco . . . ¡Oh!, no había nada . . . Acordóse de que no era aquél el sitio donde está la Custodia, sino otro más alto. Subió al altar, puso los pies en el ara santa . . . Busca por aquí, por allí . . . ¡Ah!, por fin tropezaron sus dedos con el metálico pie de la Custodia. Pero qué frío estaba, tan frío que quemaba . . . Vaciló. ¿Lo cogería, sí o no? Sí, sí mil veces; aunque muriera, era preciso cumplir. Con exquisito cuidado, mas con gran decisión, empuñó la Custodia, bajando con ella por una escalera que antes no estaba allí. Orgullo y alegría inundaron el alma de la atrevida mujer al mirar en su propia mano la representación visible de Dios . . . ¡Cómo brillaban los rayos de oro que circundan el viril, y qué misteriosa y plácida majestad la de la Hostia purísima, guardada tras el cristal, blanca, divina y con todo el aquel de persona, sin ser más que una sustancia del delicioso pan! (V, 255)

Throughout Galdós' novels point of view undergoes a process of interiorization. In that process language itself undergoes a great change. Because the reality it conveys (the level of mental activity) becomes increasingly less conceptual, abstract, rational and more emotional and irrational, language itself begins to disintegrate. Ordinary language, which reflects (in syntax, for example) the ordered patterns of the conscious mind, is increasingly incapable of revealing the state of mind of the character as it approaches the subconscious. This breakdown of language is first apparent in interior monologues and periods of insomnia, which represent states of mind somewhere between the conscious and the subconscious mind. We have previously discussed the emotive nature of the language of interior monologue (reflected in the use of interjections, questions, and incomplete sentences). As the narrative enters the character's subconscious mind, the language of ordinary discourse becomes incapable of expressing the realities found there. So the language used to describe that region of the mind is not the verbal language of the conscious mind, but the language of image and symbol. The thought patterns of the subconscious are more imagistic than verbal. Schraibman quotes Annie Edwards Dodds, who says, ". . . the dream is at once image and state of mind; it is not an allegorical description of, or allusion to, a state of mind, but the state of mind itself, living and palpitating in the image which is its body."[41] So we should not expect the language of dreams to be expressive of the character in the way that the language of interior monologue is expressive of the character. As Gullón says, to understand the dreams of Galdós' novels and the images used in them, "habremos de aceptarlas como traducción a un lenguaje diferente del cotidiano."[42]

Gullón's and Schraibman's studies reveal the complex nature and multiple function of dreams in Galdós' novels. Gullón, considering the function of dreams in relation to the dreamer (the character), discovers two and possibly three functions:[43] First, there is a compensatory function ("el sueño como compensación"). In dreams characters can realize their most cherished desires, they can become in dreams what they could never become in reality. In this way their dream life somehow compensates for the misery of their real life. Secondly, there is a premonitory function ("el sueño como premonición"). In dreams a character becomes more aware of a reality—an event, a relationship, a change in his own life—before he is aware of it consciously. In effect these dreams are symbolic projections of the character's innermost desires and fears. Finally, there is what might be called a unifying function. (Gullón suggests this but doesn't really develop the idea.) Here the dream functions as a means of self-knowledge, a means of communication with the subconscious, a bridge which unites the conscious (the rational) and the subconscious (the fantastic, the irrational). As Gullón says:[44]

> El sueño, al ponernos en comunicación con partes secretas de la naturaleza, ayuda a desentrañar el secreto de la existencia y la hace sentir como algo en que entran con análogo rango las percepciones nocturnas y las impresiones de la vigilia. El sueño según esta concepción, es un medio de conocimiento y un modo de integración, un modo de conseguir que el hombre alcance su unidad sustancial.

Schraibman, considering dreams from a stylistic or structural point of view, lists six functions: plot anticipation, plot summary, plot advancement, character enforcement, expression of the supernatural, and as a device for description.[45] It seems that, in fact, all of the functions of dreams in Galdós' novels described by Gullón and Schraibman may be reduced to one basic function: that of revealing the innermost reality of the character's mind, providing the reader the most profound psychological insight into his character. So it is, in a sense, of secondary importance that in the process, dreams may also serve the other functions described. Gullón stresses the "revelatory" function of dreams: "Galdós utiliza los sueños para revelarnos 'cosas verdaderas del otro mundo' ".[46]

The "other world" which dreams explore is that of the subconscious, the most intimate and inaccessible region of the mind. The "true things" found there in the dreams of Galdós' novels are closely related to both the world without (people and events of the real world) and the world within (fears, desires, etc.). As Gullón says, "Los sueños de los personajes galdosianos son más imaginativos que fantásticos, por lo general mantienen comunicación con la realidad, con los sucesos acontecidos en la vigilia."[47] Yet the real world is always transformed ("transfiguración de lo real")[48] in accordance with the character's inner needs, desires and fears. So it can be said that dreams in Galdós' novels reveal simultaneously two realities: that of the external world (transformed by the character's subconscious) and that of the character's subconscious (his inner reality expressed by means of images and symbols which may or may not correspond to some external reality experienced by the character.)

Some dreams clearly express the image of an external reality reflected in the character's subconscious. Here the character often relives an experience he has had while awake. But now that experience is transformed by the character's emotions and is revealed to the reader in a new light. For example, many of Luis Cadalso's dreams in *Miau* are reprises of previous experiences. As Schraibman notes, "three of Luisito's ten dreams are primarily used by the author to treat in more detail incidents already described earlier."[49] But, of course, these dreams also reveal Luis' fears of failure and inferiority and his need for love and support, expressed in his conversations with God. In these dreams God gently chides Luis for not knowing his lessons:

> Hoy no supiste la lección de Gramática. Dijiste tantos disparates, que la clase toda se reía, y con muchísima razón. ¿Qué vena te dió de decir que el participio expresa la idea del verbo en abstracto? Lo confundiste con el gerundio, y luego hiciste una ensalada de los *modos* con los *tiempos*. Es que no te fijas, y cuando estudias estás pensando en las musarañas . . .   (V, 559)

or justifies Luis' anger and resentment of the bully Posturitas:

> . . . tienes razón en quejarte de *Posturitas*. Es un ordinario, un mal criado, y ya le restregaré yo una guindilla en la lengua cuando vuelva a decirte *Miau*. Por supuesto, que esto de los motes debe llevarse con paciencia, y cuando te digan *Miau*, tú te callas y aguantas.   (V, 559)

In *La de Bringas,* dreams of the epileptic child Isabelita Bringas shed an irrational but devastatingly real light on the absurd world of the palace bureaucrats of which her parents are a part. Isabelita's dreams reveal the emptiness and meaninglessness of that society's vain posturings, its preoccupation with appearance. The best example is the dream which treats again the famous scene of the dinner for the poor on Maundy Thursday, a ceremony which supposedly celebrates that society's concern and charity for the poor. The narrator, with customary irony, had previously described the scene in detail. But the images of Isabelita's dream reveals the ceremony in a truer light as an empty spectacle, the participants as marionettes, lifeless actors in a grotesque comedy:

> Delirando más, veía la ciudad resplandeciente y esmaltada de mil colorines. Seguramente era una ciudad de muñecos; ¡pero qué muñecos! . . . Por diversos lados salían blancas pelucas, y ninguna puerta se abría en los huecos del piso segundo sin dar paso a una bonita figura de cera, estopa o porcelana; y todos corrían por los pasadizos gritando: "Ya es hora . . ." En las escaleras se cruzaban galones que subían con galones que bajaban . . . Todos los muñecos tenían prisa. A éste se le olvidaba una cosa, a aquel otro, una hebilla, una pluma, un cordón. Unos llamaban a sus mujeres para que les alcanzasen algo, y todos repetían: "La hora! . . ."
> (IV, 1586-87)

Schraibman describes in detail the function of Rosario's dreams in *Doña Perfecta*. One night Rosario dreams of the scene which she had witnessed earlier through the garden window: Caballuco and her mother's other henchmen conspiring against Pepe Rey, to foil Pepe's plans to aid Rosario to escape from her mother. The double distortion inherent in the dream (the original distortion of witnessing the scene through the garden window, plus the distortion of the dream itself) reveals the truly malevolent nature of the people and events Rosario witnessed.

In the dream Don Inocencio appears as a bird: Caballuco, as a frightening dragon; the others, as clay figures:

> El penitenciario agitaba las alas. Era una presumida avecilla que quería volar y no podía. Su pico se alargaba y se retorcía. Erizábansele las plumas con síntomas de furor, y después, recogiéndose y aplacándose, escondía la pelada cabeza bajo el ala. Luego, las figurillas de barro se agitaban, queriendo ser personas, y Frasquito Gonzáles se empeñaba en pasar por hombre.
> (IV, 479)

Schraibman quotes Vicente Gaos, who explains: "La deformación material de las imagenes que ve Rosario deja traslucir, en admirable réplica, la deformación moral de las almas de doña Perfecta y don Inocencio, lo monstruoso de su acción."[50]

Other dreams more clearly reveal the character's innermost desires and fears, "zonas de la conciencia a las que en estado de vigilia no tenemos acceso."[51] The images of these dreams are what Gullón calls "figuraciones simbólicas,"[52] which may or may not appear to be related to the character's experience of external reality. Some of these symbols seem absurd, others—the most striking—are clearly surrealistic in nature. Gullón cites, as an example, Víctor Cadalso's dream in *Miau*. Víctor dreams that he is running through an interminable series of corridors lined with mirrors, eternally pursuing a woman wearing boots with heels made of eggshells and carrying in her hand a full-size chest of drawers, which appears to Víctor as a change purse. The dream reveals Víctor's character: that of a vain, narcissistic man who gains power and influence in life through women whose favors, sexual and otherwise, are for sale. The dream symbols confirm the presentation of Víctor made throughout the novel by the narrator but also make that reality a thousand times more vivid.

Another clear case is Fortunata's dream in *Fortunata y Jacinta* in which she meets a destitute Juan in the streets of Madrid and promises to help support him in any way she can. The dream occurs at a point in the novel when Fortunata's ego has been severely wounded by her encounter with Jacinta in Guillermina's house. At the height of her rage and fury against society for what it has taken from her, and with the words of Jacinta ringing in her ears, Fortunata creates a world turned upside down: first, in her interior monologue, where she becomes Juanito's legitimate wife and Jacinta the "ladrona;" then, in the dream itself, where she and Juan change social roles. The dream begins with Fortunata's vision of herself in a hardware store, surrounded by hundreds of faucets, spigots and pipes (clearly phallic symbols). The vision reveals the need which Fortunata, frustrated by months of living with poor, impotent Maxi, feels for Juanito, and it prefigures Juanito's actual appearance in the dream (and in reality). It is significant that in her dream Fortunata first catches a glimpse of Juan across a crowded street and that her path across the street toward reunion with Juan is blocked by a collision between a carriage driven by a wealthy gentleman and a cart loaded with barrels of olive oil, a collision symbolic of the clash of social classes which is an obstacle to her union with Juan in reality. Juan's destitute appearance and Fortunata's offer of help continue the image of the world turned upside down (reversal of social roles) first noted in Fortunata's interior monologue and reveal the depth of Fortunata's desire to be wanted and needed, to justify her existence, to reassert her ego.

Dreams often reveal a reality previously hidden in the subconscious mind from the character himself as well as from the reader (Gullón's "el sueño como premonición"). Consider, for example, Maxi's dream in *Fortunata y Jacinta,* through which he becomes aware, for the first time, of Fortunata's pregnancy. An angel appears to Maxi in his dream and announces that his wife is pregnant with "el hijo del Pensamiento Puro," the only pregnancy which Maxi's knowledge of the facts can admit. Maxi consciously dismisses the dream as a *disparate,* but it is in fact true that Fortunata is pregnant. Schraibman cites the example of Fortunata's dream on her wedding night of doors opening and of men coming into her room through transparent walls, which foreshadows her reunion with Juanito the following day.[53] Gullón cites, as an example, Isidora's dream in *La desheredada,* which prefigures her downfall and in which she becomes aware, for the first time, of the destruction of her illusions of nobility and the hopelessness of ever winning her case. She dreams of her son Riquín playing with a rifle with which he shoots her, after which she is dragged through the streets while people mock her with the words "La marquesa, la marquesa." As Gullón says, "Este sentirse bofada y escarnecida por la multitud a quien detesta y que la detesta es la forma de expresar plásticamente el reconocimiento de la derrota, su vencimiento por la hostilidad del hado."[54]

In effect, then, we may consider dream sequences, because of their highly revealing nature, as structurally parallel to those passages in which language is used as image or metaphor to express the image of reality reflected in the character's conscious mind: the symbolic language of dreams expresses the image of reality reflected in the character's subconscious mind. This represents the ultimate in interiorization, the ultimate shift in point of view.

Conclusions

The purpose of this third chapter was to study carefully, at the most basic level, that of language, the words themselves, the "formula of art" which constitutes the basis of Galdosian realism, and the key role of the narrator in the implementation of that formula. Remembering George Becker's definition of realism as "a formula of art which, conceiving of reality in a certain way, undertakes to present a simulacrum of it on the basis of more or less fixed rules,"[55] and intuiting from having read Galdós' novels that reality, for Galdós, is (again, in Becker's terms), "that which has its being in some kind of relation between external phenomena and perceiving consciousness,"[56] we set out to examine those "more or less fixed rules" by which the simulacrum of reality (i.e. the relationship of perceiving consciousness to external phenomena) is conveyed. Following Ortega's theory that the novel must be perceived from within itself, we proposed that it was the narrator who was the figure through whom the novel was perceived, the consciousness through whom the reader perceived the "external phenomena" of the novel. This chapter, then, purported to show how these relationships: between narrator (and reader) and the world of the novel, between perceiving consciousness and external phenomena, were first created, at the most basic structural level of the novel, the words themselves.

What this chapter has shown is that, in fact, the relationship between perceiving consciousness and external phenomena (what has traditionally been called point of view) is determined linguistically: the language in all its functions not only determines the point of view manifest in the novel at any one moment in the novel, but indeed first creates the whole complex relationship of narrator to the world of the novel (perceiving consciousness to external phenomena). This chapter demonstrated how the narrator created the impression of a reality independent of himself in the novel through mimetic language and how the characters and their language maintained that illusion of an independent reality. In this chapter we saw that the narrator went on to establish his own point of view (presence in the novel) through his expressive language, and that similarly each of the characters established his own point of view through his own language. Here it was shown that as the language of the novel moves away from the neutrality of mimesis and becomes increasingly expressive of the narrator or one of the characters' the point of view shifts correspondingly. As language becomes increasingly expressive of the narrator, his presence (point of view) becomes more and more evident. As the narrator's language increasingly approximates that of the character, distance between them is reduced and eventually disappears completely when the narrator disappears linguistically and the narrative adopts the character's language (and point of view).

Clearly point of view in Galdós' novels is not stable, but constantly shifting from the neutrality of mimesis to the point of view of a particular character, to that of the narrator and back again to mimesis. Galdós' narrative is free flowing, moving constantly from mimetic narration and description through indirect free style to character narration to interior monologue and again to mimetic narration. The shift is seldom abrupt, often it is quite gradual but always easily discernible through linguistic clues which measure the extent of its variation from the language of the narrator in its mimetic or expressive function.

Clearly, too, point of view in Galdós' novels is multiple. In other words, reality is perceived through the consciousness of a variety of characters. Nevertheless, it is also clear that point of view in these novels is not absolute, but relative; relative to the world of the novel created by the narrator's mimesis and relative to the central perspective (point of view) established by the narrator through his expressive language. This is simply another way of expressing the narrator's dominance of the novel. The narrator does offer the reader an unlimited point of view, a multiplicity of perspective. There are passages in which he abandons the novel temporarily to allow the reader to perceive the world directly through the consciousness of another, yet he never totally abandons the novel. He always returns to manifest his presence, his point of view. His is the consciousness through which the reader perceives the world of the novel. Ultimately the world of the novel must be known and understood in terms of that consciousness.

FOOTNOTES

[1] Roman Jakobson, "Closing Statement: Linguistics and Poetics," in *Style in Language*, ed. Thomas A. Sebeok (Cambridge: Harvard University Press, 1960), p. 355.

[2] Félix Martínez-Bonati, *La estructura de la obra literaria* (Santiago de Chile: Ediciones de la Universidad de Chile, 1960) passim, pp. 45-63.

[3] *Ibid.*, p. 45.

[4] *Ibid.*, p. 45.

[5] *Ibid.*, p. 55.

[6] This does not imply that the narrator stands apart from the novelistic world: he is, indeed, an integral part of that world. He, and the reader, perceive that world from within, not from outside of the novel. An analogous situation might be a conversation between two or more people in the same room; when the person speaking uses language to describe something outside of himself, the listener's attention is drawn away from the speaker and toward the thing the speaker is describing; when the speaker uses language to express himself, the listener's attention is drawn toward the speaker, and he is only indirectly aware of the context in which the conversation takes place.

[7] Jakobson, pp. 355-357.

[8] Victor Schlovsky, "Art as Technique," in *Russian Formalist Criticism: Four Essays*, trans. and intro. Lee T. Lemon and Marion J. Rees (Lincoln: University of Nebraska Press, Regents Critics Series, 1965), p. 4.

[9] Jakobson, p. 353.

[10] Benito Pérez Galdós, *La desheredada* in *Obras completas* (Madrid: Aguilar, 6a ed., 1966), IV, p. 966. All further page references included in parentheses in the text are from *Obras completas*, IV, V (Madrid: Aguilar, 6a ed., 1966).

[11] Norman Friedman, "Point of View in Fiction: A Critical Concept," PMLA, 80 (December, 1955), p. 1169.

¹²*Ibid.*, p. 1170.
¹³*Ibid.*, p. 1170.
¹⁴The *novelas dialogadas* present a special case. Here the *acotaciones* do manifest the narrator's presence. The *acotaciones* of the *novelas dialogadas* are really the equivalent of the narrator's mimetic narrative in the other novels. The term "scene" as used by Friedman, and as used to describe certain kinds of passages in the *novelas contemporáneas* is a much broader concept than the dramatic scene of the *novelas dialogadas*. Scene refers as much to content as to form.
¹⁵Friedman, p. 1169.
¹⁶To be discussed later also in the section dealing with the characters' point of view.
¹⁷Michael Nimetz, *Humor in Galdós* (New Haven: Yale University Press, 1968), p. 101.
¹⁸Wolfgang Kayser, "Origen y crisis de la novela moderna," *Cultura universitaria* no. 47, (enero-febrero, 1955), passim.
¹⁹Nimetz, p. 101.
²⁰*Ibid.*, p. 103.
²¹*Ibid.*, p. 103.
²²*Ibid.*, p. 103.
²³*Ibid.*, p. 104.
²⁴*Ibid.*, p. 18.
²⁵*Ibid.*, p. 105.
²⁶Quoted by Nimetz, p. 21.
²⁷*Ibid.*, p. 21.
²⁸See the article by Monroe Z. Hafter, "Ironic Reprise in Galdós' Novels," PMLA, 76 (1961), pp. 233-239.
²⁹Antonio Sánchez Barbudo, "Vulgaridad y genio de Galdós," *Archivum*, 7 (diciembre-enero de 1957), p. 66.
³⁰*Ibid.*, p. 67.
³¹Nimetz, p. 180.
³²Stephen Ullman, "Reported Speech in Flaubert," in *Style in the French Novel* (Cambridge: Harvard University Press, 1957), p. 113.
³³*Ibid.*, p. 99.
³⁴*Ibid.*, passim.
³⁵Note, for example, this reported conversation between Pepeta and Rosario, tío Barret's daughter, from *La barraca:*
No; ella no era mala. Había trabajado en las fábricas, había servido a una familia como doméstica, pero al fin sus hermanas le dieron el ejemplo, cansadas de sufrir hambre; y allí estaba, recibiendo unas veces cariños y otras bofetadas, hasta que reventase para siempre. Era natural: donde no hay padre y madre, la familia termina así. De todo tenía la culpa el amo de la tierra, aquel don Salvador, que de seguro ardía en los infiernos. ¡Ah, ladrón! . . . ¡Y como había perdido a toda una familia!
Pepeta olvidó su actitud fría y reservada para unirse a la indignación de la muchacha. Verdad, todo verdad; aquel tío avaro tenía la culpa. La huerta entera lo sabía. ¡Válgame Dios, y cómo se pierde una casa! ¡Tan bueno que era tío Barret! ¡Si levantara la cabeza y viese a sus hijas. . . ." (from Vicente Blasco Ibáñez, *La barraca* (New York: Holt, Rinehart, Winston, 1960), p. 6.

[36] Note, for example, this passage representing Batiste's thoughts, from *La barraca:*

¡Cuán desgraciado era! ¡Solo contra todos. . . . Al pequeñín lo encontraría muerto al volver a su barraca; el caballo, que era su vida, inutilizado por aquellos traidores; el mal llegando a él de todas partes, surgiendo de los caminos, de las casas, de los cañares, aprovechando todas las ocasiones para herir a los suyos; y él inerme, sin poder defenderse de aquel enemigo que se desvanecía apenas intentaba resolverse contra él, cansado de sufrir.

¡Gran Dios! ¿qué había hecho él para padecer tanto? ¿No era un hombre bueno? . . .

(from Vicente Blasco Ibáñez, *La barraca,* pp. 108-109)

[37] Robert Humphreys, *Stream of Consciousness in the Modern Novel* (Berkely and Los Angeles: University of California Press, 1965), p. 24.

[38] *Ibid.,* p. 25.

[39] *Ibid.,* p. 29.

[40] *Ibid.,* p. 29.

[41] Quoted by Joseph Schraibman, *Dreams in the Novels of Galdós* (New York: Hispanic Institute, 1960), p. 178.

[42] Ricardo Gullón, *Galdó, novelista moderno* (Madrid: Editorial Gredos, 2a. 1966), p. 187.

[43] *Ibid.* pp. 177 ff.

[44] *Ibid.,* p. 183.

[45] Schraibman, p. 6.

[46] Gullón, p. 179.

[47] *Ibid.,* p. 177.

[48] *Ibid.,* p. 177.

[49] Schraibman, p. 50.

[50] Quoted by Schraibman, p. 54.

[51] Gullón, p. 183.

[52] *Ibid.,* p. 187.

[53] Schraibman, p. 24.

[54] Gullón, p. 189.

[55] George Becker, "Modern Realism as a Literary Movement," in *Documents of Modern Literary Realism* (Princeton: Princton University Press, 1963), p. 36.

[56] *Ibid.,* p. 36.

Chapter IV

DISTANCE

Some Preliminary Considerations

In any discussion of the concept of distance in a work of literature, there immediately comes to mind the idea of aesthetic distance. This concept was formulated in 1912 by Edwin Bullough in his article " 'Psychical Distance' as a Factor in Art: an Aesthetic Principle."[1] Bullough examines at length the relationship between the individual and the work of art and concludes that aesthetic distance, that distance which enables the individual to put aside his very personal, pragmatic reactions to the work, is an essential attribute of all art. In Bullough's words: "This distance appears to be between our own self and its affections, using the latter term in its broadest sense as anything which affects our being, bodily or spiritually, as sensation, perception, emotional state or idea . . . Distance lies between our own self and such objects as are the sources or vehicles of such affections."[2] He continues, "The transformation by Distance is produced by putting the phenomenon, so to speak, out of gear with our practical, actual self; by allowing it to stand outside the context of our personal needs and ends, by looking at it objectively."[3]

Bullough admits the variability of distance. It may, he says, differ not only according to the nature of the object (the work of art), but also according to the individual's capacity for maintaining a greater or lesser degree. He speaks of the effects of under-distancing, in which the individual reacts too personally to the work of art; and over-distancing, in which the work of art appears to the individual to be artificial, improbable, empty or absurd.

Bullough's concept of aesthetic distance, however, is just that—aesthetic. It does not account for the varieties of distance which may exist between the individual and the work of art, not only aesthetic, but also intellectual, psychological, moral, etc. It does not account for the fact that the degree and kind of distance existing between the individual and the work of art varies not only from one work to another, but also within the same work, from one moment to another. Finally, the concept of aesthetic distance is an extrinsic one, having to do with the relationship between the individual and the work of art. But distance may also be an intrinsic concept, having to do with the relationship between the different elements within the work itself.

Wayne Booth, in *The Rhetoric of Fiction*, discusses the complex relationships which exist between the basic elements of any narrative situation. He identifies four "participants" in the narrative situation: author, narrator, the other characters of the novel (and, by extension, the whole of the narrative itself), and the reader. These relationships can be defined by the extent and nature of the distance between each of these basic elements. As Booth explains: "In any reading experience there is an implied dialogue among author, narrator, the other characters, and the reader. Each of the four can range, in relation to each of the others, from identification to complete opposition, on any axis of value, moral, intellectual, aesthetic, and even physical."[4]

In the realistic novel in general, and more particularly in Galdós' novels, the most consistent of these relationships, as demonstrated in Chapter Three, is between the narrator and the implied author.[5] Intellectually, morally, ethically, and psychologically the distance between the narrator and the implied author of these novels is virtually nil. The result is what Booth calls the "reliable narrator," one who represents the "norms" of the novel, who consistently represents the implied author's beliefs and point of view. As Booth points out, most of the great reliable narrators indulge in a great deal of incidental irony, and are thus "unreliable" in the sense of being potentially deceptive. But the intelligent reader is not deceived, for he is aware of the fact that irony of tone is inherent in the modern novel. He does not interpret the narrator's language literally, and finds the ironic tone perfectly consistent with the norms of the novel.

The reliable narrator is, in fact, a familiar figure: the personal narrator typical of nineteenth-century fiction, who accompanies the reader as a guide through the novelistic world, introducing him to the characters, pointing out the significant features of the world, organizing and synthesizing this reality, giving it recognizable form and making it available to the reader's intelligence. The only exceptions to this prototype of the "reliable" narrator in Galdós' novels (at least within the series of *novelas contemporáneas*) are *Lo prohibido* and *El amigo Manso*. The narrators of *Lo prohibido* and *El amigo Manso* stand at the center of their own narratives. Speaking both as narrator and character, the reliability of their narration is considerably lessened.[6]

Because of the key role of the narrator in Galdós' novels, we find that distance between narrator and reader is consistently very slight.

The reader identifies closely with the narrator, perceiving the world of the novel through the narrator's eyes and mind. The distance between them increases only when the reader becomes aware of the narrator as an entity (intellectual, emotional or aesthetic) apart from himself.[7]

The relationship between the narrator and the other characters of the novel offers an even greater degree of variety and complexity. The shifting nature and degree of distance between the narrator and the other characters results in a multiple point of view, a multiplicity of perspective which greatly complicates and enriches the novel's structure. It was amply demonstrated in the previous chapter how changing psychological distance between narrator and character, as measured linguistically, creates the basic dimensions of the novel's structure.

The greatest degree of complexity is shown in the relationship between the narrator and his narrative as a whole. Here distance between the narrator and his narrative ranges from complete identification to complete opposition, and is measured on a variety of axes—temporal, spatial, psychological, emotional, intellectual, aesthetic. The distance between the narrator and his narrative in effect establishes what are, broadly conceived, the three basic structural planes of the novel, and they, in turn, determine those other characteristics—modes of narration and characterization, narrative pace, sense of time and space, and tone which constitute a novel's structure and, ultimately, its style.

The first of these narrative planes is essentially the background world of the novel—the geographical, historical, social, political and moral setting, conceived and executed intellectually, against which the central drama of the novel is played out. Here the narrator stands at a considerable distance from his narrative, playing the role of social historian or interpreter of human behavior: analyzing or generalizing upon what he sees, offering capsule versions of a character's history or personality, occasionally summarizing events taking place over a period of time. The physical world may be exhaustively described, but is never materialized: the description presupposes a previous perception of sensory details which have been recalled and "reconstructed" in an ordered fashion. Characters appear as fixed entities, as men who *are,* not as men who *exist* in time. They may be perceived as social or human types, not as individuals. Events appear as history, not as life in process.

As the narrator's distance from his narrative decreases, we enter the middleground of the novel, a vast and ill-defined area, whose only essential characteristic is its "perceptibility." Here the narrator stands immediately before the world he describes: a particular, well-defined region of time and space. What he describes of that world is what is "knowable" through the senses: thus its essentially "material" nature. Here we enter the world of material phenomena, the world of life in process. Characters are still seen from without, but they are no longer seen as fixed, "defined" entities, but as men in the process of defining themselves through their actions and dialogs with other characters. Events appear not as history but as they happen (or have just happened).

The complex nature of the middle ground results from the fact that while here the narrator's temporal and spatial distance from the narrative remains relatively constant, his psychological and emotional distance may vary considerably. The narrator's changing psychological distance tends to pull the reader alternately toward the background (dominated by the narrator) or toward the foreground (dominated by the characters). The narrator's intrusions in the narrative of the middle ground, in the form of tonal irony, imagery or interpretive commentary remind the reader that another consciousness is present, and so he is drawn away from the merely perceptual toward the intellectual character of the background. At the same time, as the characters' presence becomes more and more obvious, the reader is drawn away from the merely perceptual toward the emotional center of experience which each individual character represents.

As the distance between the narrator and his narrative decreases, we enter the foreground, a world totally dominated by the individual character as the center of experience. Here the world is not *seen* from without but is *experienced* from within. The narrator has disappeared and novelistic reality is known directly, with no mediation. The physical world appears only as reflected in the character's mind. Events are experienced simultaneously with the character's experience of them. As the narrative moves from the inner world of the character's conscious mind (outwardly directed, as he speaks to others; inwardly directed, in interior monologues) toward the inner world of the character's subconscious, it becomes increasingly emotional or experiential in character.

To understand better the nature of these levels of narration (both aesthetic and psychological) we might turn to Ortega's theories of psychological distance, as expressed in *The Dehumanization of Art*.

In a section called "A Few Drops of Phenomenology," Ortega describes a scene in which a man lies dying, surrounded by four people with varying degrees of interest in the man's death. He then goes on to discuss the psychological distance which separates each of the four people from the center of the scene. His conclusion is that although they in fact witness the same scene, they may appear to be witnessing four very different scenes. For the way in which the scene is perceived depends on the point from which it is seen, that is, on the distance between the person viewing the scene and the event he is witnessing. At the emotional center is the dying man's wife, who does not "perceive" the scene, but rather, "lives" it. She is a part of it. The doctor is in the scene, he lives it, but only with professional interest. The reporter is not a part of the scene. He merely observes it from without. His is not a personal emotional interest, for it serves only to produce an emotional response in his readers. At maximum distance stands the artist, whose interest is purely aesthetic, formal, totally devoid of human emotion.

The importance of his analysis of this scene, says Ortega, is that it establishes "a scale of emotional distances between ourselves and reality."[8] To Ortega's basic model we might add that maximum distance may well result not in an aesthetic vision of reality, but in a "conceptualized" or "intellectualized" vision of reality. Both aesthetic and intellectual distance imply some sort of previous sensory perception or observation, but the reality thus observed through the senses is subsequently transformed by the intellectual or the aesthetic consciousness.

Applying Ortega's theory to the novel, we may thus justify our observation that, because he is the basic center of consciousness in the novel, the narrator's distance from his narrative establishes several narrative planes which may be understood both psychologically and aesthetically. When the narrator, like the dying man's wife, stands at minimum distance from the center of reality, the result is a narrative plane essentially emotional or experiential, what Ortega calls "lived reality." The narrator is *in* the scene, indeed, is at the center of it. He does not observe it, but lives it. At intermediate distance the narrator, like the reporter, merely observes reality. He is not in it; he does not live it; but is nevertheless close enough (temporally and spatially) to perceive it sensorially. At maximum distance the narrator, having perceived reality through the senses, proceeds to transform it through his intellectual or aesthetic consciousness.

In aesthetic terms, this shifting distance between the narrator and his narrative creates distinct narrative planes which correspond to the psychological planes just defined: the foreground of "lived reality," the middle ground of "perceived reality" and the background of "aesthetic or intellectual reality." The psychological character of each of these narrative planes determines the aesthetic character of each (i.e. the way in which reality is presented), and this in turn determines the way in which the reader perceives or "knows" the world of the novel.

It should be pointed out that the boundaries between these structural planes are not rigidly defined. Rather, they are often blurred, for as the distance between narrator and narrative changes in degree and nature, the narrative moves from background to middle ground to foreground often quite subtly. All narrative planes are well integrated, for the worlds they represent are co-existent and ultimately inseparable. Nevertheless, we can establish a rather schematic diagram which reveals the general nature of certain structural and stylistic elements characteristic of each of the narrative planes.

	Background	Middleground	Foreground
Mode of presentation	Indirect	Mixture of direct and indirect	Direct
Pace	Slow	Fast	Slow
Time	Historical	Process; externally perceived	Simultaneous; internal; "durée"
Space		external	internal
Tone	objective, documentary; ironic	variable	intimate
Mode of characterization	abstract	perceptual	experiential

This, of course, is a greatly simplified diagrammatic representation of what is, in fact, a very complex problem. What follows is a detailed study of the variations in distance between the narrator and his narrative, as manifest in each of those basic structural elements. Its purpose is to show the key role of the narrator in creating the structure, and ultimately the style, of Galdós' novels.

Modes of Presentation

In the background world, modes of presentation are indirect. The narrator speaks directly to the reader, in his own words, acting as mediator of novelistic reality. The narrative on this plane typically takes the form of 1) the narrator's philosophical comments and speculations based on the concrete situations of the novel, or political and sociological observations; 2) the narrator's summaries of events in the life of a whole society, a particular social class, a family, or an individual; 3) the narrator's description, in the form of a well-ordered summary definition, of a particular character or group of characters (a family, for example); or his description of the habits or customs of a social class or group, presented in summary fashion (*costumbrista* type descriptions) and 4) the narrator's description of the physical setting, presented in an ordered fashion, perhaps in the course of a summary definition.

The distance at which the narrator stands allows him to see beyond what is immediately perceptible to the senses and active upon the emotions. It enables him to be objective, to abstract from and generalize upon the immediate reality, to see patterns in events and phenomena, to apply his intellect, his rational faculties, to the comprehension and ordering of reality. At the extreme, distance between the narrator and his narrative results in passages more like essays than fiction.

Consider, for example, this passage from *Fortunata y Jacinta* in which the narrator discusses the changes in social structure, the free interchange between social classes, apparent in nineteenth-century Spain:

> Es curioso observar cómo nuestra edad, por otros conceptos infeliz, nos presenta una dichosa confusión de todas las clases, mejor dicho, la concordia y reconciliación de todas ellas. En esto aventaja nuestro país a otros, donde están pendientes de sentencia los graves pleitos históricos de la igualdad. Aquí se ha resuelto el problema sencilla y pacíficamente, gracias al temple democrático de los españoles y a la escasa vehemencia de las preocupaciones nobiliarias. Un gran defecto nacional, la empleomanía, tiene también su parte en esta gran conquista. Las oficinas han sido el tronco en que se han injertado las ramas históricas, y de ellas han salido amigos el noble tronado y el plebeyo ensorbecido por un título universitario; y de amigos, pronto han pasado a parientes. Esta confusión es un bien, y gracias a ella no nos aterra el contagio de la guerra social, porque tenemos ya en la masa de la sangre un socialismo atenuado e inofensivo. . . . (V, 65)

This is clearly seen in the novel in the case of the Santa Cruz family, when friendships and familiar relationships extend over various social classes. Nor are the narrator's comments unrelated to one of the novel's major themes—the periodic but necessary vitalization of the middle and upper classes by the *pueblo* (e.g. Fortunata's giving a son and heir to the Santa Cruz family which the sterile Jacinta could not provide.)

Consider also the narrator's comments on the nature of madness, from *La desheredada*. Describing the asylum Leganés, the narrator goes on to speculate:

> . . . ¡Y considerar que aquella triste colonia no representa otra cosa que la exageración o el extremo irritativo de nuestras múltiples particularidades morales o intelectuales. . . . , que todos, cuál más, cuál menos, tenemos la inspiración, el estro de los disparates, y a poco que nos descuidemos entramos de lleno en los sombríos dominios de la ciencia alienista! Porque no, no son tan grandes las diferencias. Las ideas de estos desgraciados son nuestras ideas, pero desengarzadas, sueltas, sacadas de la misteriosa hebra que gallardamente las enfila. Estos pobres orates somos nosotros mismos que dormimos anoche nuestro pensamiento en la variedad esplendente de todas las ideas posibles, y hoy por la mañana lo despertamos en la aridez de una sola. ¡Oh Leganés! Si quisieran representarte en una ciudad teórica, a semejanza de las que antaño trazaban filósofos, santos y estampistas, para expresar un plan moral o religioso, no, no habría arquitectos ni fisiólogos que se atrevieran a marcar con segura mano tus hospitalarias paredes . . . (IV, 967)

Again, the narrator's comments reinforce one of the novel's principal themes: the heroine's (and by extension, the Spaniard's) eternal quixotism, the imposition of his ideals, his fantasies, on the real world, to the extent that all reality is excluded. Isidora and countless others who inhabit the world of *La desheredada* are no less mad than poor Tomás Rufete, whose behavior inspires the narrator's comments on madness.

Interestingly, it is only in these passages, when the narrator stands at maximum distance from his narrative, that the language of the novel loses the personal, familiar tone characteristic of most of the narrative.

The narrator's temporal distance allows him to offer histories of an entire society, a particular social class, a family, or an individual character. From this distance the life of man and society is seen as something done, finished, and not as something living, in process. Looking back, the narrator sees patterns in these events and in the relationships between people that he cannot see in the present. His distance allows him to look at reality more objectively to deal with it intellectually more than perceptually.

Consider, for example, the narrator's account of the history of Miquis' aunt, Isabel de Godoy, from *El doctor Centeno*:

> Doña Isabel y su hermana, llamada doña Piedad, fueron la única sucesión de don Gaspar Godoy, uno de los más frondosos y enhiestos ramos de aquel tronco de los Godoyes manchegos. . . . Hubo por aquellas calendas en el Quintanar un galán de hermosa presencia, tan notable por su gallardía como por sus modales y educación, hombre peregrino en aquellas tierras, a las que fue con hastío de la corte buscando un descanso a sus viajes y a las fatigas de la moda y del mundo. Doña Isabel se apasionó locamente de tal, que era de gran familia, los Herreras, de Almagro, y tenía tíos y primos en el Toboso. El le correspondía; eran públicos y honestos sus amores: parecía natural que la solución y término de esto fuera el matrimonio . . . ; mas no sucedió así. De la noche a la mañana, con pasmo y habilla de todo el pueblo, Herrera se casó, no con doña Isabel, sino con su hermana.
> (IV, 1352-53)

Or there are the histories of Juan Bou, in *La desheredada* (IV, 1078ff); of the Rubín family in *Fortunata y Jacinta* (V, 158ff); or of the Villaamil family in *Miau* (V, 588ff). In all of these examples the narrative covers an extensive period of time, and many events are mentioned only in passing. They usually form a part of an introduction to a character written in the form of a summary definition. The myriad details of a character's life have already been selected, organized and given form and meaning by the intellect, and that life appears now to be finished, defined.

In fact, few of the historical summaries in Galdós' novels are as rigidly objective as the examples might indicate. Typically, the narrator mitigates the effect of temporal distance by the personal, familiar tone of his narration, by the colloquial quality of his language, and by the presentation of history as personal history, with himself or one of the other characters as a personal witness of the events. Two very typical examples are the history of the Santa Cruz and Arnáiz families from *Fortunata y Jacinta* and the history of Isidora's life in the years intervening between parts one and two of *La desheredada*. In the former, it is Estupiñá who serves as the personal witness of the events described; in the latter, it is don José de Relimpio who tells the tale of those years. In both cases, the narrator appears only as the interlocutor of the information.

As the narrator explains, upon beginning the story of the Santa Cruz family:

> Las amistades y parentescos de las familias de Santa Cruz y Arnáiz pueden ser ejemplo de aquel feliz revoltijo de las clases sociales; mas ¿quién es el guapo que se atreve a formar estadística de las ramas de tan dilatado y laberíntico árbol, que más bien parece enredadera, cuyos vástagos se cruzan, suben, bajan y se pierden en los huecos de un follaje densísimo? Sólo se puede intentar tal empresa con la ayuda de Estupiñá, que sabe al dedillo la historia de todas las familias comerciales de Madrid y todos los enlaces que se han hecho en medio siglo. (V, 66)

And as the narrator begins his account of the events in Isidora's life between parts one and two of *La desheredada,* he explains:

> Todo lo ocurrido en ese largo espacio de treinta y cuatro meses en que ha estado Isidora fuera de nuestra vista, merece algo de historia, y para ello aprovechamos las efemérides verbales de don José de Relimpio, cuya amabilidad para el suministro de noticias es inagotable. (IV, 1065)

In effect, the history which follows clearly reveals the ephemeral style and character of don José. Consider, for example, the entry from September of 1873:

> Septiembre. — Cartagena, excursiones de las fragatas. ¡Oh! Don José les perdonaría a los cantonales en su calaverada si aprovecharan el empuje de las fragatas para irse a Gibraltar y conquistar aquel pedazo de nuestro territorio, retenido por la pérfida Inglaterra. Si viviera Méndez Núñez, otro gallo nos

> cantara. — Horrores del cura Santa Cruz. — Doña Laura, como si fuera símbolo humano de la unidad y el honor de la patria, sucumbe en aquellos tristes días . . . — Dispersión de la familia de Relimpio. Isidora vuelve a Madrid; está algo desfigurada, pero según sus cuentas, en diciembre concluirá aquello. — Castelar, ministro. El bueno de Relimpio, en quien no se había entibiado ni un punto la noble simpatía que por su ahijada sentía, se va a vivir con ella, le sirve en todo lo que puede y la acompaña cuando está sola y aburrida . . .
> (IV, 1066)

As noted above, these histories, particularly when they are a part of the summary definitions which introduce a character, sometimes take on a distinctly personal and familiar tone, as the narrator's psychological and emotional distance from his narrative decreases. Consider, for example, this excerpt from the introduction to Juan Pablo Rubín in the second volume of *Fortunata y Jacinta*. The passage relates the vicissitudes in Juan Pablo's career and his perennial lack of success:

> Durante un par de años estuvo rodando por los ferrocarriles con sus cajas de muestras. De Barcelona hasta Huelva y desde Pontevedra a Almería no le quedó rincón que no visitase, deteniéndose en Madrid todo el tiempo que podía . . . En otra temporada corrió chocolates, pañuelos y chales *galería,* conservas, devocionarios y hasta palillos de dientes. Por su diligencia, su honradez y por la puntualidad con que remitía los fondos recaudados, sus comitentes le apreciaban mucho. Pero no se sabe como se las componía, que siempre estaba *más pobre que las ratas,* y se lamentaba con amanerado pesimismo de su pícara suerte. Todas sus ganancias se le iban *por entre los dedos,* frecuentando mucho los cafés en sus ratos de descanso. . . . Rubín fue al mes siguiente inspector de Policía en no sé qué provincia. Pero su infame estrella se la había jurado; a los tres meses cambió la situación política; y a mi Rubín, cesante . . . (V, 159)

Such clichés as "más pobre que las ratas", and "todas sus ganancias se le iban por entre los dedos", as well as the narrator's intrusion of self in "mi Rubín" add a distinctly personal and familiar note to the narrative.

Summary definition of characters is another typical mode of narration on the background level of the novel. Here the primary mode of writing is description, rather than narration, by the narrator, although narration is included in the form of the historical summaries just discussed. In these passages narrator and reader view the character and his life from without and from a considerable distance, outside of any particular, perceptible situation. So the character appears as a complete entity, a portrait, as it were, apart from the contingencies of a particular moment in time and space and life in process. His personality appears fixed, "defined" in the literal sense of the word.

A few minor characters never move beyond the rigid confines of this static portrait. For others, and certainly for all major characters introduced in this fashion, summary definition serves only as a schematic outline of their personality, an outline enormously enriched by their subsequent appearances in scenes in the middle and foreground of the narrative, where these basic character traits are underlined, developed and expanded.

Nevertheless, in the summary definitions themselves, where reality is viewed apart from a particular situation in time and space, the primary appeal is to the intellect rather than to the senses. The myriad details of a character's life, his appearance and personality, have been absorbed and transformed by the narrator's intellect. There are often in the course of these summary definitions extensive descriptions of a character's physical appearance, manner of dress and speech. But, precisely because these descriptions occur outside a particular moment in time and space, outside a perceptible situation, the character is, in effect, "imagined" by the reader rather than perceived. At the very least, even in all his materiality, the character is perceived in a much less immediate way than he is in a very "immediate" scene from the novel's middle or foreground. Reading one of these summary definitions is much like looking at a portrait: both suggest much more than they state. The reader fills in which his imagination the outline drawn in the introduction. At this distance the reader may "understand" a character intellectually, but he does not perceive him sensorially nor experience him psychologically or emotionally.

The center of the summary definition of a character is often a statement by the narrator, usually expressed in abstract terms, which synthesizes a character and his personality. Whatever else may be included in the summary definition—a character's past history, his physical appearance, manner of dress, or speech and movement—functions only in support of the narrator's synthetical statement about the character. So the narrator organizes his material in direct relation to his synthetic vision of the character, then presents his material in the only way his intellectually centered approach to reality allows him: direct narration, in his own words.

Consider the following example of synthetic statements given by the narrator in the course of his summary definitions. In *La desheredada,* the narrator characterizes José de Relimpio: "Era el hombre mejor del mundo. Era un hombre que no servía para nada." (IV, 1014), and Juan Bou: "A pesar de sus baladronadas políticas y de su aspecto feroz, Juan Bou, el *ursus spoeleus* . . ." (IV, 1081). In *Tormento,* the narrator describes Bringas: "Tenía dos religiones, la de Dios y la del ahorro". (IV, 1459). In *Fortunata y Jacinta,* the narrator thus describes Guillermina Pacheco: "Era mujer que cuando se proponía algo iba a su fin, derecha como una bala . . ." (V, 76), and doña Lupe "la de los Pavos": ". . . doña Lupe era tal y como su sobrino la pintaba en aquella breve consideración; era juiciosa, razonable, se hacía cargo de todo, miraba con ojos un tanto escépticos las flaquezas humanas, y sabía perdonar las ofensas y hasta las injurias; pero lo que es una deuda, no lo perdonaba nunca. Había en ella dos personas distintas: la mujer y la prestamista." (V, 203)

The relationship between the synthetical statement and the rest of the material presented in the summary definition is perhaps best shown in the narrator's description of José de Relimpio, in *La desheredada.* Before offering his synthesis, the narrator remarks: "Rematemos este retrato con dos brochazos. Era el mejor hombre del mundo. Era un hombre que no servía para nada." (IV, 1014) Of Relimpio's past, the narrator explains, "Procedía de honorada y decentísima familia. Había sido militar en sus mocedades; pero por no servir para la milicia, vióse forzado a dejar la pesadez y estruendo de las armas . . ." (IV, 1014) Don José had been a bookkeeper, but as the narrator explains, "La familia de Relimpio vivía pobremente, porque don José, con ser tan maestro en números, no había sacado de ellos ninguna sustancia." (IV, 1015) Don José's good heart manifested itself in his love for women, and he often followed them through the streets, occasionally flattering them, but don José was so timid that his adventures never went beyond these harmless gestures. He was, says the narrator, a "libertino platónico." So anything else which appears in the summary definition serves only to underline or augment that original synthetic judgment of don José as a mixture of goodness and total uselessness.

There are countless summary definitions of families and individual characters in all of Galdós' novels; but, in general, it is used less and less as a method of characterization as Galdós' style develops and matures. Increasingly he relies on "scene" rather than summary. What follows is only a partial list, but it does give an idea of how common these passages are. From *La desheredada;* the description of José Relimpio and his family (IV, 1013ff), Juan Bou (IV, 1077ff), Joaquín Pez and his family (IV, 1032ff); from *El doctor Centeno*: the description of the priest Pedro Polo (IV, 1310ff), as well as Federico Ruiz (IV, 1341), Isabel de Godoy (IV, 1349ff), the boarders in doña Virginia's boarding house (IV, 1366ff); from *Tormento*: the description of Francisco and Rosalía Bringas (IV, 1458:), Agustín Caballero (IV, 1467ff), and the priest Nones (IV, 1503ff); from *Fortunata y Jacinta*: the description of the Santa Cruz family (V, 18ff), Estupiñá (V, 35ff), Guillermina Pacheco (V, 76ff), the Rubín family (V, 157ff), doña Lupe (V, 203ff), the Samaniego family (V, 423ff); from *Torquemada en la cruz*: the description of the Águila sisters (V, 974ff) and José Donoso (V, 995ff); from *Torquemada en el purgatorio*: the description of Torquemada himself (V, 1022-23), the pedant Zárate (V, 1040-41); from *Torquemada y San Pedro*: the description of the priest Gamborena (V, 1121ff).

In summary definition, as in historical summary, the narrator may sometimes reduce his distance from the narrative by personalizing his information: what he says about a character has a more familiar tone, and is expressed in a less formal, more colloquial language. In his description of Bringas in *Tormento,* the narrator consistently refers to his character throughout the passage (IV, 1459) as "el bueno de don Francisco," "nuestro buen señor," "este bendito varón," or "amigo nuestro queridísimo." In *Fortunata y Jacinta,* the narrator implies that it is Zalamero who provides the characterization of Guillermina Pacheco, and the language of the passage (V, 76), with such phrases as "No se reconocía con bastante paciencia para encerrarse y estar todo el día bostezando el gori gori . . ." and "Si en su camino recto encontraba espinas, las pisaba y adelante, con los pies ensangrentados" adds to the personal, familiar quality of the narrative. In the passage (also from *Fortunata y Jacinta*) describing Olimpia Samaniego, the narrator suggests that it was Ballester who was the source of information. Here, too, the colloquial informality of the language adds to the familiarity of tone:

Quería doña Casta que sus niñas tuvieran un medio de

> ganarse la vida para el día en que, por cualquier contingencia, empobreciesen, y Olimpia fue llevada al Conservatorio desde edad temprana. Siete años estuvo tecleando, y después tecleaba en casa, bajo la dirección de un reputado maestro que iba dos veces la semana . . . Pieza por la mañana, pieza por la tarde y por la noche. Ballester se la sabía ya de memoria, sin perder nota. (V, 423)

Yet, in spite of the occasionally personal tone of the narrative, these passages clearly belong to the background world: mode of presentation is still indirect, what we know of reality we know through the narrator's narration or description.

In the background world, the narrator's distance from his narrative also enables him to offer descriptions of typical patterns of behavior among social groups or of society as a whole. These are the descriptions of customs and social institutions or practices and character types usually associated with *costumbrista* literature. When the narrator stands at maximum distance, these passages appear "apart" from the narration; but the rule in Galdós' novels is that they form an integral part of the main narrative. This kind of passage occurs with much less frequency in Galdós' novels than might be suspected, and the frequency with which they do appear diminishes as Galdós' style matures. They are much less common in the *novelas contemporáneas* than in the earlier novels like *Gloria* or *La familia de León Roch,* and in the *Torquemada* series they are practically non-existent.

There are, however, several examples from the *novelas contemporáneas* which illustrate the kind of passage under consideration. From *La desheredada* comes this passage describing Christmas customs in Madrid:

> La conmemoración más grande del mundo cristiano se celebra con el desencadenamiento de todos los apetitos. Hasta el arte se encanalla. Los teatros dan mamarrachos o la caricatura del Gran Misterio en nacimientos sacrílegos. Los cómicos hacen su agosto; la gente de mal vivir, hembras inclusive, alardea de su desvergüenza; los borrachos se multiplican. Tabernas, lupanares y garitos revientan de gente, y con las palabras obscenas y chabacanas que se pronuncian estos días habría bastante ponzoña para infeccionar una generación entera. No hay más que un pensamiento; la orgía. No se puede andar por las calles, porque se triplica en ellas el tránsito de la gente

> afanada, que va y viene aprisa. Los hombres, cargados de regalos, nos atropellan, y a lo mejor se siente uno abofeteado por una cabeza de capón o pavo que a nuestro lado pasa.
> (IV, 1042)

And from *Fortunata y Jacinta* comes the description of the practice of using nicknames:

> Hay en Madrid muchos casos de esta aplicación del diminutivo o de la fórmula familiar del nombre, aun tratándose de personas que han entrado en la madurez de la vida. Hasta hace pocos años, al autor cien veces ilustre de *Pepita Jiménez* le llamaban sus amigos y los que no lo eran *Juanito* Valera. En la sociedad madrileña, la más amena del mundo, porque ha sabido combinar la cortesía con la confianza, hay algunos *Pepes, Manolitos* y *Pacos* que, aun después de haber conquistado la celebridad por diferentes conceptos, continúan nombrados con esta familiaridad democrática que demuestra la llaneza castiza del carácter español. . . . (V, 15)

All this is not to deny that Galdós' novels are a rich source of information about the very things (social customs, institutions, types) which characterize *costumbrista* literature. It is only to point out that in Galdós' novels, this information is most often presented incidentally, through scene, and not directly by the narrator. The reader is left to deduce from the scenes themselves the nature and importance of those very customs and institutions. What the reader knows of the life style of the bourgeoisie or of the very poor, he knows from having read the scenes in the first volume of *Fortunata y Jacinta*. What he knows of the bureaucracy of nineteenth-century Madrid, he knows from having followed Villaamil on his painful visits to government offices in *Miau*. What he knows of even so trivial a custom as the national lottery he knows from having read the scene in *Fortunata y Jacinta* in which don Baldomero distributes his recent winnings to all those, including the lowliest servant, who had contributed to the purchase of the winning lottery ticket.

In addition, the narrator occasionally offers direct, ordered descriptions of the physical setting of the novel. These passages clearly belong to the background world of the novel, for although they deal with a reality within the temporal-spatial dimensions of the narrative itself and are concrete rather than abstract in nature, they appear, as it were, to have been set apart from the narrative. The reality these passages describe has been removed from the context of an immediate, perceptible scene. The result is that the details of the setting appear to have been remembered and then "reconstructed" by the narrator. Consider, as an example of direct description of physical setting, this selection from a description of the Santa Cruz' house, from *Fortunata y Jacinta*:

> La casa era tan grande, que los dos matrimonios vivían en ella holgadamente y les sobraba espacio. Tenían un salón algo anticuado, con tres balcones. Seguía por la izquierda el gabinete de Barbarita, luego otro aposento, después la alcoba. A la derecha del salón estaba el despacho de Juanito, así llamado no porque éste tuviese nada que despachar allí, sino porque había mesa con tintero y dos hermosas librerías. Era una habitación muy bien puesta y cómoda. El gabinetito de Jacinta, inmediato a esta pieza, era la estancia más bonita y elegante de la casa y la única tapizada con tela; todos los demás lo estaban con colgadura de papel, de un arte dudoso, dominando los grises y tórtola con oro. . . . (V, 68)

Because of the inherent concreteness of physical setting, however, it is most often described in the context of a particular perceptible scene. And because most scenes are character-centered, the physical setting is often described from the character's point of view, that is, as the character would have seen it.[9]

As the narrator's distance from his narrative decreases, the narrative enters a kind of middle ground. Here mode of presentation may still be indirect (i.e. narration or description by the narrator), but the emphasis is perceptual rather than conceptual. As the narrator's distance decreases, the narrative falls within the spatio-temporal dimensions of a perceptible situation. The narrator stands immediately before the reality he is narrating or describing. In immediate narration or description, life is seen as open, unfinished: events are necessarily seen not as history but as process; characters are seen not as fixed, defined entities, but as people in the process of defining themselves; the material world is not something remembered and "reconstructed," but is something immediately knowable or perceptible. People, places and events of the novelistic world are still seen from without at this level, but the important point is that they are *seen*, and their immediate perceptibility materializes that world and makes it come alive.

Immediate narration and description most often occur together with dialogue in what Norman Friedman calls "scene".[10] In such passages the narrative moves freely from narration to description to dialogue and again to narration. The narrator's minimal distance from his narrative requires that he perceive all the elements of the scene—character, action, dialogue, physical setting—simultaneously. This simultaneous perception of immediate reality in turn results in the multiplicity of narrative mode typical of scene. Conversely, this minimal distance prohibits the narrator from isolating the elements of scene and relating them to common elements in other scenes, the process which precedes the organized presentation of character and event in the background world.

Compare a typical historical summary or summary definition (any of those cited above) and a typical scene. Besides the obvious reduction in the number and extent of events described, and the obvious detail with which an event is described, there is an immediacy and vividness in scene impossible to achieve in summary. This immediate quality, which reflects the narrator's minimal distance from his narrative, is effected not so much by the extent of the detail with which a character, an event or a place is described, nor so much by the concreteness of the language of the description but rather, by the way in which the material is presented. Events are seen in progress, the narration is simultaneous with the course of the action in the novel. Narrator and reader follow the characters as they move through the novelistic world and are directly witness to their interactions, in word and deed, with other characters. Characters are not defined directly by the narrator but are left to define themselves through their actions and words. A character's personality is not conceived as a whole; rather, it is seen only in fragments. Only one or a few aspects are portrayed at any one time. The physical setting is described incidentally, in the course of the narration.

Consider, as examples of scene, the passages presenting Juanito Santa Cruz' first visit to La Cava, Guillermina and Jacinta's visit to the fourth estate in search of "el Pitusín," Mauricia's "battles" with the crippled nun Sor Marcela in the convent of the Micaelas, Maxi's efforts to escape Papitos' impudent scepticism from *Fortunata y Jacinta*; passages presenting Isidora, Miquis and Juan Bou's visit to the Aransis' palace, Juan Bou's proposal of marriage to Isidora from *La desheredada;* passages presenting Rosalía and Francisco Bringas moving into their new apartment, or witnessing Amparo and Agustín's departure; the dialogue between Agustín and Pedro Polo's sister Marcela from *Tormento*.

Specifically, in the scene describing Juanito's visit to La Cava, for example, we note that what the reader perceives of the physical setting of the scene is what Juanito himself sees as he enters the building where Estupiñá lives: the number 11 on the door of the poultry shop, two women who stand arguing in the doorway, the chicken feathers and blood stains on the floor (which he immediately relates to the feathers he usually saw stuck to the soles of Estupiñá's boots), the dark stairway he must climb to reach Estupiñá's room, and in the center of the scene, the pretty young girl standing in a half-open doorway. Juanito's (and the reader's) curiosity is awakened. Together they learn the girl's name, as she flees down the stairway after only a brief appearance. What the reader knows of Juanito's character—the *señorito's* vague sense of uneasiness in the world of the *pueblo,* balanced by his curiosity and subsequent boldness in acting immediately on his desires—, or of Fortunata's character—her natural beauty, a kind of freshness and unspoiled charm, her independence, her almost innocent sensuality and the effect it has on Juanito—are apparent only through the characters' actions and words, and not through anything the narrator tells the reader directly.

As the narrative enters the foreground of the novel the narrator's psychological and emotional distance from his narrative decreases considerably and eventually becomes nil. The mode of presentation is direct and immediate, typically taking the form of dialogue, various forms of monologue on the part of the characters (soliloquies, reveries, interior monologues) and dreams. Immediate narration or description occurs in the form of 1) indirect free style, in which the narrator writes, still in third person, but using a language expressive of the character's emotions and opinions rather than his own; 2) immediate narration focused on the actions and more often the thoughts of the individual character, often freely interspersed with the character's own interior monologues; or 3) direct narration of dream sequences. These types of direct narration should be considered a part of the foreground because of their content rather than because of their form.

As the narrator's psychological and emotional distance from his narrative decreases and narrative mode becomes more direct and presentational, the narrator's presence becomes less and less obvious, until he finally disappears altogether, identifying completely with the character he is describing. As the narrator disappears, the reader begins to perceive reality directly, without the narrator's mediation (as in scenes of dialogue, for example). As the narrator moves toward a character psychologically, the reader begins to experience reality rather than merely to perceive it. He begins to experience reality as the character experiences it. That is, narrator and reader stand at the center of the novelistic world at the moment—at the center of event, character (self) and circumstance as the character experiences them. What defines the foreground of the novel is a movement toward "inner reality" (change in the subject of the narration), toward direct unmediated presentation (change in mode of narration), and toward the experience, rather than the mere perception of reality.

Narrative Pace

Narrative pace may be defined as movement through time in the novel, or the rate at which the novel's central plot moves toward its conclusion. In the background world, where the narrator stands at a great distance from his narrative, narrative pace is usually very slow. Passages typical of this narrative plane (historical summary, political, social or philosophical commentary, summary definitions) lie outside of the main flow of the narrative. Narrative movement stops completely as the narrator pauses to philosophize, to comment on social or political reality, or to take a look backward in time as he offers an historical summary. The function of these passages is essentially descriptive rather than narrative. Description is inherently static, rather than dynamic. Its object is spatial rather than temporal, so a necessary condition of description is the stoppage of movement through time. In order to be described, the world must "stand still" as it were, if only momentarily.

In description, narrator and reader cease to accompany the character through the flow of events but rather stop to contemplate reality. Contemplation is indeed an apt description of what is happening when the narrator, at maximum distance, philosophizes and offers social and political commentary, or generalizes on the concrete situations of the novel. Here he removes himself and the reality he is describing from the particular spatial-temporal dimensions of the novel. In historical summary the narrator again stops the flow of time in the novel. The period of time covered lies outside the specific temporal dimensions of the novel. Time, in these passages, is seen as history, something finished and complete, not as something moving or progressing. In summary definition, characters too have been removed from the flow of time. They are seen as complete, well-defined entities, as portraits (a spatial concept); not as beings growing and changing through action in time. Long passages describing the physical setting, for example, also slow down the flow of the narrative, for they are spatially rather than temporally conceived.

As the narrator moves closer to his narrative, stepping inside the spatial and temporal dimensions of the narrative, the pace quickens considerably. Narrative pace is perhaps most rapid in passages of immediate narration. Here the flow of the narrative is in part determined by the relationship between the length of the passage and the extent of the period of time covered. The narrator may portray the events of weeks, months or years in a single sentence or paragraph, while spending several pages in the narration of events lasting an hour or less. But beyond that, and perhaps less obviously, the narrative pace depends on the function of the passage, whether it is descriptive or dramatic in nature. Passages consisting only of immediate narration are by definition dramatic, that is, they advance the action of the novel. Passages consisting of both immediate narration and dialogue (scene) may be either dramatic or descriptive, that is, their purpose may be primarily one of delineation of character rather than one of advancing the action of the novel.

As examples of descriptive scene, consider the following passages: the scene between Miquis and Isidora in the first pages of *La desheredada* (IV, 995 ff); the scenes, written entirely as dialogue, between Isidora and Joaquín Pez, also from *La desheredada* (IV, 1090-91; IV, 1121-22 ff); scenes from *Fortunata y Jacinta* depicting the relationship between Jacinta and Juanito (V, 48 ff); or scenes from the same novel describing typical moments of life in the Santa Cruz' family, as when don Baldomero wins the lottery (V, 126-127 ff), or when Guillermina visits in search of materials or money for her latest charitable project. (V, 78-79) As examples of dramatic scene, consider the following passages: from *La desheredada*, the scene of Isidora's confrontation with the marquess of Aransis (IV, 1051 ff); or the scene portraying Sánchez Botín's angry dismissal of Isidora (IV, 1090-95); from *Tormento,* the violent second encounter between the priest Pedro Polo and Amparo (IV, 1535-47); or from *Fortunata y Jacinta,* the scene describing Fortunata's unexpected confrontation with Jacinta at Guillermina's house (V, 407 ff).

Obviously, almost any scene serves both to define and develop character, and at least to some extent, to advance the action of the novel. But the narrative pace evident in any scene depends upon its dominant function. Clearly, scenes of great dramatic intensity, where the conflict is openly and vividly expressed, move much more quickly than scenes in which conflicts are only barely apparent, as an underlying possibility, capable of future development.

To clarify, let's examine two passages from the same novel, *La desheredada*. The first, clearly descriptive in nature, is the scene between Isidora and Joaquín Pez in the second part of the novel. Joaquín has come to visit Isidora, who is now living with her second "benefactor," Sánchez Botín. Joaquín's announcement of his imminent departure for Cuba only confirms Isidora's growing suspicions of Joaquín's real intentions, so this scene does not really further plot development. The scene's primary purpose is rather to demonstrate once again how both Isidora and Joaquín stubbornly cling to an idealized vision of themselves, a stubborn belief in their "honor," eevn when apparently aware of the sordidness and emptiness of their lives. Isidora describes in detail the daily misery of her life with Sánchez Botín but stubbornly maintains throughout that she is still an honorable woman: "Nací para ser honrada," "Nací para estar arriba, muy arriba." Joaquín admits he is "un desgraciado," that he has squandered his fortune, and pursued by his creditors, must leave the country. But for both Joaquín and Isidora, it is this "reality" which is false, because it denies them the true reality they have forged for themselves in their dreams.

In contrast, the scene between Isidora and Sánchez Botín which immediately follows is clearly dramatic in nature. Here there is obvious conflict between the two characters. Sánchez Botín imposes his will and throws Isidora and all of her possessions out of the house. As a result, Isidora must leave and seek shelter elsewhere. This next step takes her one more step down her road to ruin.

In these passages of immediate narration and dialogue, then, narrative pace is fastest. Here narrator and reader stand immediately before the reality described and directly witness the passage of time. Curiously, as the narrator decreases his distance from the narrative and as the narrative is interiorized in the character's mind, narrative pace slows once again. Narrator and reader are inside the event, they experience time as it is passing, not time which has just passed. They no longer are aware of the passage of time because they are within the eternal now.

These passages are essentially descriptive in nature. Their primary function is to reveal the inner fears, hopes and dreams of the character and only indirectly to advance the action of the novel (through acts which result from the character's thoughts.) Because all of this takes place within the character's mind, all external action in the novel stops or is seen from within as narrator, reader and character experience the event simultaneously. The effect of this simultaneity of experience is to slow the pace of the narrative to such an extent that reading time appears equivalent to experienced time. Consider, as examples, Isidora's monologue "Insomnio número 50 y tantos" from *La desheredada* or Moreno-Isla's monologue in *Fortunata y Jacinta*. In these passages narrator, reader and character together experience the passage of time, the eternal now. In Isidora's monologue it is expressed in a clear consciousness of time passing (perceived sensorially). In Moreno's monologue movement through time is expressed simultaneously with movement through space.

Time

Theoretically, when the narrator stands at maximum distance from his narrative, the sense of time is totally abstract. It is measured in terms of dates on a calendar. As previously noted, events on this narrative plane are seen as history, something finished, complete, selected and ordered into a whole. In Galdós' novels, however, the sense of time is rarely totally abstract; history is rarely impersonal. The narrator habitually reduces his emotional distance from his narrative, even while maintaining temporal distance, by personalizing the history, whether it be the history of an individual character, a social group, a family or a whole society. This personalization of history in many novels takes the form of a paralleling of events in the life of the individual character with events in the life of the nation. This personalization is perhaps clearest when historical event is seen only in the context of events of personal interest to the character. In *Fortunata y Jacinta,* for example, Jacinta's mother Isabel Cordero de Arnáiz was able to remember the births of her numerous children by associating them with important dates in the reign of Isabel II:

> —Mi primer hijo—decía—nació cuando vino la tropa carlista hasta las tapias de Madrid. Mi Jacinta nació cuando se casó la reina, con pocos días de diferencia. Mi Isabelita vino al mundo el día mismo en que el cura Merino le pegó la puñalada a su majestad, y tuve a Rupertito el día de San Juan del Cincuenta y ocho, el mismo día que se inauguró la traída de aguas. (V, 31)

The narrator may further reduce his distance by presenting himself as interlocutor of "historical" information (i.e., information about a character's past given to him by another character),[11] or by allowing the character himself to relate the information. In both cases events are still seen as history, but because the events are seen from the character's point of view, history is inevitably colored by the character's personality and mode of expression, and of course, it is the character and not the narrator who has selected the events from the past and organized them into a history. So although the temporal distance remains constant, the emotional distance decreases and eventually disappears as the narrative is interiorized.

Obviously, too, as the narrative is interiorized the emotional distance between the character and his narrative is reduced, so that time and events appear less and less as something complete, finished, untouched by the present. The character may re-live the past, or selected moments of it, and there is complete interchange of past (memory) and present (emotion).

As the narrator's temporal and spatial distance from his narrative decreases, the novel enters the middle ground characterized by immediate narration and description. The immediacy of the reality being presented determines the nature of time in the middle-ground. Time here is still an external phenomenon (something observed from without rather than experienced from within) but it is now perceptual rather than conceptual. The narrative has moved from "time past" of the background world to "time passing or just passed" of the middle ground, the world of time and life in process. Time here is not measured by dates on a calendar, a chronology of events past. Rather, there are very visible (perceptible) signs of its passage: the passing of seasons, the striking of clocks, the coming of night and day, an occasional rooster's crowing, and most importantly, the flow of events occurring immediately before the reader's eyes. At this level the flow of time and events is linear and uni-directional, from past to future. This is in contrast to the essential timelessness of both the background and foreground, where, for very different reasons in each case, the unidirectional flow of time has stopped. In the middle ground the narrator may choose to speed up or slow down the flow of time, by summarizing the events of days in one sentence, or by lingering for pages over the details of a single hour, but the movement and direction of time remains clearly evident.

When the narrator stands at minimum distance from his narrative; that is, when the narrative has been interiorized in the character's mind, time ceases to be an objectively measurable or even sensorially perceptible phenomenon. It becomes, instead, a totally subjective experience. The reader experiences time and event as the character does. Consider, as an example, Isidora's monologue from *La desheredada*. (IV, 1030-31) The phenomenon of experienced temporal reality is very clear here, for time and its passage is one of the monologue's obvious themes. Isidora, in her night of insomnia, is constantly aware of the passage of time, as measured by the sights and sounds which signal its passing: Melchor's entering the house and preparing for bed at two in the morning; the clock striking three; the muffled noises entering from the street, signaling the start of a new day; the rays of the early morning sun entering her room.

Also, time in this inner world knows no limitations and is not at all subject to the linear progression from past to future characteristic of middle ground narration. A character, in his monologues and reveries often moves from past to future to present to past at will, as present emotion provokes memory of the past, which may in turn provoke future fears or hopes. This temporal confusion may be obvious and explicitly presented (as in the case of Fortunata's monologue cited in Chapter III), or it may be more subtle, but nevertheless very real.

So, in summary then, it is this simultaneity of reader-narrator-character experience and the breakdown of linear temporal progression which characterizes the sense of time in the foreground of the novel.

Space

Space, in broadest terms, may be defined as the distance or expanse between any two or more points. In the novel, space may be defined by its limits and by what is contained within those limits. Because of those limits, the question of space in the novel necessarily involves the related question of narrative focus: that is, how much of reality is seen, and how clearly it is seen. At first glance, the problem seems a relatively simple one: when the narrator stands at a great distance, narrative focus is ample, narrative space is extensive and essentially external. As the distance between the narrator and his narrative decreases, narrative focus narrows, novelistic space is reduced and becomes individualized and eventually interiorized. What, in fact, occurs is much more complex.

The overwhelmingly physical connotations of the concept of space make it extremely difficult to apply spatial concepts to some parts of the narrative. In particular, consider those passages (histories, sociological commentary, summary definition) where the narrator stands at maximum distance from his narrative. As has been pointed out, these passages appear to have been set apart from the perceptible spatial-temporal dimensions of the novelistic world. The reality on which they are based has been transformed by the narrator's intellect. So we can speak of space on this narrative plane only in the most abstract sense.

Spatial limits in the background world of the novel are determined only by the narrator's own intelligence, understanding, perceptiveness and previous experience, and by his conscious choice of subject matter (in the case of Galdós' novels, contemporary society). The nature of what fills that space is determined by the narrator's distance from his narrative, a distance which allows him to abstract from the concrete situations of the novel, to generalize about the behavior of individuals and groups, to see patterns in events in the life of men. Events become history; groups of men, society; their behavior, customs; an individual character, a portrait or even caricature of himself; his behavior, "human nature."

The novelistic space easiest to describe is that of the novel's middle ground, where the narrator, having moved closer to his narrative, stands immediately before the reality he is describing, a reality which lies within the particular spatial dimensions of the novel and so is directly perceptible by the senses. The limits of novelistic space in the middle ground are defined only by the narrator's own powers of observation and sensory perception or those of another character. The nature of what is contained in that space, again, is determined by the narrator's distance from his narrative, a distance which allows sensory perception of reality. So novelistic space of the middle ground is filled with the material phenomena of existence: the physical setting: the streets, cafes, stores and plazas of Madrid; fully materialized characters: dressing and speaking in particular ways, interacting with others, moving through the physical setting; anything, in fact, which can be known through the senses.

It should not be assumed that novelistic space at this level of scene and immediate narration is exclusively material or physical. Here the narrator has moved closer to his narrative psychologically as well as temporally and spatially, so the reader is aware of the psychological as well as the material nature of the reality before him. He is also aware of the narrator's psychological or emotional reactions to the reality he sees before him. But at this level both the character's inner reality (his thoughts and emotions, fears and hopes) and the narrator's inner reality (his psychological or emotional reaction to what he is seeing) are perceived indirectly, as they are manifest in the characters' words and actions or in the narrator's use of language as image or his use of a particular tone of irony or familiarity: phenomena that can be perceived through the senses.

The middle ground exhibits a shift from material to psychological reality, and a corresponding shift from external to internal space. This shift can be traced in the changing modes of narration, from immediate narration through indirect free style to passages in which the characters themselves speak, and finally to interior monologue.[12]

Narrative focus at this level is most often individual: that is, the narrative generally focuses on a particular character, and follows him through a scene, so that often what the reader sees of a particular reality is what the character sees, or what surrounds the character as he moves through the scene. In other words, the spatial limits of the narrative change, depending on which character is the center of the narrative at the moment.

As narrative focus narrows and the narrative centers on one or two characters, what lies in space beyond that narrow focus seems to fade, to blur and disappear; or conversely, all of novelistic reality seems to be drawn into that narrow space and becomes a part of it. As the narration centers on one character, the reader usually is less and less aware of the physical and social setting and the presence of other characters, unless the character who is the center of the narration at the moment is in conflict with something in that setting or with another character. In scenes which consist mostly of dialogue, for example, the physical or social setting is only marginally present at best, as the emphasis is on the emotional or psychological conflict between the characters.

Or, conversely, as narrative focus centers on one character, novelistic space seems defined by that character's activities, to the extent that often other characters seem to be drawn into that character-centered space. A clear example is found in *Fortunata y Jacinta,* where the narrative focus falls almost exclusively on Fortunata as the novel progresses. By the fourth book of the novel Fortunata is the center of almost all the narration, explicitly or implicitly, as it tells of Fortunata's actions or the actions of others in relation to her. The setting of the action (the space in which it occurs) is Fortunata's concrete world. As the action progresses, the space becomes even narrower: Fortunata's room in *La Cava.* Fortunata stays within this space except for one venture to Aurora's workshop. Other characters, too, function within this same setting, for it is they who come to see Fortunata. There is even one scene (V, 517 ff) is which almost all the people who have been important in Fortunata's life are present at once, sitting on the steps outside her room as they wait for her to return.

The two phenomena just described: the fading and eventual disappearance of novelistic reality lying beyond the spatial limits prescribed by narrative focus, or the apparent assumption of elements of external novelistic reality into a narrow, character-centered space, are most obvious when the narrator stands at minimum distance from his narrative: that is, when the narrative is focused exclusively on a single character's mind and the narrative is interiorized. In passages of interiorized narration narrator and reader stand together at the center of experience, the individual character's consciousness. At this level individual consciousness *is* the world of the novel. Everything has been drawn into it. Whereas in immediate narration exterior reality was perceived directly and inner reality was perceived indirectly; now, in interiorized narration, exterior reality is perceived only indirectly, as reflected in the character's consciousness,[13] and both interior and exterior reality are *experienced* directly, by narrator, reader and character together.

The key word in this discussion is experience. With psychological and emotional distance at a minimum, narrator, reader and character stand together as one, and experience the reality within them. The knowledge of one's own inner reality can only result from experience, not from perception. Perception implies a distance between "perceiver" and "perceived," a distance which does not exist when one stands at the emotional center of experience.

The inner space of the novel is at the same time severely limited and limitless. In spite of the fact that in these passages exterior space seems to have disappeared or is drawn into the narrow space of the character's mind, the spatial dimensions of the novel are not reduced, but rather are enormously expanded. Ordinary temporal and spatial dimensions simply do not apply here. The character, in his mind, may move at will from past to present to future, from "reality" to "fantasy," from the depths of despair and fear to the heights of hope. Inner space knows no limits but those imposed by the memory, the imagination and the emotional range of the individual consciousness. Also, because the narrator, through shifting point of view, presents a multiplicity of individual consciousnesses, novelistic space is expanded enormously.

Tone

The dominant tone of Galdós' *novelas contemporáneas,* as of most realistic novels, is ironic. Irony of tone is inherent in the genre itself. As both Ortega (in the *Meditaciones del Quijote*) and Harry Levin (in *The Gates of Horn*) have pointed out, irony results from the conflict between the ideal (the legacy of romance) and the real characteristic of the modern novel. The distinguishing characteristic of realist irony is its comic quality. The comic quality inherent in the modern novel results, as Ortega says, from its essentially mimetic function: "El que imita, imita para burlarse."[14] The characters of the modern novel are essentially "comic" heroes. They appear to be comic 1) because the distance between their goals and reality itself (that is, the distance between what they are and what they want to be) is so slight; and 2) because in spite of their desires to escape reality (to be heroic) they are inevitably pulled back into reality. As Ortega explains, "Como el carácter de lo heróico estriba en la voluntad de ser lo que no se es, tiene el personaje trágico medio cuerpo fuera de la realidad. Con tirarle de los pies y volverle a ella por completo, queda convertido en un carácter cómico."[15]

The irony of Galdós' novels, too, is essentially comic. What distinguishes Galdós' irony is that, although essentially comic, it is seldom cruel or grotesque; but is, rather, humane. Galdós' comic irony is always carefully balanced by a familiarity and understanding of his characters which sometimes reaches the point of true compassion and a real feeling of emotional intimacy. This tonal balance is effected by the shifting relationship of distance between the narrator and his narrative.

When the narrator stands at maximum distance from his narrative, the tone of the narrative is objective, impersonal, sometimes documentary, as the narrator plays the role of commentator of human behavior or political or social historian. Any of the passages cited above as examples of narrative commentary evidence objectivity and impersonality of tone. But, as noted there, these totally impersonal passages are relatively rare in Galdós' novels and become increasingly rarer as his style matures. Even in this kind of passage, the narrative very quickly takes on a personal quality and a change in tone from impersonality and objectivity to the characteristic irony and familiarity. Histories of characters, families and social groups present an interesting case. As noted previously, the narrator often personalizes these histories by introducing other "historians" or "chroniclers" and by presenting himself merely as the interlocutor of the information (i.e., Juan de Madrid in the *Torquemada* series, Estupiñá in *Fortunata y Jacinta*). Not only does this make the tone more personal, but the very fact that the narrator's story is called a "true history" or "chronicle" lends an ironic note in itself, for the terms "history" or "chronicle" imply a distance and objectivity which belies the intensely personal and familiar tone of the narrative. Also, the narrative at this level occasionally takes on a mock-heroic quality. The very fact that the narrator deigns to give the history of such common people or things as the bourgeoisie and their habits of dress is in itself ironic, for history is usually something pertaining to the deeds of kings and queens.

Tone is perhaps easiest to discern in passages of direct narration and description, whether these be in the background world (in summary definition) or in the middle ground (immediate narration and description). It is here that the narrator's presence is shown most clearly in the language he uses, either in images or in interpretive commentary. As pointed out in the previous chapter, Galdós' irony and his familiarity are essentially verbal, so it is to be expected that both irony and familiarity of tone are most obvious in those passages when the narrator's presence is most visible linguistically.

Irony of tone implies a considerable psychological and emotional distance between the narrator and his narrative. It also reveals a certain position which the narrator adopts vis-a-vis his characters. Valle-Inclan explained that an author could adopt one of three positions vis-a-vis his characters. If he knelt below, in awe of his characters, the result was romance; if he stood face to face with them as equals, the result was realism; and if he looked down at them from above, the result was irony. In those clearly ironic passages then, the narrator stands above his characters, not morally but psychologically and intellectually; he understands them and their foibles as they could never understand themselves; he sees clearly the chasm between what they think of themselves and what the world thinks of them, as he sees the unbridgeable gap between their ideal and what is real. A character's psychology, his way of thinking and behaving, are not shared or experienced from within, but are seen from without and from a distance. The narrator, who looks down on his character from above, tends to accentuate what Ortega calls "la vis cómica," those weakest or most laughable aspects of a character's personality. His psychological distance allows the narrator to exaggerate one or two of the character's most salient features (physical, behavioral, or both), so that the character becomes a caricature of himself. Again, the expression of irony is largely verbal, so that irony of tone clearly is the result of the narrator's consciously ironic use of language.[16]

Familiarity of tone implies a lessening of emotional, if not of psychological distance between the narrator and a character. This lessening of emotional distance has the effect of putting the narrator once again on the same level as his character, so that the narrator appears to be an integral part of the world in which his characters live. Familiarity of tone does not necessarily mean that we experience a character's psychology from within. It only indicates between narrator and character a kind of commonality of experience which both might once have shared. Familiarity is also largely verbal, and its primary function is to make narrator and reader seem a part of the novelistic world. By decreasing the vertical distance between narrator and character, familiarity in effect provides a balance to the tonal irony of most of the narrative.

The tone of those passages which are primarily dialogue is more difficult to discern. Here the narrator's presence is no longer visible (except in occasional stage directions). Irony or intimacy of tone in these passages, then, does not result from conscious use of ironic or familiar language, but rather from the relationship between the way the characters are presented here (in their own words) and the view of these same characters as presented elsewhere directly by the narrator. In all scenes, of course, the psychological distance between the narrator and the character is minimal. The difference in tone is a result, rather, of the difference in emotional distance between narrator and character evident in different scenes.

Consider, as examples, these four scenes between lovers from Galdós' *novelas contemporáneas*. The first two, from *Fortunata y Jacinta*, manifest a warmth and intimacy of tone that reflects not only the narrator's minimal emotional distance from his narrative, but the minimum emotional distance between the characters in the scene as well. The first is the scene between Jacinta and Juanito, in which the young wife's shyness and Juanito's tenderness are shown with great warmth, delicacy and charm. (V, 49 ff) The second is the scene between Maxi and Fortunata in which Fortunata's display of almost maternal concern for the suffering of her weak and impotent husband are treated with extraordinary compassion and a feeling of great warmth and intimacy. (V, 391-392) In contrast, consider the scenes between Isidora and Joaquín Pez from *La desheredada* or between José María and Eloísa from *Lo prohibido*. The ironic tone, the lack of any sense of intimacy in the first clearly evidences the narrator's emotional distance from his narration. The reader is aware of the enormous distance between the characters' view of themselves as presented in the scene and the narrator's opinion of them as manifested throughout the novel. The scene from *Lo prohibido* is presented as a burlesque of the balcony scene from *Romeo and Juliet*. The narrator's ironic distance from his narrative and the emotional distance between the two characters themselves is obvious.

In the foreground, where the narrative consists of indirect free style, character monologue, soliloquy or interior monologue, psychological and emotional distance between narrator and character is nil. Because narrator and reader experience the novel from within, as does the character, narrative tone here is determined by the emotional nature of the character's monologue, which may range from hope to fear to anger to jealousy to self-righteous indignation to greed to skepticism. The character's determination of the narrative's emotional tone begins in indirect free style, and becomes more intense as the narrative is interiorized in interior monologue.

Characterization

The narrator's distance from his narrative also determines the manner in which the characters of Galdós' novels are presented. When the narrator stands at maximum distance from his narrative, his approach is essentially intellectual. He is, as it were, outside any perceptible situation in time and space, so he must, as a result, present his characters in an abstract way. Here the primary means of characterization is the summary definition: a description of a character including his past history, physical and behavioral qualities, relationships with other people, manner of speech, dress and thought. The myriad details of a character's life have been selected and ordered by the narrator, and are usually organized around some sort of synthetical statement which "defines" the character. Narrator and reader view the character from without and from a considerable distance. The character appears as a complete entity—a portrait, apart from the contingencies of a particular moment in time and space, his identity fixed, defined in the literal sense of the word. As pointed out in the discussion of summary definition as mode of narration, detailed description of a character's physical appearance is commonly included in summary definition, but these details are never perceived, but rather seem to be recreated by the narrator from memory.

In contrast to the intellectual approach to characterization at the background level, we find that modes of characterization in the middle ground reflect the perceptual quality of immediate narration and description. When the narrator stands immediately in time and space before his narrative, characters are not "conceived" or "defined" intellectually but are perceived in the process of defining themselves. A character's personality is reflected in his words and in his behavior, and narrator and reader together perceived those words and actions and proceed to form their own definitions of the character implicit in his actions. The myriad facets of a character's life and personality are not presented in an ordered fashion, but rather are perceived one by one as they occur in the course of the narration.

At this level both major and minor characters are seen from without, so that most of what we see is their social facade, their self as seen by others. Here a character is defined implicitly in his interactions with other characters: explicitly, by what other characters say of him. Society's or other characters' opinions of him are often explicitly synthesized in the epithets they use in referring to him. Major characters, in particular, may be referred to by a multiplicity of different epithets in the course of the novel, all of which serve to reveal different aspects of his personality.

Because of the essentially external characterization at this level, many characters remain, in effect, caricatures of themselves. Presentation of their speech and behavior patterns only serves to materialize the identity laid down for them in the summary definition, and they never go beyond those rigid confines. For that reason, they usually serve a limited function in the novel. Minor characters, who remain caricatures of themselves, are often identified by some one feature: a physical defect or a quirk of behavior which synthesizes his personality. (This is typical of caricature, which so exaggerates one particular feature of a character's physical appearance or behavior that it alone is enough to suggest the character's whole being.) Consider, as example, Estupiñá, the social animal par excellence, a man who never ceases his intercourse (usually verbal) with society, and who carries a parrot-headed cane as a symbol of his character; or José Ido, who upon eating meat, immediately becomes "electrified," falls into a fit of dementia, and calls his wife an adulteress; or Torquemada, who appears in many novels only as the userer.

In all fairness, it should be added that almost all of Galdós' characters, even the most minor, have a remarkable capacity for future development, and in fact, the same character often appears in many of Galdós' novels, sometimes as a minor and sometimes as a major figure. Also, Galdós often reaches extraordinary depths of understanding in presentation of even minor figures. Only a combination of breadth and depth of presentation separates major and minor figures.

Only in the foreground do modes of characterization offer depth of understanding. Here, as the narrative is interiorized, the approach is neither intellectual nor perceptual, but experiential. Distance between narrator and character is nil, as the narrator adopts the character's point of view. Because identification is complete, the only possible approach is experiential. One cannot perceive what is within; one can only experience it.

Conclusions

In the third chapter we studied, at the most basic level, that of language, the "formula of art" which constitutes the basis of Galdosian realism. The purpose of this fourth chapter was again to study that "formula of art" as it is manifest on a level beyond the purely linguistic, a level consisting of those structural elements which define a novel's style: modes of narration and description, narrative pace, tone, modes of characterization and sense of time and space; and to study the key role of the narrator in the implementation of that formula. The first chapter showed clearly how the concept of reality basic to Galdós' novels (a reality inherent in some kind of realtionship between external phenomena and perceiving consciousness) is first created and defined aesthetically in the relationship between the narrator and the world of the novel. There we saw how the narrator, through his language, established the existence of an independent external reality and the presence of a perceiving consciousness.

This chapter demonstrated how, once having established its existence, the narrator further defines and explores the nature of the relationship between external reality and perceiving consciousness. We have seen that the nature of that relationship is defined, aesthetically, by the distance between the narrator and his narrative. Psychologically, it is determined by the mode of consciousness dominant at any moment in the novel. Consciousness, the human mind, is a complex entity: it includes the senses which perceive and transmit information from the world without; the intellect or rational mind which selects from that information, organizes and interprets it; and the emotions, which interact with the information from the outside, acting upon it as it acts upon them. So the relationship between external phenomena and perceiving consciousness must reflect the complexity of that consciousness; the reality of the novelistic world is seen by the reader alternatively as perceived by the senses, as transformed by the intellect, or as transformed by the emotions. The relationship is made even more complex by the fact that, as point of view in the novel shifts, the relationship is repeated again and again. So the reader sees the reality of the novelistic world as perceived through the senses and transformed by the intellect or emotions not only of the narrator, but of all the other characters of the novel as well.

As was pointed out in the last chapter, in spite of the fact that point of view in Galdós' novels is multiple, that is, that reality is perceived through the consciousness of a variety of characters, it is the narrator who ultimately determines the point of view evident at any one moment in the novel, and any one point of view must be judged in terms of the central perspective established by the narrator. Similarly, it can be said that although Galdós' novels offer a multi-layered vision of reality, a reality known by several different modes of consciousness, it is the narrator who, through the distance he maintains from his narrative, determines the manner in which reality is presented, and the mode of consciousness by which the reader knows that reality.

FOOTNOTES

[1] Edwin Bullough, " 'Psychical Distance' as a Factor in Art and as an Aesthetic Principle," *British Journal of Psychology*, 5 (1912), pp. 87-118.

[2] *Ibid.*, p. 89.

[3] *Ibid.*, p. 89.

[4] Wayne Booth, *The Rhetoric of Fiction* (Chicago: University of Chicago Press, 1961), p. 155.

[5] Booth defines the implied author as follows:

"The implied author (the author's second self).

—Even the novel in which no narrator is dramatized creates an implicit picture of an author who stands behind the scenes, whether as stage manager, as puppeteer, or as an indifferent God, silently paring his fingernails. This implied author is always distinct from the "real man" —whatever we may take him to be — who creates a superior version of himself, a "second self," "as he creates his work." *The Rhetoric of Fiction*, p. 151.

See also Booth's discussion of the implied author in Chapter Three of *The Rhetoric of Fiction*, pp. 71-74.

[6] These novels represent particular problems of narration, to be dealt with in Chapter V.

[7] See the discussion in Chapter III, which demonstrates how the distance between the narrator and the reader can be measured linguistically, that is, that the reader is increasingly aware of the narrator as an entity distinct from himself as the narrator becomes ever more present linguistically.

[8] José Ortega y Gasset, *The Dehumanization of Art and Other Writings on Art and Culture* (Garden City, N. Y.: Anchor Books, 1956), p. 16.

[9] See the discussion in Chapter III, which demonstrates how shift in point of view is first identified by the verb of perception in these "character-centered" scenes.

[10] See previous reference, p. 142.

[11] See p. 169, above.

[12] This process is extensively examined in Chapter III.

[13] See the discussion of Moreno-Isla's and Fortunata's interior monologues in Chapter III.

[14] José Ortega y Gasset, *Meditaciones del Quijote*, 2a ed. (Madrid: Revista de Occidente, 1966), p. 157.

[15] *Ibid.*, pp. 167-168.

[16] See the discussion of verbal irony in Chapter III.

Chapter V

THE UNRELIABLE NARRATOR

In the course of his definitive article, "Origen y crisis de la novela moderna"[1], Wolfgang Kayser characterizes the narrator typical of the modern novel. In contrast to the distant and impersonal narrator of the epic, who speaks always with the cold voice of anonymity and authority, the narrator of the modern novel is a fellow human being, one who speaks from within the realm of human experience and is thus subject to all the limitations of human knowledge. Kayser suggests that the difference corresponds to the difference in the worlds of which they are a part. The world of the epic is a world of pure essence, of absolute truth, where there is no disparity between intention and action, being and appearance, and where language unequivocally communicates the truth. The world of the novel, on the other hand, is a world intimately known by man, where consequently all is relative, a world whose essence is the conflict between reality and appearance. Kayser also points out the distinctive irony of much of the modern novel's language: an irony which reflects the dichotomy between reality and appearance essential to the modern novel and the consequent loss of faith in the ability of language to reveal reality.

We have already amply described in the preceding chapters the narrator's crucially important role in the determination and perception of novelistic reality. In addition, we may infer from Kayser's definitive description certain factors inherent in the very nature of the personal narrator which may radically affect the reader's perception of the world of the novel. Even if one assumes that the narrator speaks in good faith and that he intends to tell the truth as he sees it, he is, in fact, inherently fallible. As a human being, he is always potentially capable of error in reporting what he believes to be true.

Again, if one assumes that the narrator intends to tell the truth as he sees it, he may, and often does, consciously use language ironically. In a world where appearance is not necessarily reality, the narrator, in order to reveal the truth hidden by appearance, may use language which says just the opposite of what it appears to be saying.

Thirdly, because language no longer unequivocally reveals the truth, the narrator may be deliberately deceptive. He may consciously use language to mislead the reader, to lie about himself and the world he presents.

Then, the point of view the narrator expresses, explicitly and implicitly, may not be in accordance with the author's point of view implicit in the novel or with the "truth" as it is revealed in the interaction of character and situation in the course of the novel. In such a case, his narrative is deceptive, but not deliberately so.

Finally, the factors inherent in the character of the personal narrator are considerably exaggerated in the case of the so-called "first-person" narrator: that is, when the narrator stands at the center of his own narration. The narrator's potential deceptiveness (conscious or unconscious) is much greater when he speaks of his own life than when he speaks of others.

It is Wayne Booth in *The Rhetoric of Fiction* who first identifies and labels the problem of the "reliability" of narration: to what extent the reader can trust the narrator's vision of reality, to what extent the reader can accept the narrator as a reliable mediator of novelistic reality. As Booth points out,[2] the typical narrator of the realistic novel is indeed "reliable": he acts as the author's spokesman within the world of the novel. His vision of novelistic reality coincides with that which the author intended to present through character, situation, and theme. In Booth's terms, the reliable narrator represents the "norms" of the novel. In effect, he is the reader's guide to the world of the novel; he gives it form and meaning, as he comments upon the interprets character and event.

The personal narrator's potential fallibility here offers no barrier to the reader's accurate perception of novelistic reality. It is a part of the established convention of the modern novel and its essential perspectivism. The possible effects of the typical narrator's fallibility are lessened 1) by the fact that his role is generally that of an observer who, at best, participates only marginally in the action of the novel and thus can be more "objective;" and 2) by the fact that, as the author's reliable spokesman, his views are corroborated by the interplay of character and event in the novel.

Nor does the irony typical of the personal narrator's language necessarily offer an obstacle to accurate perception of novelistic reality. The intelligent reader is aware that irony is essential to the realistic novel, that what the narrator says is not to be taken literally. The most reliable of narrators consistently use irony to reveal truth rather than to hide it. As Booth says, "Irony alone is not sufficient to make a narrator unreliable."[3]

The question is really one of intent and the degree of directness with which an author chooses to reveal the reality of his novelistic world. He may choose to tell his story directly, to make use of the reliable narrator we have just described. The reliable narrator's intent is to tell the truth, although, as we have said, he may find that the indirectness of irony is the best means to do so.

On the other hand, an author may choose to tell his story indirectly, to make use of a narrator whose vision of novelistic reality is, for one reason or another, unreliable. The most obviously unreliable is the narrator who is deliberately deceptive, whose intent is to lie, to mislead the reader. Narrators of the nineteenth-century novel are rarely deliberately deceptive, although as Booth points out, the deliberately deceptive narrator has been an important device for more contemporary novelists like Camus in *The Fall*. Rather, says Booth, unreliability is "most often a matter of what James calls *inconscience*: the narrator is mistaken, or he believes himself to have qualities which the author himself denies him."[4]

In other words, again in Booth's terms, the narrator may stand at considerable distance from the author on any of several axes—intellectual, psychological, or ethical. The narrator may be less intelligent or less observant than the author, or his moral, ethical, political, religious or social values may be in sharp contrast to those held by the author. It is simply that the author finds that the most effective way of revealing the truth is by using a narrator whose point of view stands, obviously or subtly, in contrast to his own. The effect, of course, is the same as the effect of irony. But with the exception of the rare, deliberately deceptive narrator, the unreliable narrator in general is simply unaware of the irony of his own narration, indeed, of the irony of his whole position in the novel.

Potentially the most unreliable of narrators is the so-called "first-person" narrator, the narrator who stands at the center of his own narration. His potential unreliability arises from the conflict inherent in his dual role as narrator and character. As narrator, his language has a value of truth which the language of any one character in a novel can never obtain. In Martínez-Bonati's terms,[5] the narrator's language may be purely mimetic, while the language of a character, while it may have some mimetic function, is always primarily expressive of the character's own point of view. In more general terms, the narrator is more likely to mislead the reader, intentionally or unintentionally, when the characters and events he describes deeply affect his own life.

Unreliable Narration in Galdós' Novels

Most of the narrators of Galdós' novels are, in fact, reliable. They consistently act as his fictional spokesmen and directly voice the point of view he wishes to present in the novel. As we have seen in previous chapters, their commentary grows consistently less obtrusive as Galdós' style matures, but the narrators themselves do not deviate from the norm of reliability: their assessment of characters and events still unequivocally represents the "norms" of the novels. Although they are residents of the world they describe and are often friends of the other characters, they generally remain observers and participate only marginally in the action of the novel. Only in *La de Bringas* does the narrator's participation seem more than marginal, but even there it does not affect his reliability.

Only two of Galdós' narrators (of the *novelas contemporáneas*) are, strictly speaking, "first-person" narrators: José María Bueno de Guzmán, the cynical aristocrat of *Lo prohibido,* and Máximo Manso, the timid professor of *El amigo Manso*. Both novels are written in the form of memoirs in which the narrator and the central character are the same. As such, they cannot possibly present the ample, rich and varied view of reality presented by the observer narrators of the other novels. But, on the other hand, they are ideally suited to a study of the whole problem of the relationship of the teller and the tale, the ways in which the narrator influences the reader's perception of reality, for the basic problem is greatly exaggerated by the narrator's very unreliability. It is no coincidence that Galdós chose these two novels narrated by "first-person" unreliable narrators to examine a question so basic to his craft.

Both José María Bueno de Guzmán of *Lo prohibido* and Máximo Manso of *El amigo Manso* are unreliable narrators on two accounts. First, and most obviously, because they stand at the center of their own narration. In both cases, between the reader and novelistic reality there stands the very ambiguous personality of the narrator himself: José María, whose "madness" seriously affects the way he perceives the world; and Máximo Manso, the nature of whose very existence is so equivocal that the reader is never sure where and how the narrator stands in relation to his story. Secondly, and more subtly, both are victims of "inconscience." Throughout most of the work, their narratives are unconsciously, unwittingly ironic, **and stand in direct contrast to the norms of the novel.**

The first kind of unreliability is inherent in the "first-person" narrator, an inevitable consequence of the choice of that form of narration. The question then becomes one of why Galdós chose to make these two "first-person" narrators doubly unreliable, making their narratives unconsciously ironic. The answer lies in the very nature of the realistic novel, and of Galdós' realism, as we have previously described it. The essence of the realist novel is the conflict between appearance and reality. One of the essential characteristics of Galdós' realism is its insistence on multiple perspective and the portrayal of a multi-layered vision of reality. In first-person narration, which provides only a single perspective, the only means of portraying the conflict between appearance and reality and the multiplicity of perspective essential to Galdós' realism is through the use of ironic narration.

The effect of unreliability, particularly the unreliability of unconscious irony, on the reader is an interesting one. The reader is the reliable narrator's confidant; he participates in the latter's ironic vision, sharing the truth of reality often hidden to the other characters of the novel. In unreliable narration, alliances have shifted. The reader no longer possesses the unequivocal truth about novelistic reality. Both he and the narrator may be unaware of the truth behind reality. They may both experience together the moment of truth, the moment of *desengaño,* when the irony of the narrator's position is revealed. More likely, though, the intelligent reader will have already intuited the irony of the narrator's position, will have already suspected the truth behind the appearance of reality presented by the narrator, so that the actual moment of *desengaño,* if there is one, only confirms his earlier suspicions. In effect he will have formed a kind of secret communion with the implied author. Both of them stand together against the inconscience of the narrator.

El amigo Manso

This strange novel is, among other things, a literary *tour de force.* In 1880 Galdós wrote this prototype of the novel of interior action which some thirty years later Unamuno was to "invent" as the "nivola." Ricardo Gullón, in " 'El amigo Manso', nivola galdosiana,"[6] studies the parallels between Galdós' *El amigo Manso* and Unamuno's classic "nivola," *Niebla.* Both Máximo Manso, the protagonist of Galdós' novel, and Augusto Pérez, the protagonist of Unamuno's *Niebla,* are "entes declaradamente ficticios. Manso y el unamuniano Augusto Pérez son hombres de papel; difieren en muchas cosas, pero pertenecen a la misma especie de personajes fantasmales que sueñan y son soñados como hombres, aunque carecen de existencia verdadera."[7] Here Gullón points out the ambiguity which is the essence of Máximo Manso's character and which, as a consequence, becomes the essence of the whole novel. Elsewhere Gullón characterizes this essential ambiguity as "la dialéctica del sí y el no. . . . este ir y venir de lo positivo a lo negativo"[8] which spreads outward from Manso himself to the other characters and to the whole world of the novel.

From the very beginning Máximo Manso insists on his non-existence, his chimeric quality, declaring "Yo no existo . . . Quimera soy, sueño de sueño y sombra de sombra, sospecha de una posibilidad . . ." (IV, 1165) and referring to himself as "yo sin carne ni hueso . . ." (IV, 1165). Yet, paradoxically, from the very moment he speaks those first words "Yo no existo," he does exist, or at least he has begun to exist. Máximo Manso is a creature of fiction, but the world of fiction is a world of words, and as soon as he speaks, he exists in that world.

Máximo Manso, as the narrator, is the center of consciousness through whom the reader perceives the world of the novel, its characters and situations. Not only is his the center of consciousness, it is the only consciousness of the novel. There is only one point of view operant in the novel, and that is Máximo Manso's. But what is the nature of the consciousness that stands alone between the reader and the novel? What kinds of activities does that mind engage in as it observes the world as it appears before him in the present, remembers the world as it appeared before him in the past; imagines a world better than the one he sees, rationalizes his behavior and that of others, dreaming dreams which reveal his hopes and fears? The activities of Máximo's consciousness can be divided into two broad categories: 1) those which admit the primacy of external reality, those in which the transforming influence of Máximo's inner self is held to a minimum, and 2) those in which the inner self is primary, where external reality is displaced by imagination, or admitted only when transformed by rationalization into a reality in harmony with Máximo's inner needs.

The inherent duality of Manso's consciousness is in part a function of his dual role as both narrator and character. In Gullón's terms, he is both "el narrador-testigo" and "el narrador-personaje,"[9] he is both outside his narrative and within it. As "el narrador-testigo" he remains an observer, a witness, both of himself and others, and his narrative has an objectivity and an accuracy corroborated independently by the other characters as they speak and act. As "el narrador-personaje" he is irresistibly drawn into the action; he no longer contemplates reality from without, he lives it from within, and what he and the reader perceive is inevitably transformed by his emotions, his inner necessities.

Máximo Manso's dual role as purely ficticious narrator who sells his curious tale to the penurious author, and as the sad and timid professor, man of flesh and blood, who lives and suffers his story from within, results in a confusion of psychological distance between the narrator and his narrative. At the same time, as Gullón points out, it results in a confusion of the temporal and spatial distance between the narrator and his narrative:[10]

> La ambigüedad narrativa es obstáculo grave para averiguar desde donde narra Manso la historia. ¿Desde el limbo en que se refugia para contemplar sin riesgo el mundo? Y ¿a quién se la cuenta? Su relación con el medio en que vive . . . es esencialmente equívoca . . . Los sucesos contados en la novela son sucesos pasados, pero ¿cuándo pasaron? y ¿cuándo los cuenta? Deliberadamente se confunde al lector, que no logra calcular bien la distancia entre narración y narrador, o para ser más precisos, entre el momento en que ocurrió lo narrado y el instante en que el autor escribe.

At times he writes of things which seem to have happened in the remote past, while at other times he writes with an immediacy which makes things appear to have just happened. As narrator, he may foretell future events; as character, he appears totally surprised by the course of events.

Unconscious Irony

The nature and extent of Máximo Manso's unreliability as a narrator can perhaps best be revealed through a study of his inconscience, the unwitting irony of his tale and, indeed, of his whole character. Surely the primary consequence of the narrator's unreliability would seem to be the reader's deception: he is led to believe things about Máximo Manso and his world which are anything but true. But the deception is a dual one, for Manso succeeds equally in deceiving himself. So the reader's deception, too, is a dual one. He is not only deceived by what Manso tells him, but to the extent that he identifies with the narrator, he shares in Manso's own self deception. So to understand the unconscious irony, the mode of the reader's and of Manso's deception must be explained in purely human terms: what is there about Máximo Manso and his character which deceives the reader and Máximo himself, which interferes with their correct perception of reality?

Máximo Manso presents himself as the philosopher, the man of logic, the careful observer, the practical, methodical man whose life is ruled by the dictates of method and reason. As he describes the habits and customs of his sedentary and methodical life he appears to be "el arquetipo del profesor Krausista o institucionista . . . el hombre ejemplar modelado por Sanz del Río y Giner: austero en todo, moderado, higienista, correcto y no bohemio, sin vicios."[11] He is totally convinced the life of reason and method he has chosen give him complete mastery over himself and the world around him:

> Me propuse conseguir que mi razón fuese dueña y señora absoluta de mis actos, así de los más importantes como de los más ligeros . . . y he sabido sofocar pasioncillas . . . He conseguido una regularidad de vida que muchos me envidian, una sobriedad que lleva en sí más delicias que el desenfreno de todos los apetitos . . . El método reina en mí y ordena mis actos y movimientos con una solemnidad que tiene algo de las leyes astronómicas. (IV, 1169)

His greatest boast is that his inner self is in complete harmony with the world without:

> Constantemente me congratulo de este mi carácter templado, de la condición subalterna de mi imaginación, de mi espíritu observador y práctico, que me permite tomar las cosas como son realmente, no equivocarme jamás respecto a su verdadero tamaño, medida y peso y tener siempre bien tirantes las riendas de mí mismo. (IV, 1169)

Manso's views of himself appear to be confirmed by the opinions of other characters, like his neighbor, the widow doña Javiera: "¡Un hombre sin trapicheos, sin ningún vicio, metidito toda la mañana en su casa; un hombre que no sale más que dos veces: tempranito, a clase; por las tardes, a paseo, y que gasta poco, se cuida de la salud y no hace tonterías!" (IV, 1170) Also, his views of himself appear confirmed by the very order and clarity with which he speaks of himself and his life and by the logic and method with which he proceeds in the education of his student Manuel Peña: the careful evaluation of his student's moral and intellectual character and temperament; the winning of his student's respect and friendship; the systematic introduction of his student to all phases of human knowledge, beginning with the easiest and most amenable and proceeding to philosophy. Thirdly, Máximo's belief in his own "observant and practical spirit" appears to be confirmed in that his observations on the whole of novelistic reality with the important exceptions of Manuel and Irene, are devastatingly accurate. Máximo Manso sees the society of Restoration Spain exactly as Galdós intended to portray it: a hollow society based on appearance rather than truth, filled with the foolish and the unscrupulous, or with idealists doomed to failure. As Gullón puts it, Galdós presents "un mundillo . . . todo de pacotilla, insustancial y artificioso: la política, intriga y compadrazgo; la religión: convencionalismo y superstición; la aristocracia, arrivismo y falta de escrúpulos; la poesía, retórica y oquedad."[12] The forever-scheming gold-digger doña Cándida, the bureaucrat Pez, the cynical aristocrat Cimarra, the grotesque poet Sainz del Bardal; José María, Máximo's *nouveau riche* brother and his provincial wife and in-laws— all appear in word and deed exactly as Manso describes them. The absurdity of the "Sociedad para Socorro de los Inválidos de la Industria," the degradation of religion in the theater scene, the exploitation of women in the scene of Máximo's search for his nephew's wet-nurse—all are in accord with the norms of the novel. Fourthly, although the center of Máximo's deception is Irene, Irene herself does not appear in the novel in a way that even begins to challenge Máximo's view of her until over halfway through the work. What Máximo reveals to the reader of Irene's behavior is of such a neutral or ambiguous nature that it might be interpreted in a number of ways. So, up to that point, Irene might well have been everything Máximo said she was.

So, for all these reasons, it would appear that the reader has no reason to doubt Máximo Manso's reliability as a narrator. Indeed, it appears he has every reason to affirm it. Yet, from the beginning, the reader also has nagging doubts about the validity of Manso's vision of the world. It seems that Manso's view of himself is perhaps too pat, too smug and self-satisfied. Little inconsistencies begin to appear between Manso's view of a character and the character as he really is: first of Manuel Peña, then of Irene, finally of Manso himself. The reader watches the workings of his mind as Manso tries first to deny the inconsistency, then to rationalize in an attempt to reconcile the truth with his own point of view, finally to admit the truth to himself as he defends his illusion to the world. Reader and narrator begin to suspect the truth about Manuel Peña, Irene, and about Máximo Manso himself. There is no one moment of truth. What is portrayed is not the darkness of total deception followed by the sudden light of truth, but rather a continual dialectic of appearance and reality, of perceiving consciousness and external reality. In the course of the novel, one sees the continual conflict between the perceiving consciousness which struggles to understand and interpret what it sees in accordance with the character's inner needs, and the force of external reality, which attempts to break down the defenses that the individual mind has thrown up against an all too painful truth.

Manuel Peña

When Máximo Manso first meets Manuel Peña, he is thoroughly convinced of his pupil's intelligence and of his suitability for the kind of education Manso has in mind: "Era Manuel Peña de índole tan buena y de inteligencia tan despejada que al punto comprendí no me costaría gran trabajo quitarle sus malas mañas . . . Mi complacencia era igual a la del escultor que recibe un perfecto trozo del mármol más fino para labrar una estatua." (IV, 1173) At first it appears to Manso that his efforts with Manuel have been successful: "Contento estaba yo de mi discípulo, porque algunas de sus brillantes facultades se desarrollaban admirablemente con el estudio, mostrándome cada día nuevas riquezas." (IV, 1181), but he soon notes Manuel's preference for facile rhetoric over serious thought, his aversion to philosophy and the methodical approach of his teacher. When he discovers that Manuel's real talent is for social interaction rather than for serious scholarship, Manso says that Peña's strongest characteristic is no longer his intelligence, but his moral character, his "good heart:" "Pero lo más digno de alabanza en él era su excelente corazón, cuyas expansiones iban frecuentemente lejos de lo que los buenos términos de la generosidad piden." (IV, 1182) Manso now decides that his most decisive influence over Manuel will be in the "moral" rather than the intellectual sphere: "Yo tuve empeño en regularizar sus nobles sentimientos y su espíritu de caridad, marcándole juiciosos límites y reglas. También trabaja en corregirle el pernicioso hábito de gastar dinero tontamente . . . etc." (IV, 1182)

Manso soon recognizes the truth: that Manuel is not the philosopher that he thought him to be, but only a charming rhetorician. But he chooses to ignore that truth, to set it aside and shift his attention to another aspect of Manuel's character which, he believes, it is still possible to mold.

Manso's realization of the total implications of the truth about Manuel come slowly. The revelation comes first in the intellectual sphere. Manso notes the decreasing intellectual communication between himself and Manuel, that Manuel is struggling against being fit into the mold his teacher had prepared for him: "Nos veíamos diariamente, charlábamos de diversas cosas, y mientras procuraba llevar su espíritu a las leyes generales, él no gustaba sino de los hechos y de las particularidades, prefiriendo siempre todo lo reciente y visible." (IV, 1183) Manso and his pupil continue to drift apart as Manuel no longer comes to visit his teacher, and Manso feels himself alone again. Yet, in spite of his growing realization of the truth, Manso appears even to take some pride and consolation in Manuel's social success:

> Manuel Peña . . . fue muy bien recibido, no obstante su humilde procedencia. Pero ¿cómo no, si además de tener en su abono las tendencias igualitarias de la sociedad moderna, se redimía personalmente de su bajo origen, por ser el más simpático, el más guapo, el más listo, el más airoso, el más inteligente y dominador que podría imaginarse, en términos que descollaban sobre todos los de su edad, y no había ninguno que le igualara? (IV, 1192)

Only when Manuel confronts his teacher directly, in word and deed declaring his spiritual independence, does Manso's attitude toward him begin to change. In a café at four in the morning, Manso hears Manuel Peña proclaim his essentially active, impulsive character, in clear contrast to Manso's passivity:

> Yo quiero hacer algo, *magister*; yo necesito acción. Esta vida de tiesura social y de pasividad sosa me cansa, me aburre . . . ¡Oh maestro, por favor, no siga usted! La Filosofía me apesta. La Metafísica no entra en mí. Es un juego de palabras. ¡La Ontología! Por Dios, aparte de mi este cáliz emético. Cuando tomo una pócima de sustancia, ser y causa, estoy malo tres días. Me gustan los hechos, la vida, las particulari-

dades. No me hable usted de teorías, hábleme de sucesos; no me hable usted de sistema, hábleme de hombres. (IV, 1214)

Manuel's projected duel with the Marquis of Casa-Bojío is a direct challenge to his teacher, who had tried to teach him to live by reason, not by passion. But Manso reacts only mildly. He sees Manuel's behavior as "quizá alguna pasajera florescencia del espíritu, de esas que marcan el período culminante de la juventud . . ." (IV, 1214) He chides Manuel half-jokingly:

> Manuel, Manuel, niño, modera esos impulsitos, o será preciso ponerte un chaleco de fuerza. Estás hecho un pisaverde, un monstruo de alfeñique, un calaverilla de estos que se estilan hoy, verdaderos muñecos desvergonzados que representan el Don Juan con los trapos y la voz de Polichinela. (IV, 1215)

He half-heartedly proclaims his intention to set Manual straight, but seems too tired to carry it out; he wants only to go home to sleep. He ignores Manuel's plea for help in preparing his speech to be given before the *Sociedad*.

The real moment of climax in Manso's progressive *desengaño* about Manuel's intellectual character occurs during the evening of speeches and musical events organized by the *Sociedad*. There, Máximo Manso's well-prepared, carefully thought out and intellectually substantive speech on the nature of charity is only politely applauded. But Manuel's speech, with no intellectual content, which is little more than empty rhetoric, is given a rousing reception. On the surface, Máximo Manso appears undisturbed by his own "defeat:" "Por mi parte, debo declarar que la admiración que Manuel me causaba y el regocijo de presenciar triunfo tan grande del que había sido mi discípulo, me ponían un nudo en la garganta." (IV, 1234). He takes consolation from his own role in helping to make Manuel the brilliant success he is. Yet in the hours after the "velada," Manso is strangely quiet and withdrawn and sits alone in his room, depressed and sad. In spite of his protestations that "Se equivoca el que abribuya mi desazón a heridas del amor propio por el pasmoso éxito del discursito de Manuel Peña" (IV, 1237), it is clear that Manuel's victory over his teacher in the intellectual sphere presages Manuel's victory in another sphere. While he sits in his room that very night, Manso attributes his sadness to a premonition of his own defeat ("un presentimiento de desgracias que me dominaba") (IV, 1237), a suspicion of an as yet unknown rival in his love for Irene.

What, indeed, subconsciously disturbs Máximo Manso that night is not that he learns something about Manuel Peña's intellectual character which he did not already know. Manso was already aware of Peña's preference for facile rhetoric over intellectual discipline. What upsets him is the fact that what he knows to be the mere appearance of brilliance is accepted by society as truth, while his own truth is ignored. The truth about his society which he had seen so accurately in others and epitomized in the poet Sainz del Bardal, is now brought home to him in full force. It is for this reason that he has a premonition of his own defeat following the "velada:" in a society which prefers appearance to truth, Máximo Manso, who believes himself possesor of the truth at that point, can never win out.

The climactic moment in Manso's disillusionment with Manuel Peña occurs when he discovers that it is his former pupil who is Irene's suitor and his own rival. Manso experiences an almost physical encounter with truth. As he leaves Irene's house one day, he encounters Manuel Peña in the street near there: "Fue como un choque violentísimo con duro y pesado objeto, choque puramente moral, pues no tuve contusión, ni mi cuerpo llegó a tocar al otro, que era el de un hombre más joven que yo . . ." (IV, 1259) In his initial anger and confusion, his own self-deception is projected onto Manuel Peña, whom Manso accuses of hypocrisy and deception. But at last Manso knows the truth in a way only his senses can tell him: "Lo sospechaba, pero no lo creía; ahora lo creo, lo siento, lo veo . . ." (IV, 1260)

Manso at last accepts the truth about Peña completely, even to the extent of becoming Manuel's advocate, pleading Manuel and Irene's case before doña Javiera. But Manso never succeeds in reconciling the truth of external reality with his inner needs. He never really succeeds in conquering his own anger and disillusionment, only in pretending to the rest of the world that they do not exist.

Irene

Máximo Manso had first seen Irene when she was a child. He was impressed by Irene's early love for books and her apparent dislike for her aunt, doña Cándida (which echoed Manso's own intense dislike of the old gold-digger). On this very slight evidence, the timid and probably very lonely professor, flattered by the child's visits, creates his first ideal vision of Irene: "Hablando conmigo y respondiendo a mis preguntas sobre sus estudios, su vida y su destino probable, me mostraba un discernimiento superior a sus años. Era el bosquejo de una mujer bella, honesta, inteligente." (IV, 1179)

Some years later, Manso catches a glimpse of Irene on the street and, smitten by her pretty eyes and slender figure, he proceeds to expand on the ideal Irene he had created years before. By the time she enters Manso's brother's house as governess, she has become, in Máximo's mind, the ideal woman, the essence of everything beautiful, intelligent and good. Manso describes in detail her admirable neatness, her good taste, the regularity of her habits, her intuitive knowledge of how to deal with the children who are her charges. In essence, says Máximo Manso, "Parecía una mujer del Norte, nacida y criada lejos de nuestro enervante clima y de este dañino ambiente moral . . ." (IV, 1195) What pleases Manso most is that ". . . la imaginación tenía en ella lugar secundario. Su claro juicio sabía descartar las cosas triviales y de relumbrón, y no se pagaba de fantasmagorías, como la mayor parte de los hombres . . ." (IV, 1196) Máximo believes most of all in reason, so Irene becomes ". . . la mujer perfecta, la mujer positiva, la mujer-razón, contrapuesta a la mujer frivolidad, a la mujer capricho." (IV, 1196)

Manso describes his growing realization of what he believes to be his and Irene's shared interests, tastes and ideas, and his delight in Irene's "sensitivity:"

> . . . a medida que me iba mostrando su interior riquísimo, encontraba yo mayor consonancia y parentesco entre su alma y la mía . . . Confianza tras confianza, fue contándome poco a poco, en sucesivos paseos y sesiones interesantes, cosas de su infancia y pormenores mil, que así revelaban su talento como su exquisita sensibilidad. (IV, 1197)

When he sees a light under Irene's door late at night, he imagines her reading one of his own works. When he watches her knitting, he sees in her a model of industriousness.

As in the case of Manuel Peña, Manso's disillusionment with Irene comes slowly. As discrepancies arise between his ideal vision of Irene and the reality of her character, Máximo Manso tries to ignore the truth, or alter it to coincide with his ideal vision. At first Manso is only subconsciously aware of the disparity between reality and appearance. One afternoon Máximo and Irene take José María's children to the theater to see two plays representing the Birth of Christ and the Murder of the Innocents. Máximo reports that he and

Irene were shocked at the profanation, the degradation of religion in the staging of the two plays. Suddenly the topic of conversation changes and Irene begins to speak of her childhood and her family, her father's place in the palace of Isabel II. Máximo develops a sudden, severe headache, and as he watches the farce on stage, falls into an extremely critical state of mind. What troubles him is that his criticism, for no apparent reason, is directed at Irene. He feels intuitively, however, that his critical spirit is related to his headache, which began precisely when Irene began speaking of herself and her family. Perhaps his subconscious disillusionment with Irene manifest itself in the severe headache, and the apparently unmotivated criticism of Irene. Of course, Irene has only to say "Pobrecito Máximo," expressing her concern and affection for him, and Máximo's customary idealization returns: "Estas palabras me hicieron el efecto de un disciplinazo. Diríase que me habían despertado de un letargo. La miré; parecióme entonces tan acabada como yo torpe, malicioso y zambo de cuerpo y alma." (IV, 1199)

As little discrepancies continue to appear between Máximo's ideal vision of Irene and the "real" Irene, Manso decides to proceed with caution:

> Poniendo un freno a mis afectos, que se dejarían llevar de impetuoso movimiento, conviene seguir observando. ¿Acaso la conozco bien? No; cada día noto que hay algo en ella que permanece velado a mis ojos. Lo que más claro veo es su prodigioso tacto para no decir sino aquello que bien le cuadra, ocultando lo demás. (IV, 1205)

The first real challenge to Manso's ideal vision of Irene comes with Lica's revelation that Irene is the latest object of her husband's gallantries and with Lica's insinuation that Irene is not exactly innocent of involvement in that situation. Manso's immediate response is to defend Irene, to justify her conduct by saying she was the victim of circumstances and subject to terrible temptations. But when Lica exclaims: "¡Cuidadito con la maestra!" Manso replies: ". . . en mí habían surgido terribles desconfianzas, ¿a qué negarlo? Mi fe en Irene se había quebrantado un poco, sin ningún motivo racional." (IV, 1218) Máximo tries to justify his doubt, and proclaims that in the end it will only end up proving Irene's innocence. But in this scene there is already established the dialectic between appearance and reality, between the nagging doubts produced by the force of external reality, and the inner needs which force Manso to modify, to rationalize—a dialectic which is resolved only in his death.

As the discrepancies between appearance and reality grow, Máximo Manso continues his attempts to reconcile the two visions of Irene. At one point, no sooner has Manso praised her intelligence, than Irene asks him to provide the whole history of Spain on a single slip of paper. Máximo immediately recognizes her stupidity; but, then, he immediately begins to rationalize the truth:

> Vaya, vaya, que no es tan grande en ella el dominio de la razón; que no hay en su espíritu la fijeza que imaginé ni aquel desprecio de las frivolidades y caprichos que tanto me agradaba cuando en ella lo suponía.   (IV, 1220)

Máximo's subconscious doubts about Irene are apparent in a dream in which Irene appears entering a cheap hotel with José María, Manso's brother. Manso's overwhelming need for Irene allows him to maintain her as an ideal, in spite of her imprefections:

> ... lo extraño es que no por perder a mis ojos alguna de las raras cualidades de que la creí dotada amengua la vívisima inclinación que siento hacia ella; al contrario ... Parece que a medida que es menos perfecta es más mujer, y mientras más, y mientras más se altera y rebaja el ideal soñado, más la quiero. ....   (IV, 1220)

At last, Manso and the reader see Irene for what she really is. As Manso talks with her at doña Cándida's new apartment, Irene ceases to be the shadowy, almost incorporeal figure she has been throughout most of the novel, but is now a real girl of flesh and blood, with the characteristics of a very ordinary human being. Far from being the "mujer perfecta, mujer-razón" Máximo had created in his mind, Irene now appears "una persona de esas que llamaríamos de distinción vulgar, una dama de tantas, hecha por el patrón corriente, formada según el modelo de mediocridad en el gusto y hasta en la honradez, que constituye el relleno de la sociedad actual." (IV, 1274) Irene is not "la mujer de Norte, igual, equilibrada, seria, sin caprichos ..." (IV, 1195), but as Máximo discovers:

> ¡También santurrona! ... Era lo que me faltaba ya para el completo desengaño ... Horror del estudio; ambición de

figurar en la numerosa clase de la aristocracia ordinaria; secreto entusiasmo por cosas triviales; devoción insana que consiste en pedir a Dios carretelas, un hotelito y sanadas rentas. . . . (IV, 1274)

Once Máximo Manso becomes aware of Irene's faults, his immediate reaction is anger, but this anger is soon followed by a rationization of those same faults, a rejection of his old image, and anger with himself for having created such an image:

> Eso de la mujer-razón que tanto te entusiasmaba, ¿no será un necio juego del pensamiento? Hay retruécanos de ideas como los hay de palabras . . . Ponte en el terreno firme de la realidad y haz un estudio serio de la mujer-mujer. Estos que ahora te parecen defectos, ¿no serán las manifestaciones naturales de temperamento, de la edad, del medio ambiente? ¿De dónde sacaste aquel tipo septentrional más frío que el hielo, compuesto no de pasiones, virtudes, debilidades y prendas diferentes, sino de capítulos de libro y de hojas de Enciclopedia? Observa la verdad palpitante, y no vengas con refunfuños de una moral de cátedra a llamar graves defectos a los que en realidad son tan solo accidentes humanos, partes y modos de la verdad natural. (IV, 1275)

Here again we see the dialectic of appearance and reality established earlier in the novel. The reality of Irene impinges so strongly on Máximo's consciousness that he is forced to recognize the truth of it and to reject the appearance of his ideal vision. But at the same time his inner needs are so strong that he immediately begins to rationalize the truth to explain away Irene's defects and justify his own needs for her:

> Consistía mi nuevo mal en que al representármela despojada de aquellas perfecciones con que la vistió mi pensamiento me interesaba mucho más, la quería más, en una palabra, llegando a sentir por ella ferviente idolatría. ¡Contradicción extraña! Perfecta, la quise a la moda petrarquista, con fríos alientos sentimentales que habrían sido capaces de hacerme escribir sonetos. Imperfecta, la adoraba con nuevo y atropellado afecto, más fuerte que yo y que todas mis filosofías. (IV, 1276)

As in the case of Manuel Peña, Máximo seems to have accepted the truth of Irene's reality, to the extent that he becomes her greatest advocate, as he defends her right to marriage before Manuel Peña, and convinces doña Javiera that Irene is worthy of marrying Manuel. But again, as in the case of Manuel Peña, Manso never resolves the dialectic of appearance and reality, the conflict between the truth of external reality and his inner needs. Máximo's only solution is to try to escape the conflict. He avoids seeing Irene: "Yo me había propuesto no ver más a Irene, porque, no viéndola, estaba más tranquilo." (IV, 1285) But one day, after she and Manuel are married, Irene comes to visit Manso, who describes her visit:

> Hablamos largo rato de diversas cosas: ella me mostraba la variedad y extensión de sus imperfecciones, encendiendo más en mí, al apreciar cada defecto, el vivo desconsuelo que llenaba mi alma . . . Habló de mil tonterías graciosas, y cada una de éstas era como afilada saeta que me traspasaba. Su frívolo gozo recaía gota a gota sobre mi corazón como ponzoña. (IV, 1285-86)

Finally, the conflict is so strong that the only solution for Manso is death, that is, to change his mode of existence:

> Cada día me alejaba más de aquel centro de alegrías, que para mí era como ambiente impropio de mi espíritu enfermo. Me ahogaba en él. Además de esto, cada vez que veía delante de mí a la joven señora de Peña, mujer de mi discípulo, aunque no discípula, sino más bien maestra mía, me entraba tal congoja y abatimiento que no podía vivir . . . El influjo de estos trastornos llegó a formar en mí una nueva modalidad. Yo no era yo, o por lo menos, yo no me parecía a mí mismo. Era, a ratos, sombra desfigurada del señor Manso, como las que hace el sol a la caída de la tarde, estirando los cuerpos cual se estira una cuerda de goma. (IV, 1289)

Shortly thereafter, Máximo Manso does, indeed, die, returning to the limbo from which he had come.

Máximo Manso

The novel's greatest irony, and the narrator's greatest unreliability, lies not in Máximo Manso's deceptive vision of Irene and of Manuel Peña, but in his own self-deception. The process of his *desengaño* about himself parallels his disillusionment with Peña and Irene. Slowly, irrevocably, he is made aware that his belief in the efficacy of logic and reason and in his "practical and observant spirit" is worth naught.

As his interest in Irene grows, Máximo Manso begins to notice small changes in his own behavior and in his thoughts. He deserts his sedentary and rather solitary life of study. He now spends hours in the chaos and tumult of his brother's house, for he finds it an agreeable place to be: "Yo empezaba a formarme una segunda rutina de vida, acomodándome al medio local y atmosférico." (IV, 1200) He is surprised by his new and undisciplined way of thinking: "Y de esta situación mía nacieron pensamientos varios que a mí mismo me sorprendieron, poniéndome como fuera de mí mismo, en términos que noté un brioso movimiento de mi voluntad, la cual se encabritó como corcel no domado . . ." (IV, 1196) At the height of his passion for Irene, Máximo's usually accurate and reasonable view of others (except Irene and Manuel) is totally transformed: As Máximo explains:

> Entróme de súbito un optimismo, algo semejante al delirio que le entra al calenturiento, y todo me parecía hermoso y placentero, como proyección de mí mismo. Con todos hablé y todos se transformaban a mis ojos, que, cual los de Don Quijote, hacía de las ventas castillos. Mi hermano me parecía un Bismarck; Cimarra, se dejaba atrás a Catón; el poeta, eclipsaba a Homero. . . . (IV, 1207)

At last Máximo finds himself totally unrecognizable:

> Me ví como figura de pesadilla, o como si yo fuera otro . . . ¡Me parecía mentira! ¡Yo sentado en el banco de una buñolería a las cuatro de la mañana, teniendo delante un plato de churros y una copa de aguardiente! . . . Vamos, era para echárse a reír, y así lo hice. ¿Quién se llamará dueño de sí, quién blasonará de informar con la idea de la vida, que no se ve desmentido cuando menos lo piense, por la despótica imposición de la misma vida y por mil fatalidades que salen a sorprendernos en las encrucijadas de la sociedad, o nos secuestran como cobardes ladrones? (IV, 1213)

At one point Máximo even rebels against his usually passive self. Declaring: "Me cansaba del papel de observador que yo mismo me había impuesto" (IV, 1224), he sets off for his brother José María's house to declare his love for Irene once and for all. He explains: "Yo estaba, pues, en plena revolución, motivada por ley fatal de mi historia íntima..." (IV, 1224)

Máximo Manso, who believed he had suffocated all the little passions in his life, finds himself overwhelmed by emotions—anger, sorrow, disillusionment—which he feels on learning the truth. Indeed, he seems a different person:

> La ira que se encendió súbitamente en mí era tal, que me desconocí en aquel instante, pues en ninguna época de mi vida me había sentido transformado como entonces en un ser brutal, tosco y de vulgares inclinaciones a la venganza y a todo lo bajo y torpe. (IV, 1252)

It is the height of irony that Máximo Manso, who had scorned his society for preferring appearance to reality, not only thrives on his own illusions throughout most of the novel, but even after he learns the truth about himself, continues to prefer appearance to reality, to deny the expression of his own hurt and anger. Manso continues to hide behind "una máscara de invulnerabilidad" (IV, 1261), to pretend total disinterest: "¡Darle a conocer mi despecho, mi confusión, el estado tristísimo en que me había puesto la evidencia adquirida recientemente...!, imposible. Era preciso afectar dos cosas: conocimiento completo del asunto y poco interés en él...." (IV, 1260).

Manso continues to play the role of indifferent observer as he denies himself and acts in Manuel and Irene's behalf. This denial of the inner emotional self leads Manso to present himself as one approaching death: "Debí de reírme como los que suben al patíbulo... Sudé gotas enormes y pesadas como las del Monte Olivete, y en la oscuridad de mi alcoba, donde seguí haciendo el papel de que buscaba algo, me apabullé con mis propias manos, y grité en silencio de agonía: ¡Aniquílate, alma, antes que descubrirte!" (IV, 1262)

Interestingly, it is at this point in the novel that Manso imagines his own death; he sees himself curiously detached, witnessing the scene from afar, from another world:

> Antojóseme que iba a amanecer muerto, y me entretenía en considerar la sorpresa que recibirían mis amigos al saber la triste nueva y el duelo que harían las personas que verdadera-

mente me estimaban. ¡Y yo, tranquilo, observando este duelo y aquella sorpresa desde el ámbito misterioso de la muerte; Figurábame estar absolutamente ausente de todo lo conocido hasta ahora, pero continuando conocedor de mí mismo en una esfera, región o espacio competamente privado de las propiedades generales de la Física . . .   (IV, 1263)

After his dream in which he imagines himself (perhaps the emotional self) dead, Manso feels refreshed, alive again as the man of thought and reason. He feels he has regained his moral energy. He begins to rationalize his defeat by Manuel Peña, when he said that the man of reason knows when to yield to the man of action, but that the man of reason will win out in the end. Here again we see the dialectic of appearance and reality, as the conflict between external reality and inner needs manifests itself. Manso's reason struggles to reassert itself, to dominate his mind and deny his emotional needs. But reality again overwhelms him and his reason, as he finds himself behaving in ways contrary to all reason:

. . . ahora trae mi narración cosas tan estupendas, que no las creerá nadie. Y no porque en ellas entre ni un adarme de ingrediente maravilloso, ni tenga el artificio más parte que la necesaria para presentar agradable y bien ataviada la verdad, sino proque ésta, haciéndose tan juguetona como la loca de la casa, dispuso una serie de acontecimientos aparentemente contrarios a las propias leyes de ella, de la misma verdad, con la que padecí nuevas confusiones.   (IV, 1265)

Máximo Manso, as he stood before Irene and at last saw her in all her mediocridad, had proclaimed: "Observa la verdad palpitante . . ." But Manso can never merely observe "la verdad palpitante" about Irene, about Manuel or about himself. When he sees Irene, Manso is always caught up in the dialectic of external reality and his own inner needs, which still continue to transform and modify external reality in order to reconcile it with those same inner needs.

Nor does Máximo Manso ever succeed in accepting his own truth. After learning the truth about Irene, he continues to play the part of disinterested observer, to deny his own inner needs, to refuse to express his anger and hurt. In effect he is again using reason to modify or deny his own inner reality, as before he had used reason to modify external reality.

In the last moments of the novel, Máximo Manso finds it increasingly difficult to endure the conflict and begins to withdraw once again from reality. He consistently avoids seeing Irene, for she still provokes in him the old conflict:

> Cada vez que veía delante de mí a la joven señora de Peña . . . me entraba tal congoja y abatimiento que no podía vivir. Y si por acaso la conversación me hacía encontrar en ella un nuevo defectillo, el descubrimiento era combustible añadido a mi llama interior. Cuanto menos perfecta, más humana, y cuanto más humana, más divinizada por mi loco espíritu, al cual había desquiciado para siempre de sus fijos polos aquel fanatismo idolátrico, bárbara adoración hacia un fetiche con alma. Todos los días buscaba mil pretextos para no bajar a comer, para no asistir a reuniones, para no acompañarlos a paseo, porque verla y sentirme cambiado y lleno de tonterías y debilidades era una misma cosa. . . .
> (IV, 1289)

But beyond that, Irene represents a real threat that his inner reality will be revealed. What disturbs Manso most of all is the thought that Irene knows of his "pasioncilla," which he had thought he had rid himself of. He imagines Irene thinking:

> No cuela, Mansito, no cuela. Conste que perdiste la chaveta como el último de los estudiantes, y ahora, no con toda la filosofía del mundo me has de hacer creer otra cosa. Las maestras de escuela sabemos más que los metafísicos, y éstos no engañan ya a nadie más que a sí mismos. (IV, 1286)

For Máximo Manso, the only escape from this dual reality, the inevitable conflict between his inner self and the world as it is, and the threatened revelation of his inner reality—is death. No sooner has Manso imagined the revelation of his inner reality, than he becomes ill, and soon afterward, he dies, returning to that painless limbo from which he had come.

We had said previously that the process of Manso's *desengaño* is a slow one. As the novel progresses, the reader is constantly led to believe that the final moment of truth is at hand. But as the reader soon discovers, for Máximo Manso there is no ultimate *desengaño*. To the end, there exists that dialectic between perceiving consciousness and external reality of which we spoke. Only in the end—death, for Manso; the end of the novel for the reader—can the dialectic be resolved.

It is evident that Máximo Manso's unreliability as a narrator has multiple implications, both thematically and aesthetically. Manso clearly does not represent the thematic norms of the novel. As Gullón pointed out, Galdós chose to reflect an empty society, a society based on appearance rather than reality, in the mind of a narrator who is himself only the "appearance" of reality. As we have seen, Máximo Manso is admittedly a ficticious being, a nonentity. But beyond that, Manso's whole narrative is unconsciously ironic: he criticizes his society for what he himself is—a man who is first unaware of reality, and who then ignores and denies that reality once he is aware of it.

But Máximo Manso is not only the timid professor who, as character, lives and suffers through the events of the novel; he is also a narrator with a tale to tell. As narrator, he is just as clearly in opposition to the aesthetic norms of the novel. Máximo Manso, as he describes himself and as he would like to have been, is the man of method and reason, confident of his general ideas and concepts. As he begins his tale, he imposes his own concepts on characters and situations of the novel. As we have seen, throughout much of the novel these characters seldom appear in person, speaking and acting independently of Manso's view of them. Irene, at one point, even says to Manso: "Yo no haré sino lo que usted mande." (IV, 1206)

But, in fact, as the novel progresses, Irene and Manuel do appear independently of Manso, and neither of them acts as Manso would have them act. As characters and situations become increasingly independent of the narrator, he never knows what is going to happen next. He cannot even control his own behavior, let alone that of others. The narrator is forced to revise continually his view of the world, to abandon his preconceived vision of the world and enter the dialectic of external reality and perceiving consciousness.

Robert Russell, in his article *"El amigo Manso:* Galdós with a Mirror,"[13] sees this novel as a metaphor for the creative process and as an important fictional statement of Galdós' aesthetic creed. Russell sees what happens in *El amigo Manso,* the movement from the ideal to the real, as symbolic of what happens in Galdós' novels throughout his career: his novels become increasingly less symbolic of ideas and more "realistic." Russell notes Galdós' abandonment of the *novelas de tesis,* with their relatively rigid characters; and Galdós' development of the *novelas contemporáneas,* with less rigidly defined characters who are allowed to grow and change, and a narrator who is less actively involved in his tale.

In our own terms, the aesthetic significance of Máximo Manso's inconscience as narrator is Galdós' abandonment of a narrator who *a priori* imposed his consciousness on reality, in favor of a narrator who enters fully into the dialectic of perceiving consciousness and external reality.

Lo prohibido

Like Máximo Manso, José María Bueno de Guzmán, the narrator of *Lo prohibido,* stands at the center of his own narration. To comprehend fully the nature of his unreliability, we must first examine the character of the consciousness which stands alone between the reader and the world of the novel, and can thus so radically affect the reader's perception of that world. Again, like Máximo Manso, the narrator of *Lo prohibido* is characterized by an essential duality: José María, both idealist and materialist, thus reflects the essence of the modern novel and is the prototype of the comic hero of that novel. As described by Ortega in the *Meditaciones del Quijote*,[14] although the modern novel is essentially a presentation of contemporary, daily reality, there is always implicit within it the world of myth, of the ideal. The hero of the modern novel, like Don Quijote, tries to impose his ideal vision on reality and to raise himself up to the level of the ideal, to escape and to deny the real world around him. But reality is always stronger, and inevitably pulls him down once again to the level of reality. What characterizes the hero of the modern novel, and makes him appear so comic and pathetic, is the minimal distance between his ideal and the reality he is trying to escape. His imagination is often so limited that his ideal is expressed in terms of his own ordinary reality.

José María: Idealist and Materialist

It seems strange, indeed, to label José María Bueno de Guzmán, a jaded, decadent, cynical aristocrat whose total time, energies and resources in the course of the novel are dedicated exclusively to the pursuit and conquest of his three married cousins, an idealist, in any sense of the word. His eroticism, however, always takes a particular form: an attraction to women who are in some way prohibited. His three cousins, for example, are doubly taboo: his attraction for them is both adulterous and incestuous. They exist just beyond his grasp, in the realm of the "prohibited." As each of them becomes the object of his attraction, she becomes in his mind an ideal, and each ceases to be that ideal only when she is no longer prohibited. It is clear, then, that José María's "entusiasmos faldamentarios" are nothing more or less than his longing for the ideal, his desire to enter the prohibited kingdom. However ordinary, gross or vulgar the nature of his ideal, it is still an ideal and represents a desire to escape reality and himself.

José María's longing for the ideal is shared by most of the other characters in the novel: all desire in some way to escape the mediocracy of their society, to break out of the narrow confines of their existence. All have "entusiasmos:" Eloísa's "entusiasmos caseros," Carrillo's "entusiasmos políticos," María Juana's "entusiasmos sociales," or Raimundo's "entusiasmos artísticos y literarios."

Under the influence of his idealism, his "entusiasmos," José María gives free reign to his imagination. With "vehemencia romántica" he transforms each of his cousins, successively, into an ideal. He is subject to a kind of "ilusión de mozalbete," erotic fantasies in which he imagines himself in romantic situations with Eloísa and Camila. What reality denies him, he supplies through his imagination: "Mi fantasía enferma, mi contrariada pasión, buscaban refugio en la idealidad. Lo que los hechos me negaban asimilábamelo yo con el pensamiento . . ." (IV, 1792). María Juana, his self-styled confidante, warns him that his passion (in this case for Camila) is totally distorting his view of reality, and is making him see the world through "telarañas," or rather "falsos prismas." (IV, 1810)

At the same time, José María is a materialist who espouses all the dogma of determinism and positivism then fashionable in his society. From the beginning of the novel, he carefully defines the various factors, which according to Taine, determine the course of a man's life: *race, moment,* and *milieu*. The history of the family illness, as told by José María's uncle Rafael, together with details of his own and his parents' life supplied by José María, delineate the character of the *race*. José María then proceeds to establish the physical, social, psychological and intellectual *milieu* and fixes the precise historical *moment* when all of these influences converge to produce a crisis in his personal life. He states explicitly that he is "un producto de la edad en que vivo;" he finds himself "en fatal armonía con el medio en que vivo." He has within him "los componentes que corresponden al origen y al espacio." (IV, 1776)

José María sees himself as a passive being, completely without a will of his own, the victim of his own passions, his actions completely determined by the situations in which he finds himself: ". . . mi ser moral se funda más en la arena de las circunstancias que en la roca de un sentir puro, superior y anterior a toda contingencia. No domino yo las situaciones en que me ponen los sucesos y mi debilidad, no. Ellas me dominan a mí . . ." (IV, 1777) His belief that his behavior is totally determined by circumstance, and predictable once the circumstances are known, extends to other characters as well. He denies to them, as well as to himself, any possibility of self-transcendence. To the extent that his determinism identifies man with his circumstances, it reduces him to the level of the material, for it subjects him to the same laws which rule the material world. José María's materialism is evident throughout the novel. It is implicit in his incorrigible cynicism, which consistently reduces man to a physiological being, an animal, or even an object; which reduces the hero of literary or classical tradition to a grotesque figure, a caricature of the prototype; which reduces human relationships to a poor comedy in which men are only actors who play a multitude of roles. It is implicit in a burlesque tone which takes nothing "serious" seriously, and which raises the trivial to the level of the transcendent.

Together with this determinist vision of the world there is José María's positivist vision of a world ultimately reducible to pure matter, a world known only through the senses, capable of being ordered by fixed rules and ultimately comprehensible by human logic. Reality reduced to the level of the material is manageable, and comprehensible, only through the material. So to José María, his control, and comprehension, of the world is symbolized in his control of the economic order, his possession of money and material wealth. At the height of his "entusiasmos" for both Eloísa and Camila he spends extravagantly, and more than once reaches the point of economic ruin. To combat his idealism, he must have recourse to logic and reason, symbolized in Arithmetic, the magic power of numbers. In other words, he must re-establish economic order.

During José María's and Eloísa's trip to Biarritz, for example, José María is aware for the first time of his own economic extravagance in his impassioned pursuit of Eloísa: "Era la primera vez en mi vida que me sorprendí en flagrante delito contra las agustas leyes de la Aritmética." (IV, 1718) In a dream shortly thereafter, he becomes aware of the remedy for his extravagance, the means to re-establish reason and logic in his life: "Vi la clara imagen de la diosa Cantidad, alta severa, con una luz en la mano que, al modo de faro, me alumbraba para que no naufragase. . . ." (IV, 1718)

José María is aware of the essential duality of his character, which he expresses in terms of his dual racial heritage:

> En mí se hallarán los caracteres de la familia a que pertenezco y el aire que respiro. De mi madre saqué un cierto espíritu de rectitud, idea de orden; de mi padre, fragilidad, propensión a lo que mi tío Serafín llama entusiasmos faldamentarios. Lo demás me lo hicieron, primero, mi residencia en Inglaterra; luego, mi largo aprendizaje comercial, y por fin, mi navegación por este mar de Madrid, aguas turbias y tracioneras que a ningunas otras se parecen. (IV, 1776)

José María continues to experience the conflict between these two aspects of his character, which is expressed throughout the novel as a conflict between his maternal and his paternal heritage. In the midst of his passion and his extravagant pursuit of Eloísa, José María explains: "En aquel período mi salud se resintió algo. Zumbáronme los oídos ... La aptitud de los números se eclipsó en mí. Mi dualismo estaba desequilibrado; mi madre dormía, y la sangre andaluza de mi padre era lo que mangoneaba entonces en mí." (IV, 1737) And in a strong reaction against Eloísa's extravagance and his own indulgence of her, José María explains: "La apreciación de los números despertaba en mí con fiera energía, proporcionada al largo tiempo del eclipse que había sufrido. En mí renacía de súbito el hijo de mi madre, el inglés ... Mi padre huía de mí como en el teatro echa a correr el diablo cuando se presenta el ángel. ..." (IV, 1744)

For José María, his idealism, his "entusiasmos," is a kind of madness. It gives free reign to his imagination, and interferes with his correct perception of reality. It makes him lose control of the order of his life and leads him toward economic ruin. He struggles against his madness, as we have seen, in various ways, all designed to correct the view of the world his madness presents to him. But his madness has a curious variation. José María suffers from a strange, rather ill-defined illness, sometimes taking the form of nausea, at other times of a strange ringing of the ears, a buzzing in the head which becomes like a chorus of human voices murmuring something indistinguishable. José María ringing of the ears is but a variation of the illness which afflicts all those of his family: his uncle Rafael's feeling of being permanently suspended in mid-air; Eloísa's sensation of a feather caught in her throat; María Juana's sensation of a piece of cloth between her teeth; Raimundo's "softening of the brain."

José María's illness is but a physiological manifestation of a spiritual uncertainty or uneasiness, a questioning of the vision of the world supplied by his own materialism. As José María suffers for his "mal" he laments:

> ¡Otra vez en mí aquel terror inexplicable, aquel azoramiento, aquella previsión fatigosa de peligros irremediables! ¡Qué esfuerzos hacían mi voluntad y mi razón para vencer esta tontería! "Pero, ¿a qué tengo yo miedo, a qué, vamos a ver?", me decía, tratando de corregirme y aun de avergonzarme como si hablara con un chiquillo. Nada conseguía con este sermoneo de maestro de escuela. (IV, 1695)

So José María's "mal" represents the opposite side of the coin of his madness. Both his "entusiasmos" and his "mal" serve to enable José María to break out of the narrow confines of logic and reason, of the purely material. Unconsciously, José María's "mal," his feeling of spiritual uncertainty and uneasiness serves to "correct" the vision of the world presented by his reason, just as his cynicism and logic served to correct the vision of the world offered to him through his imagination.

José María as Narrator

The same essential duality is evident on the aesthetic level in José María's role as narrator of *Lo prohibido*. There is in *Lo prohibido* an interesting interior duplication of the figure of the narrator: between the reader and novelistic reality there stands not only the ambiguous personality of José María Bueno de Guzmán, but also the strange figure of the amanuensis José Ido del Sagrario, who is hired to transcribe José María's memoirs. Readers of Galdós' novels will remember José Ido as the "hacedor de novelas" in life as well as in literature, who, in *Fortunata y Jacinta,* invents the whole tale of *el Pitusín* to deceive poor Jacinta, by using her maternal longings for his own benefit. In *Lo prohibido,* José Ido's character is briefly but clearly defined. José Ido's unbridled imagination is reflected in his handwriting, which the narrator describes: "Tenía una letra clara, hermosa, si bien un poco floreada y como con tendencias a criar pelo por los infinitos rasgos que por arriba y por abajo salían de los renglones." (IV, 1888)

José Ido's fantasy, his unbridled imagination and his tendency toward literary rhetoric stand in direct contrast to the narrator's (José María's) own clearly defined aesthetic creed. José María intends his memoirs to be a "true history," a faithful observation of "real" reality as opposed to literary reality. Throughout the novel, he makes a clear distinction between literature and life, between "real" and "literary" reality. In no way must his work be a work of imagination which reflects a "literary" reality: "Por ningún caso introduciría en mis *Memorias* invención alguna. Puedo asegurar que nada hay aquí que no sea escrupuloso traslado de la verdad." (IV, 1888) Near the end of the novel, as he outlines the aesthetic purposes of his work, the narrator imagines a series of possible "literary" endings to his story, which would have enabled him to "hacer la moral de la fábula." But in accordance with his aesthetic creed, that is impossible. He declares that:

> No me habría sido difícil, sobre todo contando con la experta mano de mi inteligente pendolista, alterar la verdad dentro de lo verosímil en beneficio del interés . . . bien quisiera, repito, que en este campo de la fresca verdad nacieran todas estas hierbas, que son el forraje de que se apacientan los necios; pero no puede ser, y lo escrito, escrito está. (IV, 1889)

José Ido's function, then, is to serve as a figure whose aesthetic creed stands in exact contrast to the narrator's own. The two narrators—one dominated by reason and a desire to tell the truth; the other dominated by imagination—represent, on the aesthetic level, an exact parallel to the two aspects inherent in the character of José María himself. José María insists that he knows how to manage and control the imagination of his scribe:

> Decíame Ido que él era del oficio; que si yo le dejara meter su cucharada, añadiría a mi relato perfiles y toques de maestro que él sabía dar muy bien; pero no se lo permití. Por ningún caso introduciría yo en mis Memorias invención alguna, ni aun siendo tan llamativa como todas las que brotaban del fecundísimo cacumen de mi escribiente. Yo ponía mis cinco sentidos en el manuscrito, temeroso siempre de que él se dejara arrastrar de su desbocada fantasía, y puedo asegurar que no hay nada que no sea escrupuloso traslado de la verdad. (IV, 1888)

Although it seems that José Ido has added nothing to the story and, in accordance with the narrator's aesthetic creed, has told only "sucesos que en nada se diferencian de los que llenan y constituyen la vida de los hombres" (IV, 1888), the novel is full of literary, classical, historical and Biblical allusions which do not fit the "estilo llano" the narrator proposed. These literary illusions, however, are all used with ironic intent. In all his "técnica desmitificadora" the narrator corrects José Ido's fantasy. Again, the conflict between the two narrators and their divergent styles parallels the conflict between the two aspects of José María's character.

The same essential duality is manifest in the conflict between José María's role as character and as narrator. As the main character, José María lives his own story from within, and, as such, his view of the world is subject to alteration by his own inner needs. In María Juana's words, he sees the world through the "cobwebs," or rather, the "false prisms" of his passion. As narrator, as the author writing the memoirs of his past "madness" form the relative "sanity" of the present, José María can step outside of the narrative to look at the world objectively, to correct the vision of the world presented to the reader through the "false prisms" of his passion. Like Máximo Manso, José María is both "el narrador-testigo" and "el narrador-personaje."

José María describes in detail the genesis of his memoirs. He carefully explains his reason for writing them, and in so doing clearly attempts to distinguish himself as narrator from himself as character:

> . . . de aquel anhelo de distracción nacieron estas Memorias, que, empezadas como pasatiempo, pararon pronto en verdadera lección que me daba a mí mismo . . . Proponíame hacer un esfuerzo de sinceridad y contar todo como realmente era, sin esconder ni disimular lo desfavorable, ni omitir nada . . . Tuve especial empeño en describir las falsas apreciaciones que hice de Eloísa, alucinado por la criminal pasión que me inspiró; dí a conocer el pueril entusiasmo, el desatino con que me representaba todas las cosas, viéndolas distintas de como efectivamente eran; y poco a poco las fuí trayendo a su ser natural, descubriendo su formación íntima conforme los hechos las iban descarnando. . . . (IV, 1791)

His purpose, says José María, is "to tell things as they were." His memoirs must be a faithful observation of reality. Yet, the memoirs were written in various stages, representing various stages in José María's understanding of the nature of his "madness." So, if in fact the memoirs are intended as a faithful observation of reality, they must reflect the development of his "madness," the process by which he reaches "sanity," and in so doing, they must present reality as it appeared to José María at any one given moment. As José María himself says: ". . . poco a poco las fuí trayendo a su ser natural, descubriendo su formación íntima conforme los hechos las iban descarnando . . ."

As "el narrador-personaje," at the height of his "entusiasmo" for Eloísa, José María can see her only as "aquella divinidad . . . aquella perla de las primas," (IV, 1682) full of "los signos más hermosos del alma humana: sentimiento, piedad, querer y soñar." (IV, 1682) During a period of illness, imagination overcomes his reason, and José María finds that "se me pegó la manía de pensar y de figurar cosas y sucesos ideales, si bien nunca completamente absurdas." (IV, 1699) As Eloísa fusses over him one night during his illness, José María seems certain that she is his wife.

All his time, energy and resources were dedicated to courting her. Yet once his interest in her begins to wane, José María, as "el narrador-testigo" can see the truth of his illusion, that Eloísa, his first beloved, is the product of his imagination: ". . . la miraba como miraría el artista su obra maestra. No es esto, no, lo que quiero decir: mirábala como una planta que yo había regado con mi aliento, abrigado con mi calor y fertilizado con mi dinero. . . ." (IV, 1716) In fact, she is not the *product* of his imagination but a *reality transformed* by his own imagination to conform to his own inner needs.

Throughout the novel, José María continues to play the role of both "el narrador-testigo" and "el narrador-personaje," reflecting the duality of his own character. The reader identifies with José María in all of this and experiences with him the continuing dialectic between the two parts of his character, or between the "subjectivity" of the "narrador-personaje" and the relative "objectivity" of the "narrador-testigo." The dialectic remains unresolved until the end of the novel. José María and the reader together discover the truth, and the conflict between the "narrador-personaje" and the "narrador-testigo" is resolved. All of this is simply another way of saying that the reader cannot trust the veracity of any "reality" presented in the novel, except in the context of the work as a whole. The reality described is not a static reality, but rather a dynamic reality in the process of becoming, a reality changing continuously as the elements of which it is made up change. The reader can only judge that reality, that is he can only accept or reject the narrator's view of it as accurate, when it no longer exists as a reality.

Like Máximo Manso, then José María Bueno de Guzmán is an unreliable narrator whose unreliability is clearly the result of the essential duality of his own character. And like Máximo Manso, José María's unreliability is compounded by his "inconscience," by the fact that he stands, both as character and narrator, in clear contrast to the norms of the novel. But unlike Máximo Manso, José María's unreliability is doubly compounded by the peculiar nature of his inconscience. For José María's narrative is consciously and unconsciously ironic. Máximo Manso provides a direct, if deceptive, vision of reality. He believes he is telling the truth, and he chooses to do it directly, and for the most part, with great seriousness. José María, on the other hand, provides an oblique, or indirect, if deceptive, vision of reality. He also believes he is telling the truth, but he chooses to do it indirectly, consciously using the language of irony and a cynical, mocking tone to reveal the truth, the emptiness behind the facade. The reader of the realist novel has been led to expect this kind of irony as an accepted convention, and is thus lulled into a sense of community with this ironic narrator. He believes that he understands the narrator's irony, that the two of them share the true vision of reality, as opposed to the other "deluded" characters. But the reader has been deceived, for in *Lo prohibido* there is unconscious irony in that very apparent irony and cynicism. José María's materialistic vision of the world, his tendency to reduce everything to the level of pure matter and to deny the spirit, stands in direct contrast to the norms of the novel. In José María's terms, his longing for "lo prohibido," and his vague uncertainty and uneasiness constitute madness, while his materialism, positivism and determinism constitute logic and sanity. Ironically, it is his "sanity," his materialistic vision of the world, which ultmately turns against him, and according to the norms of the novel, is shown to be his real madness.

José María: the Technique of Demythification

The nature of José María's inconscience and the process by which the unconscious irony of his narrative is revealed is best approached through the problem of style. In the style which José María employs in telling his story, there is a constant tendency toward the materialization of reality. This kind of total materialization is the ultimate consequence of the de-mythicizing process of realism which Ortega speaks of in *Las meditaciones del Quijote*:[15] "He aquí lo que llamamos realismo: traer las cosas a una distancia, ponerlas bajo una luz, inclinarlas de modo que se acentúe la vertiente de ellas que baja hasta la pura materialidad."

The result of this materialization is that man is reduced to a merely physiological being, to an animal, or to an object; that the hero of literary or historical tradition is reduced to a grotesque caricature of himself; and that imagination is limited to the realm of the ordinary and the vulgar. The narrative has a burlesque tone which takes nothing "serious" seriously, and which treats seriously what has traditionally been considered comic or frivolous. This burlesque tone reduces human relations to a kind of poor comedy, and all too real "sainete" in which men are only actors playing a multitude of parts.

Throughout the novel, the narrator explains his own or other character's psychological or moral sufferings in purely physiological terms: the origin of their suffering is physiological or it manifests itself physiologically. Carrillo's illness, in fact a physiological manifestation of his troubled state of mind is, for the narrator, the result of "alguna perturbación nutritiva." (IV, 1723) Raimundo, whose comments throughout the novel constitute a kind of caricature of the doctrines of determinism and positivism, offers a physiological explanation of his own illness. Although Raimundo realizes that "es la inacción que me mata" (IV, 1691), he rationalizes by explaining it as "reblandecimiento de la médula." (IV, 1691) José María explains: "Dióme una lección de fisiología, en la cual habló de la *piamáter, del canal raquídeo,* de la *sustancia gris,* de las perturbaciones *vasomotoras* con otros terminachos que no recuerdo." (IV, 1691) Ramimundo's dilettantism is explained as "la afasia, la pérdida de la palabra." (IV, 1691) The characters' psychological illnesses and suffering become physiological illnesses. José María's strange and indefinable fear and uneasiness takes the form of a ringing in his ears or of his stomach's "refusal" to digest properly.

While psychological illness is associated with physiological illness, psychological peace and well-being are associated with the health of the body. Camila and Constantino, who in the second half of the novel become José María's idols, are examples of perfect health. They are perfect physical specimens. They have an enormous appetite for life. As the narrator describes them in their "country idylls:" "Ambos tenían coloración tostada y encendida, por efecto del sol, del agua de mar y de aquel apetito de la Edad de Oro. Ambos revelaban el aspecto de la salud y del vigor físico, así como el grado culminante de la alegría, que es consecuencia de aquel feliz estado." (IV, 1795) José María, on the other hand, a psychological and moral weakling, is in Camila's words, "el tísico."

Moral decadence is always accompanied by physical decay. Perhaps the phenomenon is clearest in the case of Eloísa. Intoxicated by her desire for luxury, Eloísa finally comes to sell herself in order to maintain even the appearance of luxury. The particular variation of the family illness from which Elena suffers is the sensation of a feather stuck in her throat. As it becomes more and more difficult for her to maintain the appearance of luxury and Eloísa's moral standards fall, she imagines that the feather has become a bird, and finally a whole aviary. Eloísa's moral decadence is accompanied by an illness in which her throat becomes grotesquely deformed.

José María's own moral and psychological crisis is manifested in a slow deterioration of both his mental and physical faculties. It seems to him that he is growing old, that he is suffering from premature senility. At the very moment of crisis, he suffers a stroke which leaves him half-paralyzed and speechless. He must be cared for like a sick, dirty child. As the narrator describes his own physiological state:

> Mi pena fue horrible. Tremendo rato aquel en que la conciencia física me acusó con pavorosa austeridad, en que me rebelé contra la sentencia fisiológica y contra Dios que la daba o la consentía, ¡no sé! . . . Aun me faltaba la más negra . . . Intenté decir una expresión clara y no dije sino ¡*mah, mah, mah*! Causóme tal horror mi propio lenguaje, que resolví enmudecer. Me daba vergüenza hablar de aquella manera. ¡Ser la mitad de lo que fuimos, sentir uno que su derecha viva tiene que echarse a cuestas a la izquierda *cadáver*, y por añadidura pensar como un hombre y expresarse como los animales es cosa bien triste . . . !
> (IV, 1876)

In the end, then, as the passage reveals, José María's materialistic tendency to reduce man to a merely physiological being turns against him, as he himself becomes a victim of "la sentencia fisiológica."

At the same time that he reduces man to a physiological being, the narrator consistently presents man as an animal. In the beginning of the novel, the references to man as an animal have only a humorous or perhaps a familiarizing purpose. For example, the narrator refers to Eloísa's child as "aquel cachorro de hombre." (IV, 1687)

The unaffected, natural, vital Camila, who in the second part of the novel becomes José María's ideal, is called "la borriquita." Her husband, Constantino, an eminently physical man of animal force, who "sólo entendía de hacer planchas gimnásticas, tirar al florete y montar a caballo," is called "el burrito" or "el asno del Toboso." Their naturalness and their complete enjoyment of the physical life is expressed in their burro-like characters. Note the narrator's description of Camila and Constantino during the country idylls:

> Cuando salíamos al campo, Camila se embriagaba de aire puro y de luz, corría por las praderas como una loca, se tendía en el césped, saltaba zanjas . . . Nunca había visto a mi borriquita dar tanto y tanto brinco. En su frenesí llegó a decir, tirándose al suelo:
> —Me dan ganas de comer hierba.
> Por su parte, Constantino hacía los mismos disparates, acomodándolos a su natural rudo y atlético. Daba vueltas de carnero y saltos mortales, hacía flexiones y planchas en la rama de un roble, andaba con las palmas de las manos, cantaba a gritos, relinchaba. . . .   (IV, 1791)

At the same time, however, man's animal nature represents moral, intellectual and physical decadence. In the climactic moments of his personal crisis, José María insists on his own animal nature. It is not only that he seems an animal, he *is* an animal. When he realizes that he has become the victim of "la sentencia fisiológica," he declares: "Yo era una cosa más bien que una persona, un pobre animal moribundo que ladraba, pero que ya no podía morder." (IV, 1878) In his state of paralysis, it occurs to José María that he is a dog, a miserable animal. Like a dog, he is even given strichnine. Later he compares himself to a pig: "Acuérdate, Camila—le decía yo con el pensamiento—de cómo te quiso ese cerdo cuando era hombre." (IV, 1880)

Like Raimundo, José María most regrets his loss of speech, symbolic of the loss of his whole way of thinking. More than the misery of his animal-like state, he is bothered by the fact that he can no longer communicate with other human beings. Rather than "bark," he prefers not to speak.

The relationship between José María's fall into an animal state and the loss of his proud and pretentious metaphysical position is clearly seen in the Biblical references which the narrator uses to describe the scenes of his illness. José María compares himself to Nebuchadnezzar, the Babylonian king condemned, because of his pride, to live among the animals and to become like an animal. Terrified by the sound of his own voice, his "espeluznante ¡mah, mah, mah!," José María resolves to keep silent forever and "no ofrecer a la estupefacción de oyente alguno . . . aquel bramido de Nabucodonosor condenado a arrastrarse por el suelo y a comer hierba. . . ." (IV, 1876) Once again, José María's aesthetic and his materialistic vision has turned against him. As he reduces others to animals, even in jest, he himself is reduced to an animal.

José María's determinism, when it subjects man to the same laws which rule the physical universe, equates the human world with the world of objects, and effectively erases the line between them. Not only does it reduce man to an object, but it also makes objects acquire an existence of their own. For example, as he describes Eloísa's Thursday gatherings, the house and the people who came to these gatherings, the narrator says "Pero dejemos las cosas que parecían personas, y vamos a las personas que parecían cosas." (IV, 1727)

In the relationship between men and objects manifest in the novel, the world of objects ends up imposing itself on men. At first it seems that objects only reflect a man's character. The narrator explains, for example, how Camila's capriciousness is reflected in her house: "La casa de Camila era digna de estudiar por el desorden que en ella reinaba. *Sicut domus homo,* se podía decir allí con más razón que en parte alguna." (IV, 1709) Later, objects seem to define man's character. When he returns to Madrid, José María explains how much he enjoyed being in a familiar world once again:

> ¡Qué gusto ver mi casa, el semblante amigo de mis muebles y entregarme a la rutina de aquellas comodidades adquiridas con mi dinero, y que tanta parte tenían en mis propias costumbres! Eran las costras, digámoslo así, de mi carácter. Como a ciertos moluscos, se nos puede clasificar a los humanos por el hueco de nuestras viviendas, molde infalible de nuestras personas.　　　　　　　　　　　　(IV, 1694)

The world of objects, the material world, is the mold in which the individual's character is formed. So rooted is this concept in José María's mind that he comes to believe that if he returns to his former physical surroundings, he can recover the normal psychological state he enjoyed while living in those surroundings. The remedy for his madness is to work in familiar physical surroundings: "Si yo tuviera mi escritorio, como lo tenía en Jerez, y además mis viñas y mis bodegas, estaría muy entretenido todo al año y no pensaría las mil tonterías que ahora pienso. . . ." (IV, 1805) When José María begins to lose interest in Eloísa, the very idea of entering Eloísa's physical surroundings is repugnant to him.

Objects have such power that they may even seem more real than the characters themselves. In his description of Eloísa's Thursday gatherings, José María describes two paintings hanging on the living-room wall. One was of a poor old man, perhaps a "cesante." The narrator says of him, ". . . no vi jamás pintura moderna en que el Arte suplantara a la Naturaleza con más gallardía. El toque era allí perfecto símil de la superficie de las cosas." (IV, 1727) The other painting was of a "chula," who in the narrator's words, "no era una ficción, era la vida misma." (IV, 1727)

At last objects appear to have replaced human beings. When José María fails to attract Camila, his ideal, into his physical surroundings, he puts a pair of her boots in her place. The significance of these objects is manifest in the narrator's words:

> . . . trájome el maestro . . . las botas de Camila, que eran finísimas, de charol, con caña de cuero amarillo. Ramón las puso casualmente sobre una mesa frontera a mi cama, y los ojos no se me apartaban de ellas. ¡Oh dulces prendas! . . . Una falta les encontraba, y era que no teniendo huellas de uso, carecían de la impresión de la persona. Pero hablaron bastante aquellos mudos objetos y me decían mil cositas elocuentes y cariñosas. Yo no les quitaba los ojos, y de noche, durante aquellos fatigosos insomnios, ¡qué gusto me daba mirarlas, una junto a otra, haciendo graciosa pareja, con sus puntas vueltas hacia mí como si fueran a dar pasos hacia donde yo estaba! (IV, 1857-58)

These idealized, personified objects exist at the same level as man, who has been "objectified" to such an extent that it is sometimes impossible to distinguish man from object. In this description of Eloísa's Thursday gatherings, the narrator speaks of "las cosas que parecen personas" and "las personas que parecen cosas." (IV, 1727) And at the climactic moment of his personal crisis, José María himself, in his own words, is no longer a person, but a thing. Once again,

José María has become the victim of his own materialization. His irony again falls unconsciously on himself.[16]

The materialization of reality is repeated in the demythicizing of the literary or classical hero. This demythicizing is but the ultimate consequence of the determinist-positivist view of the world which metaphysically reduces the spirit to pure matter, and aesthetically, reduces the ideal to a poor, ridiculous imitation of itself. In his desire to demythicize, the narrator employs caricature, parody and epithets to produce the desired irony and mocking tone of the narrative.

The technique is most clearly seen in the epithets the narrator uses to describe the other characters. The most obvious example is Eloísa. At first Eloísa appears to José María as "una obra maestra," but "una obra maestra de carne mortal." When he helps her furnish her new apartment, she becomes "la Musa del Buen Gusto." Her desire for luxury is represented as the temptation of Eve, in this case tempted not by the evil serpent but a salesman who offers her a few glass beads. When Eloísa returns from an evening at the theater to find her husband dying, in her feigned sorrow she seems to José María "una elegante pastora del pequeño Trianón llorando ausencias de algún pastor de peluca." (IV, 1740)

In addition to caricatures of famous mythical figures, the narrator offers parodies of famous scenes from literary and classical tradition. The most obvious example is the love scene between Eloísa and José María which is, in the narrator's words, "una parodia grotesca de *Romeo y Julieta*." The two lovers have spent the afternoon in José María's apartment imagining themselves in another world and scarcely noticing the passage of time. As the moment of separation draws closer, the narrator comments: "Con tales tonterías se pasaba el tiempo, y por fin la adusta hora de la separación llegó. Hubo parodias grotescas de Romeo y Julieta." (IV, 1750) The balcony scene from *Romeo and Juliet,* and Romeo's famous soliloquy comparing Juliet to the sun is the basis for parody:

> José María:—Esa claridad mortecina no es, como dices, la del gas, sino la del crepúsculo. El cielo, teñido de rojo, celebra con siniestro esplendor las exequias del día. Es la seudoaurora que este año da tanto que hablar a la gente supersticiosa . . .
> Eloísa:—No; es el gas, el gas. Ya el mensajero de la noche, corriendo de farol en farol con un palo en la mano, va colgando luces en las ramas de los árboles . . .
> José María—Te digo que es la tarde . . .

>   Eloísa:—Te digo que es la noche . . .
>   José María:—Un rato más . . .
>   Eloísa:—¡Horror de los horrores; las siete!

Instead of "A thousand times good night" and "Parting is such sweet sorrow," we have:

>   Señora . . .
>   —Encantada de conocer a usted . . . Me parece usted algo tímido. No se decide . . .
>   —Señora, usted se me antoja una sílfide, una hada sin consistencia corpórea, sin realidad física . . .
>   —¡Burlón!, otro abrazo. Tu amor o la muerte . . .
>   Que te espero . . .
>   —¡Eh!, sinvergüenza, no pelizques.
>   . . .
>   Abur, abur . . . Largo de aquí . . .
>   —Feo, apunte, mamarracho, adiós. (IV, 1750)

Also, the scene in Eloísa's bedroom during her illness is a grotesque parody of scenes from classical literature. Her bed appears as "un féretro pagano." As José María describes the scene:

>   En vez del cobertor ordinario, la cama ostentaba una colcha riquísima de raso azul bordado de oro . . . la viuda de Carrillo . . . yacía entre sábanas, envuelta la cabeza en aquel tul de seda que yo había visto poco antes, dispuesto con graciosos y elegantes pliegues. Al través de la diáfana tela se veía el rostro de la enferma. Los ojos lucían; pero las deformidades de la garganta quedaban esfumadas y como perdidas en los cambiantes y tornasoles de la tela . . . Alrededor de la cabeza . . . habían puesto flores, muchas flores . . . afectando lo que los retóricos llamaban un *bello desorden* . . . Yo no tenía idea, hasta entonces, de la *coquetería mortuoria*.
>   (IV, 1838-39)

Eloísa, too, is aware of the classical antecedents of the scene: "¿Qué te has creído al entrar? Ello debe de parecer cosa antigua, del paganismo, así como cuando van a enterrar a una ninfa o a quemarla viva. . . ." (IV, 1839)

Raimundo points out the concrete models of the scene and its theatrical quality: "A Raimundo, que vino un poco más tarde, parecióle excesivamente teatral, y sacó a relucir a Ofelia, Beatrice Cenci, Ifigenia y otras muertas célebres." (IV, 1839)

The description of Eloísa's Thursday gatherings offers a good example of the ridiculizing effect of the narrator's "técnica desmitificadora," the contamination of the ideal by a vulgar reality. Eloísa engages a bourgeois painter to create a mural for her salon. The painter describes his idea for the painting:

> Sería una procesión de figuras helénicas representando todos los ideales del manudo antiguo y los prodigios del moderno: la Filosofía peripatética y el Teléfono de Edison, las Matemáticas de Euclides y la Educación física de Spencer, el Osirios egipcio y la Vacuna de Jenner, la Geografía de Herodoto y el Cosmos de Humboldt, el barco de Jason y el acorazado de Zamuda, los Vedas y el Darvinismo, Euterpe y Wagner. . . . (IV, 1730)

This technique of materialization and demythicizing produces a mocking tone which permeates all levels of the novel, and makes it impossible to take anything seriously. Rather, it treats everything serious as a joke, and treats the trivial very seriously. Raimundo embodies this mocking tone. He makes fun of everything. His letters reveal in concrete form his vision of the world. As the narrator says of Raimundo's letters: ". . . escribíalas en estilo espeluznante cuando me contaba alguna trivialidad, y en el más ligero cuando me transmitía noticias de importancia." (IV, 1694) Raimundo's own illness, the dissipation of his mental faculties, is cured by "el triple trapecio," a verbal exercise, a tongue-twister, which he takes very seriously and which represents for him real mental discipline. When Raimundo takes seriously his ridiculous "mapa moral geográfico de España," he makes fun of all serious intellectual endeavour. His ideas are a caricature of the doctrines of determinism and positivism. He carries to an extreme the consequences of those doctrines adhered to by his society, and thus makes fun of it as well. José María and the others can accept him only as a fool. They cannot take him seriously, for his jokes threaten the very basis of their world view.

This burlesque tone is a reflection of determinism, which, when it takes away from man his will and makes him a product of the situations in which he finds himself, makes of him a poor actor playing a role, which anyone else might play, in the comedy of life. Determinism, on taking away man's will, deprives him of his individuality. Now he can no longer define himself; he is defined by circumstance. He is no longer a unique individual, but an anybody, "un cualquiera." Lacking his own essence, man adapts himself to his surroundings. Noting, for example, that María Juana had adopted "una postura académica y teológica como se adopta un color o un perfume" (IV, 1861), the narrator thinks that "la vida es un constante trabajo de asimilación en todos los órdenes." (IV, 1861)

The motif of human situations as a poor comedy and of man as an actor in that comedy is found throughout the novel. Eloísa's Thursday gatherings seem "una comedia, o mejor, aristocrático sainete." (IV, 1724) The scenes between José María and Eloísa are "disparatones más disparates que los disparates del teatro." (IV, 1748) As his madness progresses, José María begins to suspect that he is "un cualquiera." At first, to be just anybody implies only a sense of inferiority. But later he begins to believe that he is only "un cualquiera," that he plays a role which circumstance has imposed on him: "En medio de tanta indolencia, una idea me inquietaba de cuando en cuando . . . Era la idea de que el buen rato que yo pasaba, lo pudiera pasar otra persona. . . ." (IV, 1748)

After his fall and the subsequent attack which cripple him physically and mentally, José María feels that he is less than a man, not even "un cualquiera." When he at last realizes the ultimate consequences of his materialism, he also realizes the real significance of what Raimundo was saying. He no longer finds Raimundo's jokes amusing. What Raimundo, in his jokes, implies, is not a joke, and there is nothing to laugh at. Again, the burlesque tone, like the irony, has turned against the narrator; the joke is on him.

It may be argued that José María's irony and cynicism are consciously directed as much against himself as against others. But it may also be demonstrated that José María does not realize until the end of the novel the implications of the materialistic view of the world which his cynicism reflects. And even more significantly ironic, it is at the hands of Camila herself, who had come to represent for José María the ideal incarnate of his materialism, that his materialistic view of the world is shown to be invalid, that is, that his point of view is shown to be in clear contrast to the norms of the novel.

Implicitly and explicitly, the narrator makes use of the Cervantine tradition of *Don Quijote* to present the problem of reality and his relationship to it. In both novels, the author puts the protagonist, with his vision of the world already well defined, into contact with reality so that the two contradictory forces—man who wishes to impose his vision on reality and reality itself which resists and ultimately ends up imposing itself on man's ideals—are forced to interact. Although Don Quijote and José María Bueno de Guzmán enter the world with very different world views, both must undergo similar experience, and both end up adjusting their vision of reality.

Don Quijote goes out to encounter the world with his head full of the humanistic heritage of the Renaissance, as presented in the ideal characters of the books of chivalry he has read. From his reading of these books comes his idealism, based on a concept of a mythical world, an epic world where nothing is impossible. He tries to impose his world view, the ideal, on the world of matter. As Ortega says, because his will toward the ideal is an active one, reality resists him actively

José María, on the other hand, goes out to encounter reality with his head full of the dual heritage of his past: the vestiges of his youthful quixotism, the idealistic heritage of his Spanish father, and the materialism of his intellectual formation in the doctrines of determinism and positivism. In José María's case, then, there are two stages in the resolution of the conflict between his idealism and his materialism. At the beginning of the novel, he is more influenced by the idealism, which he later describes as "el idealismo falso," of his Spanish heritage. But his past life, he says, "no me había presentado ocasiones de desplegar mis energías iniciales propias." (IV, 1703) For that reason, he feels like "un soldado que ha estado sirviendo mucho tiempo sin ver jamás un campo de batalla. Pero al venir a Madrid, cuando menos lo pensaba, el humo de la batalla me envolvía. Pronto se vería quién era yo y cuál era el valor de mi valor, o dejando a un lado el símil, qué realidad tenían mis convicciones." (IV, 1703)

Searching for an ideal, he seems to find it in the form of Eloísa. As the narrator says: "En su perfección creí ver impresos los signos más hermosos del alma humana: sentimientos, piedad, querer y soñar." (IV, 1682) All of his relationship with Eloísa is characterized by "entusiasmos caballerescos," "vehemencia romántica," "ilusión de mozalbete." But he is soon aware of the false idealism which Eloísa represents. In fact, Eloísa is as much, or more, of a materialist than José María. What José María attempts to do with his Arithmetic and numbers is not only to re-establish economic order, but to raise Eloísa once again to the level of the ideal. But after she falls into temptation (of material wealth), she is contaminated by the material world and cannot maintain her ideal state. Eloísa represents the false idealism of the surface, an idealism which is compatible neither with reason nor with reality.

José María's "idealism" contained the seeds of its own destruction. Like the student Sansón Carrasco, José María had a very superficial understanding of quixotism. And, in accordance with the materialism of his age, it is natural that José María would be deceived in identifying appearance with reality. It is also logical that his idealism, as he understood it, could not co-exist with his materialism. Thus it is that he abandons idealism and becomes a kind of anti-Quijote, dedicated to overthrowing the ideals in which Cervantes' Don Quijote had believed, and to imposing his own materialistic vision of the world.

After his experience with Eloísa, the determinist-positivist side of José María is triumphant. The moment of triumph occurs at the beginning of the second half of the novel, where the doctrines of determinism and positivism are openly expressed. His false idealism has been destroyed and he is bored with Eloísa. In his celebration of the material world, he is enchanted with Camila, a very corporeal being ("la borriquita"), who suddenly becomes his new ideal. She and her husband Constantino, in their physical perfection, are the ideals of a new, material Golden Age. In a curious reversal of his "técnica desmitificadora," the narrator idealizes these eminently natural, material beings. Camila is "la borriquita;" Constantino is "aquel rebuzno mío," "el asno del Toboso." The ass, a traditionally humble animal profoundly rooted in common reality, becomes the symbol of a new ideal. In Christian tradition, "el hermano asno" is the body, that is, man's animal nature. When José María idealizes Camila and Constantino, the basis of his idealism is the vitality and naturalness of these beings, the result of their physical perfection and their enjoyment of their animal nature.

Materialism carried to the level of an ideal by José María also contains the seeds of its own destruction, a phenomenon we have seen present throughout the novel. José María persists in believing that Camila, the ideal incarnate of his materialism, will fall into temptation, according to the laws of human relationships: that she will eventually succumb to his efforts to seduce her. But belief is not sufficient. Ultimately he has to test his belief. This, as with Don Quijote, is his fatal mistake. In a scene which offers a clear parallel with the episode in the second part of the *Quijote* when the knight puts to a test his faith in the ideal character of Dulcinea, José María goes up to Camila's apartment to demand that she love him, that is, that she behave according to the laws of human relationships. As in the case of Don Quijote, the girl he sees is not the one he wants to see. Seeing Camila's spiritual nature (when she resists falling into temptation, that is, the material) is for José María as traumatic an experience as seeing Dulcinea (or the village girl whom Sancho presents as Dulcinea) is for Don Quijote. As "Dulcinea's" material resistance to Don Quijote's ideal has profound psychological effects on Don Quijote; so Camila's spiritual resistance to José María's materialism has profound physical, as well as psychological, effects on José María.

Like Don Quijote, who is punished physically when he attempts to impose his ideal will on reality, José María is punished physically by Camila when he attempts to impose his materialistic will on her spiritual reality. When, in desperation, José María says to Camila: "Quiéreme, o te mato" (IV, 1851) and tries to drag her physically to his own level, Camila reacts with physical violence. The narrator explains:

> La vi encenderse en verdadera cólera. Aquel manojito de gracias, aquel ramillete de chistes, nunca se había presentado a mis ojos en la transformación fisiológica de la ira. En tal instante miréla por la primera vez airada, y me acobardé cual no me he acobardado nunca. La vi palidecer, dar una fuerte patada; le oí tartamudear dos o tres palabras; levantó la pierna derecha, quitóse con rápido movimiento una de aquellas enormes botas, la esgrimió en la mano derecha, y me sentó la suela en la cara una, dos, tres veces . . . Yo cerré los ojos y aguanté. (IV, 1851-52)

In the days which follow, José María is not the same man. His physical and mental decadence is accelerated. He can no longer manage his business affairs. Not even Raimundo's "triple trapecio" or the "wise" María Juana's efforts can save him. There follows a few weeks later the incident of his fall down the stairwell, at the moment of climax in the novel. When his entry into Camila's and Constantino's earthly paradise through a false door is prohibited, José María falls down the stairs and into an unconscious state, which he compares to "aquella lóbrega cisterna, simulacro de los abismos de la muerte." (IV, 1875) That is, he has to die and be re-born to pass once again through certain ontological and biological steps in order to arrive at a new vision of the world which admits the presence of the spirit. The motif of death and symbolic rebirth in the "lóbrega cisterna" has a certain parallel with the episode of the Cave of Montesinos in the *Quijote*. Don Quijote, in the Cave of Montesinos, also has to suffer a kind of death and rebirth. Both José María and Don Quijote suffer a radical change: they have to reconcile their world view with reality. Like Don Quijote, who had to admit the force of the material world, José María has to admit the strength of the spirit, of the soul.

At last, in the miserable, animal-like existence of his convalescence, José María realizes the ultimate consequence, the true significance of his deterministic vision: materialism alone is as false as idealism alone (the "misticismo falso" of which Raimundo speaks). José María's tendency to reduce everything to matter, to reduce man to an animal, turns against him. The only thing that saves him from being completely an animal is his awareness of his own soul:

> Absolutamente privado de toda facultad sensoria que no era el placer de comer, pensaba en lo ideal que se había vuelto mi amor para Camila. Por esto, gracias a Dios, yo no era completamente bestia. Si aquello me faltara, hubiera andado a cuatro pies, siempre que el izquierdo y la mano del mismo lado lo consintieran. Pero conservaba mi alma, aunque desquiciada, y en mi alma aquella chispa divina, por la cual me creía con derecho a reclamar un sitio en el mundo espiritual, cuando la bestia cayese por entero en el inorgánico. La conciencia de aquella chispa me consolaba de tener cara de idiota, voz como un ladrido, cuerpo de palo, y de sentir caer las babas de mi boca. (IV, 1880)

José María's materialistic vision of the world has been proved wrong. The unconscious irony of his position is at last revealed to him. As José María himself says "Yo no decía más que la mitad de la verdad, y la mitad de la verdad suele ser tan falsa como la mentira misma..." (IV, 1860)

As in the case of Máximo Manso, José María's unreliability as a narrator has multiple implications, both thematically and aesthetically. Clearly, José María does not represent the thematic norms of the novel. To point out the weaknesses in the doctrines of determinism and positivism and the emptiness of the society which accepted them as dogma, Galdós chose a narrator whose narrative is in fact a caricature of those same doctrines.

Just as clearly, José María stands in contrast to the aesthetic norms of the novel. He sets out to write a "true history" and to destroy the convention of the literary hero. Yet, in writing his "true history," José María employs an ironic, cynical tone and a "técnica desmitificadora" which, as we have seen, consistently turn against him. His style enabled him to reveal a "truth" which was only a "half-truth," as much a lie as the "literary" truth he set out to destroy.

To replace the literary heroes he destroys with his demythicizing, José María invents a new "natural" or "material" hero. Yet the new heroine, Camila, actively resists being fit into this mold.

The wider aesthetic implications are evident. In *Lo prohibido*, Galdós' protests the excesses of naturalism and the philosophical materialism inherent in that literary style. He rejects it as a kind of half-truth and opts for his own "naturalismo espiritual," the title of one of the chapters of the third volume of *Fortunata y Jacinta*, the novel which immediately followed *Lo prohibido*.

Conclusions

Our study has shown that unreliable narration in Galdós' novels is limited to his two works written in the form of memoirs, where unreliability is most obviously an inevitable consequence of the "first-person" mode of narration. We discovered that less obviously, but more significantly, the unreliable narration of these two novels is the result of "inconscience," an unconsciously ironic narrative. This unconscious irony and the resultant unreliability is necessary to maintain the dialectic of appearance and reality, of perceiving consciousness and external reality characteristic of Galdós' realism.

FOOTNOTES

[1] Wolfgang Kayser, "Origen y crisis de la novela moderna," *Cultura universitaria*, no. 47 (enero-febrero, 1955), passim.

[2] Wayne Booth, *The Rhetoric of Fiction* (Chicago: University of Chicago Press, 1961), p. 158.

[3] *Ibid.*, p. 159.

[4] *Ibid.*, p. 159.

[5] Félix Martínez-Bonati, *La estructura de la obra literaria*, (Santiago de Chile: Ediciones de la Universidad de Chile, 1960), passim, pp. 45-63. Martínez-Bonati's theory of linguistic function is described at length in Chapter III.

[6] Ricardo Gullón, " 'El amigo Manso', nivola galdosiana," *Mundo nuevo*, Nos. 4 y 5 (octubre y noviembre de 1966).

[7] *Ibid.*, p. 8.

[8] *Ibid.*, p. 13.

[9] *Ibid.*, pp. 12-13.

¹⁰*Ibid.*, p. 14.
¹¹*Ibid.*, p. 5.
¹²*Ibid.*, p. 4.
¹³Robert Russell, "El amigo Manso: Galdós with a Mirror," *Modern Language Notes*, (1963), pp. 761-168.
¹⁴José Ortega y Gasset. *Meditaciones del Quijote*, 2a. ed., (Madrid: Revista de Occidente, 1966), passim.
¹⁵*Ibid.*, p. 154.
¹⁶Galdós' criticism of the treatment of men as objects in *Lo prohibido* results from the fact that he sees this vision as revealing only a half-truth. In accord with the Hegelian dialectic, Galdós stresses the importance of a synthesis of the material and the spiritual. Basically, then, his attitude toward the interrelationship between the organic and the inorganic is a positive one.

Chapter VI

CONCLUSIONS

This study has grown out of a basic dissatisfaction with traditional views of realism as a literary style which tend to define realism as the approximation of literary to external reality, that is, those definitions which offer a very literal interpretation of Aristotle's concept of mimesis.

These traditional views of realism are descriptively true, but they are neither definitive nor explanatory. The statement that realism is "the objective representation of contemporary social reality" is certainly an accurate description of much of historical realism (the realist novel of the nineteenth century), but it alone does not distinguish those works from many twentieth-century novels which do give a picture of contemporary social reality, yet which are somehow basically different from the novels of the nineteenth century. Nor does the statement offer an explanation of why realism is concerned with representation of contemporary reality.

This study instead attempts the formation of a theory of realism which might be both definitive and aesthetically valid, that is, consistent with the nature of the novel as a literary genre: in fact, a theory of realism which might serve to distinguish the realistic novel from its successors, and which might offer an aesthetically valid theoretical explanation of what earlier observers of the nature of realism had intuitively and correctly described.

The theories of the novel as a literary genre expressed in José Ortega y Gasset's *Meditaciones del Quijote* and *Ideas sobre la novela,* Ian Watt's *The Rise of the Novel* and Wolfgang Kayser's "Origen y crisis de la novela moderna" revealed the inadequacies of traditional definitions of realism and provided the basis for a new theory of realism as a literary style. They are in accord with the traditional belief that the modern novel is, in fact, an essentially realistic genre, presenting a particular kind of reality: observable, contemporary social reality. But they go on to point out that this is a necessary consequence of the novel's form, the key element of which is the personal narrator. They point out that the modern novel, with its distinguishing characteristic, the personal narrator, arose in an historical period in which philosophy took the position that truth (i.e. reality) can be discovered by the individual through his senses, and that it is only natural that a literary form arising in that period would present the circumstances attendant upon the life of an individual human being, and that it would depict truth, or reality, as it is seen by the individual.

Ortega's theories point out that precisely because it is a realistic genre, the reality of the modern novel cannot stand comparison with the real world. To avoid that implicit comparison, to establish the primacy of its own inner world over the surrounding one, the novel must be perceived from within itself. This study attempted to show that the key figure in the perception of the novel's reality is the personal narrator, who is the primary "center of consciousness" in the novel and who acts as reader's guide and interpreter of novelistic reality. For the narrator in effect duplicates within the novel the experience of reality as the reader has known it in the real world where he, himself, is the center of his own universe. Or, put another way, through identification with the narrator as the mediator of novelistic reality, the reader duplicates within the world of the novel his experience of reality in the world without.

This study attempted to show that this shared consciousness of reader and narrator, who together enter into the dialectic of external reality and perceiving consciousness, constitutes the psychological basis of the novel's realism. Any valid theory of realism must account for that psychological concept in aesthetic terms; so we set about a careful study of the *Novelas contemporáneas* of Benito Pérez Goldós, whose works are by far the best and most representative produced by Spanish realism, in order to show how the dialectic of perceiving consciousness and external reality basic to realism is established and elaborated upon. The narrator's language, in its multiple functions, first creates an external reality independent of the narrator, then establishes the presence of a perceiving consciousness (that of the narrator). The narrator, through language, creates a complex web of relationships with other characters in the novel which results in a multiplicity of perspective, or point of view; that is, a potentially infinite multiplication of the dialectic of perceiving consciousness and external reality.

Once the dialectic of perceiving consciousness and external reality is established, the nature of that relationship is further examined. Consciousness, the human mind, is a complex entity, including the senses which perceive and transmit information from without; the intellect, or rational mind, which selects from that information, organizes and interprets it; and the emotions, which interact with the information from the outside, and act upon it as it acts upon them. So to say that the reader enters into shared consciousness with the narrator in his perception of the novelistic world, is to say that the reader shares modes of consciousness with the narrator. The result, as we have seen, is that reality is stratified; it is perceived at many levels: intellectually, from afar; emotionally, from within; perceptually, from immediately before reality. This multi-layered vision of reality is the function of the distance between the narrator and his narration, a distance which sets up levels of narration (background, middle ground, and foreground), which are the stylistic counterparts of the psychological levels determined by mode of consciousness.

To say that Galdós' realism is based on a dialectic of perceiving consciousness and external reality is to affirm the novel's essential perspectivism. Perspective implies the discovery of the subject-object duality and the identification of a point from which reality is viewed. Secondly it implies distance between the subject and the object and the resultant stratification of reality into distinct levels. Certainly the discovery of perspective—the affirmation of the individual, subjective point of view and the stratification of reality—does not belong exclusively to realism, nor even to the novel as a literary genre. But perhaps the function of perspective may characterize realism in the novel. We have said that Galdós' novels offer a multiplicity both of perspective and of levels of reality. That is, both horizontally and vertically, his novels offer a comprehensive vision of reality. Secondly, we have noted that even in spite of the multiplicity of perspective, all points of view must ultimately be judged in terms of the narrator's point of view; that, although these novels offer a multi-layered vision of reality, a reality known by several modes of consciousness, it is the narrator who determines the manner in which reality is presented and the mode of consciousness by which the reader knows that reality. In other words, this multi-faceted, multi-layered reality is filtered through the consciousness of one individual. This filtering of reality through a single consciousness (present in all modes) provides a coherent vision of reality. These two factors—comprehensiveness and coherence—characterize Galdós' realism, and perhaps by extension, all nineteenth-century realism.

We have at this point provided a satisfactory description of Galdós' realism and a theoretical explanation of it. But have we defined it? Have we distinguished it, both from its predecessors and its successors? Only an exhaustive comparative and contrastive study can answer the question satisfactorily. But I would suggest that these two characteristics—comprehensiveness and coherence of vision—may indeed best define the realistic novel and distinguish it from other kinds of novels.

SELECTED BIBLIOGRAPHY

I. Works by Benito Pérez Galdós
Pérez Galdós, Benito. *Obras completas*, Vol. IV-V 6a ed. Madrid: Aguilar, 1966. Includes:
1. *Novelas de la primera época*
   La Fontana de Oro, 1867-68
   La sombra, 1870
   El audaz: historia de un radical de antaño, 1871
   Doña Perfecta, 1876
   Gloria, 1876-77
   Marianela, 1878
   La familia de León Roch, 1878
2. *Novelas contemporáneas*
   La desheredada, 1881
   El amigo Manso, 1882
   El doctor Centeno, 1883
   Tormento, 1884
   La de Bringas, 1884
   Lo prohibido, 1884-85
   Fortunata y Jacinta, 1886-87
   Miau, 1888
   La incógnita, 1888-89
   Torquemada en la hoguera, 1889
   Realidad, 1889
   Angel Guerra, 1890-91
   Tristana, 1892
   La loca de la casa, 1892
   Torquemada en la cruz, 1893
   Torquemada en el Purgatorio, 1894
   Torquemada y San Pedro, 1895
   Nazarín, 1895
   Halma, 1895
   Misericordia, 1897

II. Works about Benito Pérez Galdós
   A. General Studies
Alonso, Amado. "Lo español y lo universal en la obra de Galdós." in *Materia y forma en poesía*. Madrid: Gredos, 1955, 230-256 .
Ayala, Francisco. *Experiencia e invención*. Madrid: Tauras, 1960.
Baquero Goyanes, Mariano. *Perspectivismo y contraste*. Madrid: Gredos, 1963.
_____. *Proceso de la novela actual*. Madrid: Rialp, 1963.
Brenan, Gerald. *The Literature of the Spanish People*. Cleveland and New York: World Publishing Company, 1957.
Del Río, Angel. *Historia de la literatura española*. New York: Holt, Rinehart, Winston, 1963.
Eoff, Sherman H. *The Modern Spanish Novel*. New York: New York University Press, 1961.
Gaos, Vicente. *Temas y problemas de literatura española*. Madrid: Guadarrama, 1959.

Hurtado y Palencia, Juan. *Historia de la literatura española.* Madrid: 1932.
Madariaga, Salvador de. *Semblanzas literarias contemporáneas.* Barcelona: Ediciones Cervantes, 1924.
Marías, Julián. *Al margen de estos clásicos: Autores españoles del siglo XX.* Madrid: Aguado, 1966.
Menéndez y Pelayo, Marcelino. *Estudios de crítica literaria, V.* Madrid: 1908.
Montesinos, José F. *Costumbrismo y novela: Ensayo sobre el redescubrimiento de la realidad española.* Madrid: Castalia, 1960.
Romera-Navarro, Miguel. *Historia de la literatura española.* Boston: D. C. Heath, 1928.
Salinas, Pedro. *Ensayos de literatura hispánica.* Madrid: Aguilar, 1958.
Serrano Poncela, Segundo. *Introducción a la literatura española.* Caracas: Universidad Central de Venezuela, 1969.
Stamm, James. *A Short History of Spanish Literature.* Garden City, N. Y.: Doubleday, 1967.
Torres Bodet, Jaime. *Tres inventores de realidad: Stendhal, Dostoyevski, Pérez Galdós.* México: Universitaria, 1955.

B. Books

Alas, Leopoldo (Clarín). *Galdós* in his *Obras completas, I.* Madrid: Renacimiento, 1912.
Berkowitz, H. Ch. *Pérez Galdós, Spanish Liberal Crusader.* Madison: University of Wisconsin Press, 1948.
Casalduero, Joaquín. *Vida y obra de Galdós.* 2a ed. Madrid: Gredos, 1966.
Correa, Gustavo. *Realidad, ficción y símbolo en las novelas de Pérez Galdós.* Bogotá: Instituto Caro y Cuervo, 1967.
Del Río, Angel. *Estudios galdosianos.* Zaragoza: 1953.
Eoff, Sherman H. *The Novels of Pérez Galdós.* Saint Louis, Washington University Studies, 1954.
Gullón, Ricardo. *Galdós, novelista moderno.* 2a ed. Madrid: Gredos, 1966.
Montesinos, José F. *Galdós.* Madrid: Castalia, 1969.
Nimetz, Michael. *Humor in Galdós.* New Haven: Yale University Press, 1968.
Pattison, Walter J. *Benito Pérez Galdós and the Creative Process.* Minneapolis: University of Minnesota Press, 1954.
Ricard, Robert. *Aspects de Galdós.* Paris: Presses Universitaires de France, 1963.
_____. *Galdós et ses Romans.* Paris: L'Institut d'Etudes Hispaniques, 1961.
Schraibman, Joseph. *Dreams in the Novels of Galdós.* New York: Hispanic Institute, 1960.
Shoemaker, William H. *Estudios sobre Galdós: Homenaje ofrecido al Profesor William H. Shoemaker.* Madrid: Castalia, 1970.
Walton, L. B. *Pérez Galdós and the Spanish Novel of the Nineteenth Century.* London: J. M. Dent and Sons, Ltd., 1927.

C. Articles

Arroyo, Ciriaco M. "Galdós y Ortega y Gasset, Historia de un silencio." *Anales galdosianos,* I (1966), 143-50.
Ayala, Francisco. "Sobre el realismo en literatura con referencia a Galdós." *La Torre,* núm. 26, San Juan de Puerto Rico (abril-junio, 1959), 91-121.

Bacarisse, S. "The Realism of Galdós: Some Reflections on Language and the Perception of Reality." *Bulletin of Hispanic Studies*, 42 (1965), 139-250.
Bosch, Rafael. "Galdós y la teoría de la novela de Lukács." *Anales galdosianos*, 2 (1967), 169-84.
Casalduero, Joaquín. "La sombra." *Anales galdosianos*, 1 (1966), 33-38.
Davidson, Ned J. "Galdós' Conception of Beauty, Truth and Reality in Art." *Hispania*, 38 (1955), 52-54.
Del Río, Angel. "Galdós: el hombre y el novelista." Introduction to *Torquemada en la hoguera*. New York: Las Américas, 1962.
Eoff, Sherman H. "Galdós y los impedimentos del realismo." *Hispanófila*, 5, 14 (enero de 1962), 51-54.
Gillespie, Gerald. "Reality and Fiction in the Novels of Galdós." *Anales galdosianos*, 1 (1966), 11-31.
Gilman, Stephen A. "Realism and the Epic in Galdós' *Zaragoza*." in *Estudios Hispánicos, Homenaje a Archer M. Huntington*. Wellesley, 1952, 171-92.
_____. "Review of Eoff, Sherman H. *The Novels of Pérez Galdós*." Romanische Forschungen, 70 (1958), 455-65.
Gullón, Ricardo. " 'El amigo Manso', nivola galdosiana." *Mundo nuevo*, nos. 4 y 5 (octubre y noviembre, 1966), 3-17.
Hafter, Monroe Z. "Ironic Reprise in Galdós' Novels." *PMLA*, 76 (1961), 233-39.
Latorre, Mariano. "Cervantes y Galdós." *Atenea*, 86 (septiembre de 1958), 11-40.
Livingstone, L. "Interior Duplication and the Problem of Form in the Modern Spanish Novel." *PMLA*, 73 (1958), 393-406.
Montesinos, José F. "Galdós en busca de la novela." *Insula*, 18, 202 (septiembre de 1963), 1, 16.
Portnoff, G. "The Beginning of the New Idealism in the Works of Tolstoy and Galdós." *Romanic Review*, 23 (1932), 33-37.
Russell, Robert. *"El amigo Manso:* Galdós with a Mirror." *Modern Language Notes*, 78 (1963), 161-168.
Sánchez Barbudo, Antonio. "Vulgaridad y genio de Galdós." *Archivum*, 7 (diciembre-enero de 1957), 48-75.
Yañez, Agustín. "La novela de Pérez Galdós." *Universidad Nacional de Colombia*, 10 (sept-oct-nov, 1947), 29-35.

III. Works on the Theory of the Novel
A. Books

Booth, Wayne. *The Rhetoric of Fiction*. Chicago: University of Chicago Press, 1961.
Daiches, David. *The Novel and the Modern World*. Rev. ed. Chicago, 1960.
Forster, E. M. *Aspects of the Novel*. New York: Harcourt, Brace and World, 1954.
Girard, René. *Deceit, Desire and the Novel: Self and Other in Literary Structure*. Trans. by Yvonne Freccero. Baltimore: Johns Hopkins Press, 1965.
Humphreys, Robert. *Stream of Consciousness in the Modern Novel*. Berkeley and Los Angeles: University of California Press, 1965
Langer, Suzanne K. *Feeling and Form*. New York: Charles Scribner's Sons, 1953.

Lubbock, Percy. *The Craft of Fiction.* New York: Viking Press, 1957.
Lukács, Georg. *Teoría de la novela.* Prólogo de Lucien Goldmann. Traducción de Juan José Sevreli. Buenos Aires: Ediciones Siglo Veinte, 1966.
Muir, Edwin. *The Structure of the Novel.* London: Hogarth Press, 1963.
Martínez-Bonati, Félix. *La estructura de la obra literaria.* Santiago de Chile: Ediciones de la universidad de Chile, 1960.
Ortega y Gasset, José. *The Dehumanization of Art and Other Writings on Art and Culture.* Garden City, N. Y.: Anchor Books, 1956.
─────────. *Meditaciones del Quijote.* 2a ed. Madrid: Revista de Occidente, 1966.
Rader, Melvin. *A Modern Book of Aesthetics.* Rev. ed. New York, 1952.
Scholes, Robert. Ed. *Approaches to the Novel.* San Francisco: Chandler Press, 1966.
Stevick, Phillip. Ed. *The Theory of the Novel.* New York: The Free Press, 1967.
Watt, Ian. *The Rise of the Novel.* Berkeley and Los Angeles: University of California Press, 1967.

B. Articles

Adams, Ken. "Notes on Concretization." *British Journal of Aesthetics,* 4 (1964), 115-25.
Barnes, Hazel. "Modes of Aesthetic Consciousness in Fiction." *Bucknell Review,* 3 (March, 1964), 81-92.
Bullough, Edward. " 'Psychical Distance' as a Factor in Art and as an Aesthetic Principle." *British Journal of Psychology,* 5 (1912), 87-118.
Cook, Albert. "The Beginning of Fiction: Cervantes." *Journal of Aesthetics and Art Criticism,* 17 (June, 1959), 463-72.
De Man, Paul. "Georg Lukács' *Theory of the Novel.*" *Modern Language Notes,* 81 (1966), 527-41.
Friedman, Norman. "Point of View in Fiction: The Development of a Critical Concept." PMLA, 70 (December, 1955), 1160-84.
Jakobson, Roman. "Concluding Statement: Linguistics and Poetics." in *Style in Language,* ed. Thomas A. Sebeok. Cambridge: MIT Press, 1960, 350-78.
Kayser, Wolfgang. "Origen y crisis de la novela moderna." *Cultura universitaria,* no. 47 (enero-febrero, 1955), 5-50.
Schlovsky, Víctor. "Art as Technique." in *Russian Formalist Criticism: Four Essays,* Translated and with an Introduction by Lee T. Lemon and Marion J. Rees. Lincoln: University of Nebraska Press, Regents Critics Series, 1956, 3-24.
Ullman, Stephen, "Reported Speech in Flaubert." in *Style in the French Novel.* Cambridge: Harvard University Press, 1957, 94-120.

IV. Works on Realism

A. Books

Auerbach, Erich. *Mimesis: The Representation of Reality in Western Literature.* Trans. Willard Trask. Garden City, N. Y.: Doubleday, 1957.
Becker, George. *Documents of Modern Literary Realism.* Princeton, Princeton University Press, 1963.

Hauser, Arnold. *The Social History of Art.* Trans. Stanley Godman. New York: Vintage Books, 1951.
Levin, Harry. *The Gates of Horn: A Study of Five French Realists.* New York: Oxford University Press, 1963.
Lukács, Georg. *Ensayos sobre el realismo.* Traducción de Juan José Sebreli. Buenos Aires: Ediciones Siglo Veinte, 1965.
_____. *Studies in European Realism: A Sociological Study of the Writings of Balzac, Stendhal, Zola, Tolstoy, Gorki and Others.* London: Hillway Publishing Co., 1950.
  B. Articles
Durán, Manuel and Antonio Regalado García. "Harry Levin y su exploración de la novela realista." *Anales galdosianos,* 1 (1966), 117-23.
Gold, Herbert. "Truth and Falsity in the Novel." *Hudson Review,* 8 (1955), 410-422.
Levin, Harry, Ed. "A Symposium on Realism." *Comparative Literature,* 3 (Summer, 1951), 193-199.
Lewis, C. S. "On Realisms" in *An Experiment in Criticism.* Cambridge: Cambridge University Press, 1969, 57-73.
Sorenson, Virginia. "Is it True? The Novelist and his Materials." *Western Humanities Review,* 7 (1953), 283-92.
Wellek, René. "The Concept of Realism in Literary Scholarship" in *Concepts of Criticism.* Ed. Stephen G. Nichols, Jr. New Haven and London: Yale University Press, 1963, 222-256.
Woodman, Ross. "Literature and Life." *Queens Quarterly,* 68 (1962), 621-31.

The Department of Romance Studies Digital Arts and Collaboration Lab at the University of North Carolina at Chapel Hill is proud to support the digitization of the North Carolina Studies in the Romance Languages and Literatures series.

www.ingramcontent.com/pod-product-compliance
Lightning Source LLC
Chambersburg PA
CBHW022020220426
43663CB00007B/1156